Ae

Adobe
After Effects CC
2017 release

CLASSROOM IN A BOOK®
The official training workbook from Adobe

Brie Gyncild and Lisa Fridsma

WHERE ARE THE LESSON FILES?

Purchase of this Classroom in a Book in any format gives you access to the lesson files you'll need to complete the exercises in the book.

You'll find the files you need on your **Account** page at peachpit.com on the **Registered Products** tab.

1 Go to www.peachpit.com/register.

2 Sign in or create a new account.

3 Enter the ISBN: 9780134665320.

4 Answer the questions as proof of purchase.

5 The lesson files can be accessed through the Registered Products tab on your Account page.

6 Click the Access Bonus Content link below the title of your product to proceed to the download page. Click the lesson file links to download them to your computer.

CONTENTS

GETTING STARTED

Adobe After Effects CC provides a comprehensive set of 2D and 3D tools for compositing, animation, and effects that motion-graphics professionals, visual effects artists, web designers, and film and video professionals need. After Effects is widely used for digital post-production of film, video, DVD, and the web. You can composite layers in various ways, apply and combine sophisticated visual and audio effects, and animate both objects and effects.

About Classroom in a Book

Adobe After Effects CC Classroom in a Book (2017 release) is part of the official training series for Adobe graphics and publishing software, developed with the support of Adobe product experts. The lessons are designed to let you learn at your own pace. If you're new to Adobe After Effects, you'll learn the fundamental concepts and features you'll need to master the program. And if you've been using Adobe After Effects for a while, you'll find that Classroom in a Book teaches many advanced features, including tips and techniques for using the latest version.

Although each lesson provides step-by-step instructions for creating a specific project, there's room for exploration and experimentation. You can follow the book from start to finish, or do only the lessons that match your interests and needs. Each lesson concludes with a review section summarizing what you've covered.

Prerequisites

Before beginning to use *Adobe After Effects CC Classroom in a Book (2017 release)*, make sure that your system is set up correctly and that you've installed the required software and hardware. You should have a working knowledge of your computer and operating system. You should know how to use the mouse and standard menus and commands, and also how to open, save, and close files. If you need to review these techniques, see the printed or online documentation included with your Microsoft® Windows® or Apple® Mac® OS software.

To complete the lessons in this book, you'll need to have both Adobe After Effects CC (2017 release) and Adobe Bridge CC installed. The exercises in this book are based on After Effects CC (2017 release).

Installing After Effects and Bridge

Adobe After Effects CC is not included with the book; you must purchase it separately from Adobe Creative Cloud. For system requirements and complete instructions on installing the software, visit www.adobe.com/support. Note that After Effects CC requires a 64-bit operating system and OpenGL 3.3 support. To view QuickTime movies on Mac OS, you must also have Apple QuickTime 7.6.6 or later installed on your system.

Some of the lessons in this book use Adobe Bridge. After Effects and Bridge use separate installers. You must install these applications from Adobe Creative Cloud (adobe.com) onto your hard disk. Follow the onscreen instructions.

Optimizing performance

Creating movies is memory-intensive work for a desktop computer. After Effects CC (2017 release) requires a minimum of 4GB of RAM. The more RAM that is available to After Effects, the faster the application will work for you. For information about optimizing memory, cache, and other settings for After Effects, see "Improve performance" in After Effects Help.

Restoring default preferences

The preferences files control the way the After Effects user interface appears on your screen. The instructions in this book assume that you see the default interface when they describe the appearance of tools, options, windows, panels, and so forth. Therefore, it's a good idea to restore the default preferences, especially if you are new to After Effects.

Each time you quit After Effects, the panel positions and certain command settings are recorded in the preferences files. To restore the original default settings, press Ctrl+Alt+Shift (Windows) or Command+Option+Shift (Mac OS) while starting After Effects. (After Effects creates new preferences files if they don't already exist the next time you start the program.)

Restoring the default preferences can be especially helpful if someone has already customized After Effects on your computer. If your copy of After Effects hasn't been used yet, these files won't exist, so this procedure is unnecessary.

Important: If you want to save the current settings, you can rename a preferences file instead of deleting it. When you are ready to restore those settings, change the name back, and make sure that the file is located in the correct preferences folder.

1 Locate the After Effects preferences folder on your computer:

- **For Windows:** .../Users/*<user name>*/AppData/Roaming/Adobe/ AfterEffects/14.0

- **For Mac OS:** .../Users/*<user name>*/Library/Preferences/Adobe/ After Effects/14.0

2 Rename any preferences files you want to preserve, and then restart After Effects.

Online content

● **Note:** In Mac OS 10.7 and later, the user library folder is hidden by default. To see it, in the Finder, choose Go > Go To Folder. In the Go To Folder dialog box, type **~/Library**, and then click Go.

Your purchase of this Classroom in a Book includes online materials provided by way of your Account page on peachpit.com. These include:

Lesson files

To work through the projects in this book, you will need to download the lesson files from peachpit.com. You can download the files for individual lessons or it may be possible to download them all in a single file.

Web Edition

The Web Edition is an online interactive version of the book providing an enhanced learning experience. Your Web Edition can be accessed from any device with a connection to the Internet and it contains:

- The complete text of the book

- Hours of instructional video keyed to the text

- Interactive quizzes

In addition, the Web Edition may be updated when Adobe adds significant feature updates between major Creative Cloud releases. To accommodate the changes, sections of the online book may be updated or new sections may be added.

Accessing the lesson files and Web Edition

If you purchased an eBook from peachpit.com or adobepress.com, your Web Edition will automatically appear under the Digital Purchases tab on your Account page. Click the **Launch** link to access the product. Continue reading to learn how to register your product to get access to the lesson files.

If you purchased an eBook from a different vendor or you bought a print book, you must **register** your purchase on peachpit.com in order to access the online content:

1 Go to www.peachpit.com/register.

2 Sign in or create a new account.

3 Enter ISBN: 9780134665320.

4 Answer the questions as proof of purchase.

5 The **Web Edition** will appear under the Digital Purchases tab on your Account page. Click the **Launch** link to access the product.

The **Lesson Files** can be accessed through the Registered Products tab on your Account page. Click the Access Bonus Content link below the title of your product to proceed to the download page. Click the lesson file links to download them to your computer.

Organizing the lesson files

The files are compressed into ZIP archives to speed download time and protect the contents from damage during transfer. You must uncompress (or "unzip") the files to restore them to their original size and format before you use them with the book. Modern Mac and Windows systems are set up to open ZIP archives by simply double-clicking.

1 On your hard drive, create a new folder in a convenient location and give it the name "Lessons," following the standard procedure for your operating system:

 • In Windows, right-click, and choose New > Folder. Then enter the new name for your folder.

 • In Mac OS, in the Finder, choose File > New Folder. Type the new name, and drag the folder to the location you want to use.

Note: If for any reason you need to download fresh copies of the lesson files, you can download them from your account again at any time.

2 Drag the unzipped Lessons folder (which contains folders named Lesson01, Lesson02, and so on) that you downloaded onto your hard drive to your new Lessons folder. When you begin each lesson, navigate to the folder with that lesson number to access all the assets you need to complete the lesson.

About copying the sample movies and projects

You will create and render one or more movies in some lessons in this book. The files in the Sample_Movies folders are examples that you can use to see the end results of each lesson and to compare them with your own results.

The files in the End_Project_File folders are samples of the completed project for each lesson. Use these files for reference if you want to compare your work in progress with the project files used to generate the sample movies. These end-project files vary in size from relatively small to a couple of megabytes, so you can either download them all now if you have ample storage space, or download just the end-project file for each lesson as needed, and then delete it when you finish that lesson.

How to use these lessons

Each lesson in this book provides step-by-step instructions for creating one or more specific elements of a real-world project. The lessons build on each other in terms of concepts and skills, so the best way to learn from this book is to proceed through the lessons in sequential order. In this book, some techniques and processes are explained and described in detail only the first few times you perform them.

Many aspects of the After Effects application can be controlled by multiple techniques, such as a menu command, a button, dragging, and a keyboard shortcut. Only one or two of the methods are described in any given procedure, so that you can learn different ways of working even when the task is one you've done before.

The organization of the lessons is also design-oriented rather than feature-oriented. That means, for example, that you'll work with layers and effects on real-world design projects over several lessons, rather than in just one lesson.

Additional resources

Adobe After Effects CC Classroom in a Book (2017 release) is not meant to replace documentation that comes with the program or to be a comprehensive reference for every feature. Only the commands and options used in the lessons are explained in this book. For comprehensive information about program features and tutorials, refer to these resources:

- **Adobe After Effects Learn & Support:** helpx.adobe.com/after-effects.html is where you can find and browse tutorials, help, and support on Adobe.com.

- **After Effects Forums:** forums.adobe.com/community/aftereffects_general_ discussion lets you tap into peer-to-peer discussions, and questions and answers about After Effects.

- **Adobe *Create* Magazine:** create.adobe.com offers thoughtful articles on design and design issues, a gallery showcasing the work of top-notch designers, tutorials, and more.

- **Resources for educators:** www.adobe.com/education and edex.adobe.com offer a treasure trove of information for instructors who teach classes on Adobe software. Find solutions for education at all levels, including free curricula that use an integrated approach to teaching Adobe software and can be used to prepare for the Adobe Certified Associate exams.

Also check out these useful links:

- **Adobe Add-ons:** creative.adobe.com/addons is a central resource for finding tools, services, extensions, code samples, and more to supplement and extend your Adobe products.
- **Adobe After Effects CC product home page:** www.adobe.com/products/aftereffects

Adobe Authorized Training Centers

Adobe Authorized Training Centers offer instructor-led courses and training on Adobe products. A directory of AATCs is available at training.adobe.com/trainingpartners.

1 GETTING TO KNOW THE WORKFLOW

Lesson overview

In this lesson, you'll learn how to do the following:

- Create a project and import footage.

- Create compositions and arrange layers.

- Navigate the Adobe After Effects interface.

- Use the Project, Composition, and Timeline panels.

- Transform layer properties.

- Apply basic effects.

- Create keyframes.

- Preview your work.

- Customize the workspace.

- Adjust preferences related to the user interface.

- Find additional resources for using After Effects.

 This lesson will take about an hour to complete. Download the project files for this lesson, following the instructions in the Getting Started section under "Accessing the lesson files and Web Edition," if you haven't already done so. As you work on this lesson, you'll preserve the start files. If you need to restore the start files, download them from your Account page.

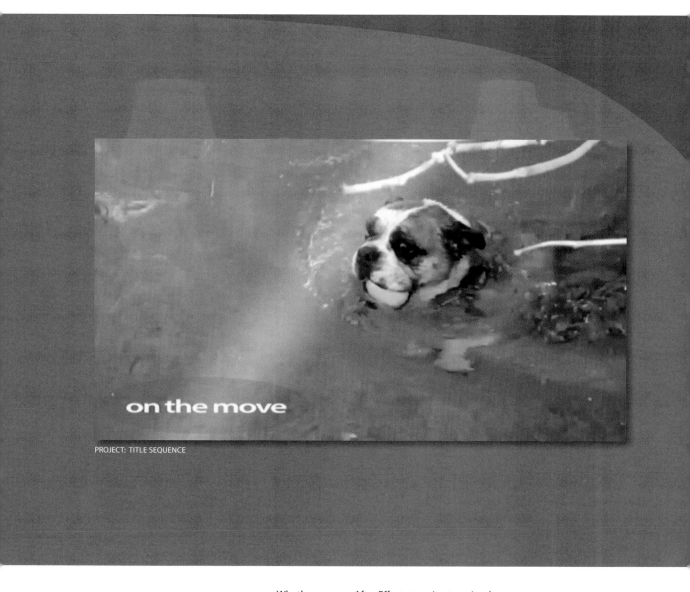

on the move

PROJECT: TITLE SEQUENCE

Whether you use After Effects to animate a simple DVD title sequence or to create complex special effects, you generally follow the same basic workflow. The After Effects interface facilitates your work and adapts to each stage of production.

About the After Effects work area

After Effects offers a flexible, customizable work area. The main window of the program is called the *application window*. Panels are organized in this window in an arrangement called a *workspace*. The default workspace contains stacked panels as well as panels that stand alone, as shown below.

A. *Application window* **B.** *Workspace bar* **C.** *Tools panel* **D.** *Project panel* **E.** *Composition panel* **F.** *Timeline panel* **G.** *Stacked panels* **H.** *Time graph*

You customize a workspace by dragging the panels into the configuration that best suits your working style. You can drag panels to new locations, change the order of stacked panels, move panels into or out of a group, place panels alongside each other, stack panels, and undock a panel so that it floats in a new window above the application window. As you rearrange panels, the other panels resize automatically to fit the window.

When you drag a panel by its tab to relocate it, the area where you can drop it—called a *drop zone*—becomes highlighted. The drop zone determines where and how the panel is inserted into the workspace. Dragging a panel to a drop zone either docks it, groups it, or stacks it.

If you drop a panel along the edge of another panel, group, or window, it will dock next to the existing group, resizing all groups to accommodate the new panel.

If you drop a panel in the middle of another panel or group, or along the tab area of a panel, it will be added to the existing group and be placed at the top of the stack. Grouping a panel does not resize other groups.

You can also open a panel in a floating window. To do so, select the panel, and then choose Undock Panel or Undock Frame from the panel menu. Or, drag the panel or group outside the application window.

Getting started

A basic After Effects workflow follows six steps: importing and organizing footage, creating compositions and arranging layers, adding effects, animating elements, previewing your work, and rendering and outputting the final composition so that it can be viewed by others. In this lesson, you will create a simple animated video using this workflow, and along the way, you'll learn your way around the After Effects interface.

First, you'll preview the final movie to see what you'll create in this lesson.

1 Make sure the following files are in the Lessons/Lesson01 folder on your hard disk, or download them from your Account page at www.peachpit.com now:

 • In the Assets folder: movement.mp3, swimming_dog.mp4, title.psd

 • In the Sample_Movies folder: Lesson01.avi, Lesson01.mov

2 Open and play the Lesson01.avi sample movie in Windows Media Player or the Lesson01.mov sample movie in QuickTime Player to see what you will create in this lesson. When you are done, close Windows Media Player or QuickTime Player. You may delete the sample movies from your hard disk if you have limited storage space.

Creating a project and importing footage

When you begin each lesson of this book, it's a good idea to restore the default preferences for After Effects. (For more information, see "Restoring default preferences" on page 2.) You can do this with a simple keyboard shortcut.

1 Start After Effects, and then immediately hold down Ctrl+Alt+Shift (Windows) or Command+Option+Shift (Mac OS) to restore default preferences settings. When prompted, click OK to delete your preferences.

2 Close the Start window.

▶ **Tip:** Restoring default preferences can be tricky in Windows, especially if you're working on a fast system. Press the keys after you double-click the application icon but before After Effects begins to list the files it's activating. Alternatively, you can choose Edit > [your Creative Cloud account username] > Clear Settings, and then restart the application.

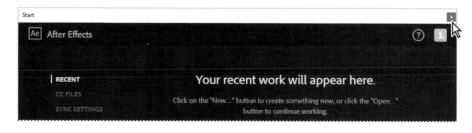

After Effects opens to display an empty, untitled project.

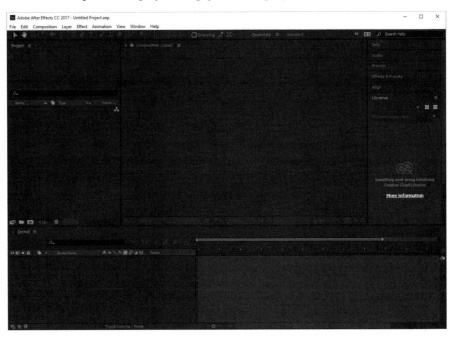

▶ **Tip:** To quickly
maximize a panel,
double-click the panel
tab. To return it to its
original size, double-
click the tab again.

An After Effects project is a single file that stores references to all the footage
you use in that project. It also contains *compositions*, which are the individual
containers used to combine footage, apply effects, and, ultimately, drive the output.

When you begin a project, often the first thing you'll do is add footage to it.

3 Choose File > Import > File.

4 Navigate to the Assets folder in your Lessons/Lesson01 folder. Shift-click to select
 the movement.mp3 and swimming_dog.mp4 files. Then click Import or Open.

A *footage item* is the basic unit in an After Effects project. You can import many types of footage items, including moving-image files, still-image files, still-image sequences, audio files, layered files from Adobe Photoshop and Adobe Illustrator, other After Effects projects, and projects created in Adobe Premiere® Pro. You can import footage items at any time.

As you import assets, After Effects reports its progress in the Info panel.

Because one of the footage items for this project is a multilayer Photoshop file, you'll import it separately as a composition.

5 Double-click in the lower area of the Project panel to open the Import File dialog box.

▶ **Tip:** You can also choose File > Import > Multiple Files to select files located in different folders, or drag and drop files from Explorer or the Finder. You can use Adobe Bridge to search for, manage, preview, and import footage.

6 Navigate to the Lesson01/Assets folder again, and select the title.psd file. Choose Composition from the Import As menu. (In Mac OS, you may need to click Options to see the Import As menu). Then click Import or Open.

After Effects opens an additional dialog box that displays options for the file you are importing.

7 In the title.psd dialog box, choose Composition from the Import Kind menu to import the layered Photoshop file as a composition. Select Editable Layer Styles in the Layer Options area, and then click OK.

The footage items appear in the Project panel.

8 In the Project panel, click to select different footage items. Notice that a thumbnail preview appears at the top of the Project panel. You can also see the file type and size, as well as other information about each item, in the Project panel columns.

When you import files, After Effects doesn't copy the video and audio data itself into your project. Instead, each footage item in the Project panel contains a reference link to the source files. When After Effects needs to retrieve image or audio data, it reads it from the source file. This keeps the project file small, and allows you to update source files in another application without modifying the project.

If you move a file or if After Effects can't access its location, it will report that the file is missing. To find missing files, choose File > Dependencies > Find Missing Footage. You can also type **Missing Footage** into the Search box in the Project panel to look for the missing assets.

▶ **Tip:** You can locate missing fonts or effects the same way. Choose File > Dependencies, and then choose Find Missing Fonts or Find Missing Effects. Or just type **Missing Fonts** or **Missing Effects** into the Search box in the Project panel.

To save time and minimize the size and complexity of a project, you'll usually import a footage item once even if you're using it multiple times in a composition. However, you may sometimes need to import a source file more than once, such as if you want to use it at two different frame rates.

After you've imported footage, it's a good time to save the project.

9 Choose File > Save. In the Save As dialog box, navigate to the Lessons/ Lesson01/Finished_Project folder. Name the project **Lesson01_Finished.aep**, and then click Save.

Creating a composition and arranging layers

The next step of the workflow is to create a composition. You create all animation, layering, and effects in a composition. An After Effects composition has both spatial dimensions and a temporal dimension (time).

Compositions include one or more layers, arranged in the Composition panel and in the Timeline panel. Any item that you add to a composition—such as a still image, moving-image file, audio file, light layer, camera layer, or even another composition—becomes a new layer. Simple projects may include only one composition, while elaborate projects may include several compositions to organize large amounts of footage or intricate effects sequences.

To create a composition, you'll drag the footage items into the Timeline panel, and After Effects will create layers for them.

1 In the Project panel, Shift-click to select the movement.mp3, swimming_dog.mp4, and title assets. Don't select the title Layers folder.

2 Drag the selected footage items into the Timeline panel. The New Composition From Selection dialog box appears.

After Effects bases the dimensions of the new composition on the selected footage. In this example, all of the footage is sized identically, so you'll accept the default settings for the composition.

3 Select swimming_dog.mp4 in the Use Dimensions From menu, and then click OK to create the new composition.

The footage items appear as layers in the Timeline panel, and After Effects displays the composition, named swimming_dog, in the Composition panel.

When you add a footage item to a composition, the footage becomes the source for a new layer. A composition can have any number of layers, and you can also include a composition as a layer in another composition, which is called *nesting*.

Some of the assets are longer than others, but you want them all to continue only as long as the swimming dog is on the screen. You'll change the length of the entire composition to 7:00 to match the dog clip.

4 Choose Composition > Composition Settings.

5 In the Composition Settings dialog box, rename the composition **movement**, type **7:00** for the Duration, and then click OK.

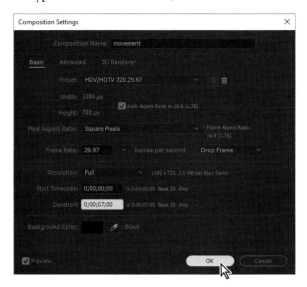

The Timeline panel displays the same duration for each of the layers.

In this composition, there are three footage items, and therefore three layers in the Timeline panel. Depending on the order in which the elements were selected when you imported them, your layer stack may differ from the one shown on the previous page. The layers need to be in a specific order as you add effects and animations, however, so you'll rearrange them now.

About layers

Layers are the components you use to build a composition. Any item that you add to a composition—such as a still image, moving-image file, audio file, light layer, camera layer, or even another composition—becomes a new layer. Without layers, a composition consists only of an empty frame.

Using layers, you can work with specific footage items in a composition without affecting any other footage. For example, you can move, rotate, and draw masks for one layer without disturbing any other layers in the composition, or you can use the same footage in more than one layer and use it differently in each instance. In general, the layer order in the Timeline panel corresponds to the stacking order in the Composition panel.

● **Note:** You may need to click a blank area of the Timeline panel or press F2 to deselect layers before you can select an individual layer.

6 Click an empty area of the Timeline panel to deselect the layers, and then drag the title layer to the top of the layer stack, if it is not already there. Drag the movement.mp3 layer to the bottom of the layer stack.

7 Choose File > Save to save your project so far.

Adding effects and modifying layer properties

● **Note:** This exercise is just the tip of the iceberg. You will learn more about effects and animation presets in Lesson 2, "Creating a Basic Animation Using Effects and Presets," and throughout the rest of this book.

Now that your composition is set up, you can start having fun—applying effects, making transformations, and adding animation. You can add any combination of effects and modify any of a layer's properties, such as size, placement, and opacity. Using effects, you can alter a layer's appearance or sound, and even generate visual elements from scratch. The easiest way to start is to apply any of the hundreds of effects included with After Effects.

Transforming layer properties

The title is currently in the center of the screen, obscuring the dog and distracting from the action. You'll move it to the lower left corner, where it will remain visible but not in the way.

1 Select the title layer (layer 1) in the Timeline panel. Notice that layer handles appear around the layer in the Composition panel.

2 Click the triangle to the left of the layer number to expand the layer, and then expand the layer's Transform properties: Anchor Point, Position, Scale, Rotation, and Opacity.

3 If you can't see the properties, scroll down the Timeline panel using the scroll bar at the right side of the panel. Better yet, select the title layer name again, and press P.

This keyboard shortcut displays only the Position property, which is the only property you want to change for this exercise. You'll move this layer to the lower left corner.

4 Change the coordinates for the Position property to **265, 635**. Or use the Selection tool to drag the title to the lower left corner of the screen.

5 Press P to hide the Position property and keep the timeline neat.

Adding an effect to correct color

After Effects includes several effects to correct or modify color in your projects. You'll use the Auto Contrast effect to adjust the overall contrast in the clip and intensify the color of the water.

1 Select the swimming_dog layer in the Timeline panel.

2 Click the Effects & Presets panel (in the panel stack at the right side of the application window) to open it, and type **contrast** in the search box.

● **Note:** If you double-click a layer in the Timeline panel, After Effects opens the layer in the Layer panel. To return to the Composition panel, click the Composition tab.

After Effects searches for effects and presets that contain the letters you type, and displays the results interactively. Before you have finished typing, the Auto Contrast effect—located in the Color Correction category—appears in the panel.

3 Drag the Auto Contrast effect onto the swimming_dog layer in the Timeline panel.

After Effects applies the effect and automatically opens the Effect Controls panel in the upper left area of the workspace.

The contrast intensifies colors a little more than we need. You'll customize the settings to reduce the effect.

4 In the Effect Controls panel, click the number next to Blend With Original, type **20%**, and press Enter or Return to accept the new value.

Adding a stylistic effect

After Effects also includes many stylistic effects. You'll add a beam of light to the clip to add an artistic touch. You'll change the settings of this effect to modify the angle and intensity of the light.

1 Click the *x* in the search box in the Effects & Presets panel to clear it, and then locate the CC Light Sweep effect by doing one of the following:

- Type **CC Light** in the search box.

- Click the triangle next to Generate to expand the category in alphabetical order.

2 Drag the CC Light Sweep effect in the Generate category onto the swimming_ dog layer name in the Timeline panel. After Effects adds the CC Light Sweep settings to the Effect Controls panel under the Auto Contrast effect.

3 In the Effect Controls panel, click the triangle next to the Auto Contrast effect to hide those settings so that you can see the CC Light Sweep settings more easily.

First, you'll change the angle of the light.

4 For Direction, type **37**°.

5 From the Shape menu, choose Smooth to widen and soften the light beam.

6 For Width, type **68** to widen the beam a bit more.

7 Change the Sweep Intensity value to **20** to make the beam a little more subtle.

8 Choose File > Save to save your work so far.

Animating the composition

So far, you've started a project, created a composition, imported footage, and applied some effects. It all looks great, but how about some movement? You've applied only static effects.

In After Effects, you can change any combination of a layer's properties over time using conventional keyframing, expressions, or keyframe assistants. You'll explore many of these methods throughout the lessons of this book. For this project, you'll apply an animation preset to introduce the title to the screen, and you'll animate the title's color over time.

Preparing the text composition

In this exercise, you'll work with a separate composition—the one you imported from a layered Photoshop file.

● **Note:** If the Project tab isn't visible, choose Window > Project to open the Project panel.

1 Select the Project tab to display the Project panel, and then double-click the title composition to open it as a composition in its own Timeline panel.

This composition is the layered Photoshop file you imported. Two layers—Title Here and Ellipse 1—appear in the Timeline panel. The Title Here layer contains placeholder text that was created in Photoshop.

At the top of the Composition panel is the Composition Navigator bar, which displays the relationship between the main composition (movement) and the current composition (title), which is nested within the main composition.

You can nest multiple compositions within each other; the Composition Navigator bar displays the entire composition path. Arrows between the composition names indicate the direction in which information flows.

Before you can replace the text, you need to make the layer editable.

● **Note:** If you see a warning about missing fonts or layer dependencies, click OK.

2 Select the Title Here layer (layer 1) in the Timeline panel, and then choose Layer > Convert To Editable Text.

A T icon appears next to the layer name in the Timeline panel, indicating that it is now an editable text layer. The layer is also selected in the Composition panel, ready for you to edit.

The blue lines at the top, bottom, and sides of the Composition panel indicate title-safe and action-safe zones. Television sets enlarge a video image and allow some portion of its outer edges to be cut off by the edge of the screen. This is known as *overscan*. The amount of overscan is not consistent between television sets, so you should keep important parts of a video image, such as action or titles, within margins called *safe zones*. Keep your text inside the inner blue guides to ensure that it is in the title-safe zone, and keep important scene elements inside the outer blue guides to ensure that they are in the action-safe zone.

About the Tools panel

As soon as you create a composition, the tools in the Tools panel in the upper left corner of the After Effects application window become available. After Effects includes tools that enable you to modify elements of your composition. Some of these tools—the Selection tool and the Hand tool, for example—will be familiar to you if you use other Adobe applications, such as Photoshop. Others will be new.

A. Selection B. Hand C. Zoom D. Rotation E. Camera tools F. Pan Behind G. Mask and Shape tools H. Pen tools I. Type tools J. Brush K. Clone Stamp L. Eraser M. Roto Brush and Refine Edge tools N. Puppet tools

When you hover the pointer over any button in the Tools panel, a tool tip identifies the tool and its keyboard shortcut. A small triangle in the lower right corner of the button indicates that one or more additional tools are hidden behind it. Click and hold the button to display the hidden tools, and then select the tool you want to use.

Editing text

You'll start by replacing the placeholder text with real text. Then you'll format it to fit the space better.

1 Select the Horizontal Type tool (T) in the Tools panel, and drag over the placeholder text in the Composition panel to select it. Then type **on the move**.

● **Note:** After Effects offers robust character and paragraph formatting controls, but the default settings—whatever typeface appears when you type—should be fine for this project. You'll learn more about type in Lesson 3, "Animating Text."

2 Select the text again. Then, in the Character panel (docked on the right side of the screen), change the text size to **100 px** and the tracking to **-50**.

Animating text with animation presets

Now that the text is formatted, you can apply an animation preset. You'll use the Fade Up Words preset, so the words will appear in order over time.

1 Select the Title Here layer in the Timeline panel again, and make sure you're at the first frame of the animation by doing one of the following:

 • Drag the current-time indicator all the way to the left of the time ruler, to 0:00.

 • Press the Home key on your keyboard.

2 Select the Effects & Presets tab to display the Effects & Presets panel. Then type **fade up words** in the search box.

3 Select the Fade Up Words effect in the Animate In category, and drag it onto the **on the move** text in the Composition panel.

After Effects adds the effect. Because it's a simple effect, there are no settings in the Effect Controls panel.

4 Manually preview the effect by dragging the current-time indicator from 0:00 to 1:00. The words fade in, so that they are all onscreen by 1:00.

About timecode and duration

The primary concept related to time is *duration*, or length. Each footage item, layer, and composition in a project has its own duration, which is reflected in the beginning and ending times displayed in the time rulers in the Composition, Layer, and Timeline panels.

The way you view and specify time in After Effects depends on the display style, or unit of measure, that you use to describe time. By default, After Effects displays time in Society of Motion Picture and Television Engineers (SMPTE) timecode: hours, minutes, seconds, and frames. Note that the figures are separated by semicolons in the After Effects interface, representing drop-frame timecode (which adjusts for the real-time frame rate), but this book uses a colon to represent non-drop-frame timecode.

To learn when and how to change to another system of time display, such as frames, or feet and frames of film, see After Effects Help.

About the Timeline panel

Use the Timeline panel to animate layer properties and set In and Out points for a layer. (In and Out points are the points at which a layer begins and ends in the composition.) Many of the Timeline panel controls are organized in columns of related functions. By default, the Timeline panel contains a number of columns and controls, as shown here:

A. Current time **B.** Composition name **C.** Timeline panel menu **D.** Audio/Video Switches column
E. Source Name/Layer Name column **F.** Layer switches **G.** Time graph/Graph Editor area

Understanding the time graph

The time graph portion of the Timeline panel (the right side) contains a time ruler, markers to indicate specific times, and duration bars for the layers in your composition.

A. Time navigator start and end brackets
B. Work area start and end brackets
C. Time zoom slider
D. Time ruler
E. Composition marker bin
F. Composition button

Before delving too deeply into animation, it will help to understand at least some of these controls. The duration of a composition, a layer, or a footage item is represented visually in the time graph. On the time ruler, the current-time indicator marks the frame you are viewing or editing, and the frame appears in the Composition panel.

The work area start and end brackets indicate the part of the composition that will be rendered for previews or final output. When you work on a composition, you may want to render only a portion of it by specifying a segment of the composition time ruler as a work area.

A composition's current time appears in the upper left corner of the Timeline panel. To move to a different time, drag the current-time indicator in the time ruler—or click the current-time field in the Timeline panel or Composition panel, type a new time, and click OK.

For more information about the Timeline panel, see After Effects Help.

Animating effects using keyframes

You'll add an effect to the type layer, but this time, you'll animate its settings using keyframes.

1 Go to the beginning of the time ruler by doing one of the following:

 • Drag the current-time indicator to the left in the time ruler so that it's positioned at 0:00.

 • Click the Current Time field in the Timeline panel or Composition panel, and type **00**. If you clicked in the Current Time field in the Composition panel, click OK to close the Go To Time dialog box.

2 Type **channel blur** in the search box in the Effects & Presets panel.

3 Drag the Channel Blur effect onto the Title Here layer in the Timeline panel.

After Effects adds the Channel Blur effect to the layer and displays its settings in the Effect Controls panel. The Channel Blur effect individually blurs the red, green, blue, and alpha channels in a layer. It will create an interesting look for the title.

4 In the Effect Controls panel, set the Red Blurriness, Green Blurriness, Blue Blurriness, and Alpha Blurriness values to **50**.

5 Click the stopwatch icon next to each of the settings you changed to create initial keyframes. The text will be blurred as it first appears.

Keyframes are used to create and control animation, effects, audio properties, and many other kinds of changes that occur over time. A keyframe marks the point in time where you specify a value, such as spatial position, opacity, or audio volume. Values between keyframes are *interpolated*. When you use keyframes to create a change over time, you must use at least two keyframes—one for the state at the beginning of the change, and one for the state at the end of the change.

6 From the Blur Dimensions menu, choose Vertical.

7 Go to 1:00 in the timeline.

8 Change the values to the following:

- Red Blurriness: **0**

- Green Blurriness: **0**

- Blue Blurriness: **0**

- Alpha Blurriness: **0**

9 Manually preview the effect by moving the current-time indicator from 0 to 1:00.

Changing the opacity of the background

The title looks good, but the ellipse is too bright. You'll change its opacity so that the water in the video shows through.

1 In the Timeline panel, select the Ellipse 1 layer.

2 Press T to reveal the layer's Opacity property.

3 Change the Opacity value to **20%**.

▶ **Tip:** To remember the keyboard shortcut for the Opacity property, think of it as *transparency*.

▶ **Tip:** To see how the title appears over the water, click the movement tab in the Timeline panel.

Previewing your work

You're probably eager to see the results of your work. You can preview your composition using the Preview panel, which is in the stacked panels on the right side of the application window in the default workspace. To preview your composition, click the Play/Stop button in the Preview panel, or press the spacebar on your keyboard.

1 In the title Timeline panel, hide all layer properties, and deselect all layers.

2 Make sure that the Video switch (👁) is selected for the layers that you want to preview—in this case, the Title Here and Ellipse 1 layers.

3 Press the Home key to go to the beginning of the time ruler.

4 Do one of the following:

- Click the Play/Stop button (▶) in the Preview panel.
- Press the spacebar.

5 To stop the preview, do one of the following:

- Click the Play/Stop button in the Preview panel.
- Press the spacebar.

▶ **Tip:** Verify that the work area brackets include all the frames you want to preview.

You've previewed a simple animation, so it probably played back in real time.

When you press the spacebar or click the Play/Stop button, After Effects caches the composition and allocates enough RAM to play the preview (with audio) as fast as the system allows, up to the frame rate of the composition. The number of frames played depends on the amount of RAM available to the application. Often, the preview will play in real time only after After Effects has cached all the included frames.

In the Timeline panel, the preview plays either the span of time you specify as the work area, or from the beginning of the time ruler. In the Layer and Footage panels, the preview plays only untrimmed footage. Before you preview, check which frames are designated as the work area.

Now you'll preview the entire composition—the animated text plus graphic effects.

6 Click the movement tab in the Timeline panel to bring it forward.

7 Make sure that the Video switch () is turned on for all of the layers in the composition except the audio layer, and press F2 to deselect all layers.

8 Drag the current-time indicator to the beginning of the time ruler, or press the Home key.

9 To start the preview, click the Play/Stop button (▶) in the Preview panel, or press the spacebar.

A green progress bar indicates which frames are cached to RAM. When all of the frames in the work area are cached, the preview plays back in real time. Until all the frames are cached, the playback may be slower and the audio may drag.

The more detail and precision you want to preview, the more RAM is required. You can control the amount of detail shown by changing the resolution, magnification, and preview quality of your composition. You can also limit the number of layers previewed by turning off the Video switch for certain layers, or limit the number of frames previewed by adjusting the composition's work area.

10 Press the spacebar to stop the preview.

11 Choose File > Save to save your project.

Optimizing performance in After Effects

How you configure After Effects and your computer determines how quickly After Effects renders projects. Complex compositions can require a large amount of memory to render, and the rendered movies can take a large amount of disk space to store. Search for "Improve Performance" in After Effects Help for tips that can help you configure your system, After Effects preferences, and your projects for better performance.

Rendering and exporting your composition

When you're finished with your masterpiece—as you are now—you can render and export it at the quality settings you choose, and create movies in the formats that you specify. You will learn about exporting compositions in subsequent lessons, especially in Lesson 14, "Rendering and Outputting."

Customizing workspaces

In the course of this project, you may have resized or repositioned some panels or opened new ones. As you modify a workspace, After Effects saves those modifications, so the next time you open the project, the most recent version of a workspace is used. However, you can choose to restore the original workspace at any time by choosing Window > Workspace > Reset "Essentials" To Saved Layout.

Alternatively, if you find yourself frequently using panels that aren't part of the Essentials workspace, or if you like to resize or group panels for different types of projects, you can save time by customizing the workspace to suit your needs. You can save any workspace configuration, or use any of the preset workspaces that come with After Effects. These predefined workspaces are suitable for different types of workflows, such as animation or effects work.

Using predefined workspaces

Take a minute to explore the predefined workspaces in After Effects.

1 If you closed the Lesson01_Finished.aep project, open it—or any other project—
 to explore the workspaces.

2 Click Animation in the Workspace bar, which is next to the Tools panel. Click
 the double arrows (>>) to see workspaces that don't fit in the Workspace bar.

After Effects opens the following panels at the right side of the application window:
Info, Preview, Effects & Presets, Motion Sketch, Wiggler, Smoother, and Audio.

You can also change workspaces using the Workspace menu.

3 Choose Window > Workspace > Motion Tracking.

Different panels open. The Info, Preview, and Tracker panels give you easy access
to the tools and controls you need to focus on tracking objects in your compositions.

Saving a custom workspace

You can save any workspace, at any time, as a custom workspace. Once saved,
new and edited workspaces appear in the Window > Workspace submenu and
in the Workspace bar at the top of the application window. If a project with
a custom workspace is opened on a system other than the one on which it was
created, After Effects looks for a workspace with a matching name. If After Effects
finds a match (and the monitor configuration matches), it uses that workspace;
if it can't find a match (or the monitor configuration doesn't match), it opens the
project using the current local workspace.

1 Close a panel by choosing Close Panel from its panel menu.

2 Choose Window > Effects & Presets to open another panel.

The Effects & Presets panel is added to the panel stack.

3 Choose Window > Workspace > Save As New Workspace. Enter a name for the workspace, and click OK to save it, or click Cancel if you don't want to save it.

4 Click Essentials in the Workspace bar.

Controlling the brightness of the user interface

You can brighten or darken the After Effects user interface. Changing the brightness preference affects panels, windows, and dialog boxes.

1 Choose Edit > Preferences > Appearance (Windows) or After Effects CC> Preferences > Appearance (Mac OS).

2 Drag the Brightness slider to the left or right, and notice how the screen changes.

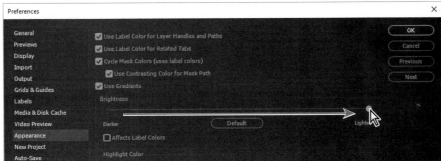

3 Click OK to save the new brightness setting or Cancel to leave your preferences unchanged. You can click Default to restore the default brightness setting.

4 Close the file without saving any changes.

Finding resources for using After Effects

For complete and up-to-date information about using After Effects panels, tools, and other application features, visit the Adobe website. To search for information in After Effects Help and support documents, as well as on other websites relevant to After Effects users, simply enter a search term in the Search Help box in the upper right corner of the application window. You can narrow the results to view only Adobe Help and support documents.

The Start window that appears when you open the application provides access to video tutorials and other information to help you get the most out of After Effects.

For additional resources, such as tips and techniques and the latest product information, check out the After Effects Help And Support page at helpx.adobe.com/after-effects.html.

Congratulations! You've finished Lesson 1. Now that you're acquainted with the After Effects workspace, you can continue to Lesson 2 to learn how to create and animate compositions using effects and preset animations, or you can proceed to another lesson in this book.

Review questions

1 What are the basic components of the After Effects workflow?

2 What is a composition?

3 How can you find missing footage?

4 How can you preview your work in After Effects?

5 How can you customize an After Effects workspace?

Review answers

1 Most After Effects workflows include these steps: importing and organizing footage, creating compositions and arranging layers, adding effects, animating elements, previewing your work, and rendering and exporting the final composition.

2 A composition is where you create all animation, layering, and effects. An After Effects composition has both spatial and temporal (time) dimensions. Compositions include one or more layers—video, audio, still images—arranged in the Composition panel and in the Timeline panel. Simple projects may include only one composition, while elaborate projects may include several compositions to organize large amounts of footage or intricate effects sequences.

3 To locate missing footage, choose File > Dependencies > Find Missing Footage. Or type **Missing Footage** into the Search field in the Project panel.

4 You can manually preview your work in After Effects by moving the current-time indicator, or you can press the spacebar or click the Play/Stop button in the Preview panel to preview your composition from the current-time indicator to the end of the composition. After Effects allocates enough RAM to play the preview (with audio) as fast as the system allows, up to the frame rate of the composition.

5 You can customize an After Effects workspace by dragging the panels into the configuration that best suits your working style. You can drag panels to new locations, move panels into or out of groups, place panels alongside each other, stack panels, and undock a panel so that it floats above the application window. As you rearrange panels, the other panels resize automatically to fit the application window. You can save custom workspaces by choosing Window > Workspace > Save As New Workspace.

2 CREATING A BASIC ANIMATION USING EFFECTS AND PRESETS

Lesson overview

In this lesson, you'll learn how to do the following:

- Use Adobe Bridge to preview and import footage items.
- Work with the layers of an imported Adobe Illustrator file.
- Apply drop-shadow and emboss effects.
- Apply a text animation preset.
- Adjust the time range of a text animation preset.
- Precompose layers.
- Apply a dissolve transition effect.
- Adjust the transparency of a layer.
- Render an animation for broadcast use.

 This lesson will take about an hour to complete. Download the project files for this lesson, following the instructions in the Getting Started section under "Accessing the lesson files and Web Edition," if you haven't already done so. As you work on this lesson, you'll preserve the start files. If you need to restore the start files, download them from your Account page.

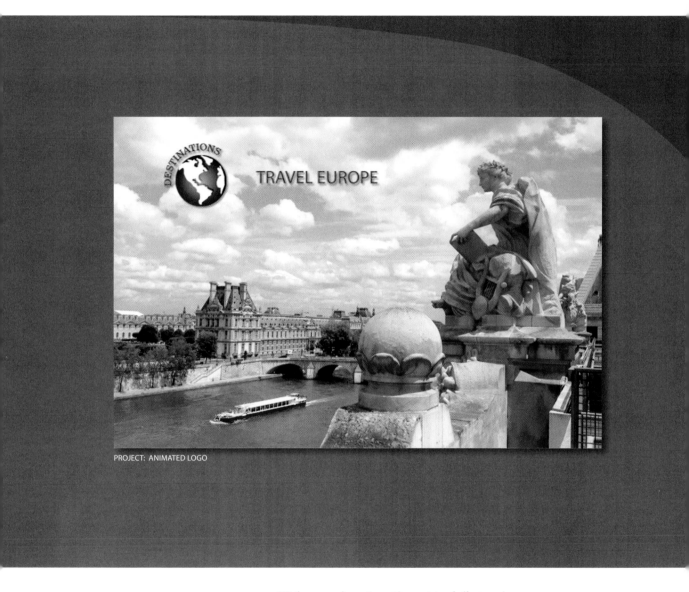

PROJECT: ANIMATED LOGO

Hit the ground running with a variety of effects and animation presets in After Effects. You can use them to create great-looking animations quickly and easily.

Getting started

In this lesson, you will become more familiar with the Adobe After Effects project workflow. You'll learn new ways to accomplish basic tasks as you create a simple identification graphic for a fictional travel show called "Travel Europe" on the fictional Destinations cable network. You will animate the travel show ID so that it fades to become a watermark that can appear in the lower right corner of the screen during other TV programs. Then you'll export the ID for use in broadcast output.

First, take a look at the final project files to see what you'll be doing.

1 Make sure the following files are in the Lessons/Lesson02 folder on your hard disk, or download them from your Account page at www.peachpit.com now:

- In the Assets folder: destinations_logo.ai, ParisRiver.jpg

- In the Sample_Movies folder: Lesson02.avi, Lesson02.mov

2 Open and play the Lesson02.avi sample movie in Windows Media Player or the Lesson02.mov sample movie in QuickTime Player to see what you will create in this lesson. When you are done, close Windows Media Player or QuickTime Player. You may delete the sample movies from your hard disk if you have limited storage space.

Before you begin the lesson, you'll restore the default application settings for After Effects. See "Restoring default preferences" on page 2 for more information.

3 Start After Effects, and then immediately hold down Ctrl+Alt+Shift (Windows) or Command+Option+Shift (Mac OS) to restore default preferences settings. When prompted, click OK to delete your preferences.

4 In the Start window, click New Project.

After Effects opens to display a blank, untitled project.

5 Choose File > Save As > Save As.

6 In the Save As dialog box, navigate to the Lessons/Lesson02/ Finished_Project folder.

7 Name the project **Lesson02_Finished.aep**, and then click Save.

Importing footage using Adobe Bridge

In Lesson 1, you chose File > Import > File to import footage. However, you can also use Adobe Bridge: a powerful, flexible tool for organizing, browsing, and locating the assets you need to create content for print, web, television, DVD, film, and mobile devices. Adobe Bridge keeps native Adobe files (such as PSD and PDF files) as well as non-Adobe application files available for easy access. You can drag assets into your layouts, projects, and compositions as needed; preview your assets; and even add metadata (file information) to assets to make files easier to locate.

Adobe Bridge is not automatically installed with After Effects CC. You'll need to install it separately. If Bridge is not installed, you'll be prompted to install it when you choose File > Browse In Bridge.

In this exercise, you will jump to Adobe Bridge to import the still image that will serve as the background of your composition.

Tip: You can use Adobe Bridge separately to manage your files. To open Adobe Bridge directly, choose Adobe Bridge from the Start menu (Windows) or double-click the Adobe Bridge icon in the Applications / Adobe Bridge folder (Mac OS).

1 Choose File > Browse In Bridge. If you receive a message about enabling an extension to Adobe Bridge, click Yes.

Adobe Bridge opens, displaying a collection of panels, menus, and buttons.

2 Click the Folders tab in the upper left corner of Adobe Bridge.

3 In the Folders panel, navigate to the Lessons/Lesson02/Assets folder. Click the arrows to open nested folders. You can also double-click folder thumbnail icons in the Content panel.

Note: We're using the Essentials workspace, which is the default workspace in Bridge.

The Content panel updates interactively. For example, when you select the Assets folder in the Folders panel, thumbnail previews of the folder's contents appear in the Content panel. Adobe Bridge displays previews of image files such as those in PSD, TIFF, and JPEG formats, as well as Illustrator vector files, multipage Adobe PDF files, QuickTime movie files, and more.

Tip: To prioritize different information in Adobe Bridge, change the workspace: Choose Window > Workspace, and then select a workspace. See Adobe Bridge Help to learn about customizing Adobe Bridge.

4 Drag the thumbnail slider at the bottom of the Adobe Bridge window to enlarge the thumbnail previews.

5 Select the ParisRiver.jpg file in the Content panel, and notice that it appears in the Preview panel as well. Information about the file, including its creation date, bit depth, and file size, appears in the Metadata panel.

6 Double-click the ParisRiver.jpg thumbnail in the Content panel to place the file in your After Effects project. Alternatively, you can drag the ParisRiver.jpg thumbnail into the Project panel in After Effects.

7 Return to After Effects, if you're not already there.

You can close Adobe Bridge if you'd like. You won't be using it again during this lesson.

Creating a new composition

Following the After Effects workflow you learned in Lesson 1, the next step to building the travel show ID is to create a new composition. In Lesson 1, you created the composition based on footage items that were selected in the Project panel. You can also create an empty composition, and then add your footage items to it.

1 Create a new composition by doing one of the following:

- Click the Create A New Composition button (▣) at the bottom of the Project panel.

- Choose Composition > New Composition.

- Press Ctrl+N (Windows) or Command+N (Mac OS).

2 In the Composition Settings dialog box, do the following:

- Name the composition **Destinations**.

- Choose NTSC D1 from the Preset pop-up menu. NTSC D1 is the resolution for standard-definition television in the United States and some other countries. This preset automatically sets the width, height, pixel aspect ratio, and frame rate for the composition to NTSC standards.

- In the Duration field, type **300** to specify 3 seconds.

- Click OK.

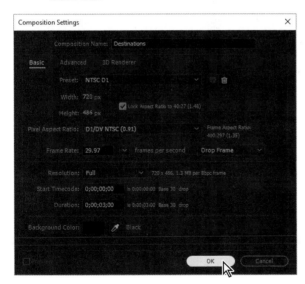

After Effects displays an empty composition named Destinations in the Composition panel and in the Timeline panel. Now, you'll add the background.

3 Drag the ParisRiver.jpg footage item from the Project panel to the Timeline panel to add it to the Destinations composition.

▶ **Tip:** The keyboard shortcut for fitting a layer to a composition is Ctrl+Alt+F (Windows) or Command+Option+F (Mac OS).

4 With the ParisRiver layer selected in the Timeline panel, choose Layer > Transform > Fit To Comp to scale the background image to the dimensions of the composition.

Importing the foreground element

Your background is now in place. The foreground object you'll use is a layered vector graphic that was created in Illustrator.

1 Choose File > Import > File.

2 In the Import File dialog box, select the destinations_logo.ai file in the Lessons/Lesson02/Assets folder. (The file appears as destinations_logo if file extensions are hidden.)

3 Choose Composition from the Import As menu. (In Mac OS, you may need to click Options to display the Import As menu). Then click Import or Open.

The Illustrator file is added to the Project panel as a composition named destinations_logo. A folder named destinations_logo Layers also appears. This folder contains the three individual layers of the Illustrator file. Click the triangle to open the folder and see its contents if you like.

4 Drag the destinations_logo composition file from the Project panel into the Timeline panel above the ParisRiver layer.

You should now see both the background image and the logo in the Composition panel and in the Timeline panel.

Working with imported Illustrator layers

The destinations_logo graphic was created in Illustrator; your job in After Effects is to add text and animate it. To work with the layers of the Illustrator file independently of the background footage, you'll open the destinations_logo composition in its own Timeline and Composition panels.

1 Double-click the destinations_logo composition in the Project panel. The composition opens in its own Timeline and Composition panels.

2 Select the Horizontal Type tool (T) in the Tools panel, and click in the Composition panel.

3 Type **TRAVEL EUROPE**, all capital letters, and then select all of the text you just entered.

4 In the Character panel, select a sans serif typeface such as Myriad Pro, and change the font size to **24** pixels. Click the eyedropper in the Character panel, and click the rotated "Destinations" text on the logo to select the green color. After Effects applies it to the text you typed. Leave all other options in the Character panel at their defaults.

● **Note:** If the Character panel isn't open, choose Window > Character. You may need to expand the width of the panel to see the eyedropper.

You'll learn more about working with text in Lesson 3, "Animating Text."

5 Select the Selection tool (▶), and then drag the text in the Composition panel to position it as it appears in the following figure. Notice that when you switch to the Selection tool, the generic Text 1 layer name in the Timeline panel changes to TRAVEL EUROPE, the text you typed.

▶ **Tip:** Choose View > Show Grid to make the nonprinting grid visible to help you position objects. Choose View > Show Grid again to hide the grid later.

Applying effects to a layer

Now you will return to the main composition, Destinations, and apply an effect to the destinations_logo layer. This will apply the effect to all of the layers nested in the destinations_logo composition.

1 Click the Destinations tab in the Timeline panel, and then select the destinations_logo layer.

The effect you create next will be applied only to the logo elements, not to the background image of the river.

2 Choose Effect > Perspective > Drop Shadow.

A soft-edged shadow appears behind the nested layers of the destinations_logo layer—the logo graphic, the rotated type, and the words *Travel Europe*—in the Composition panel. You can customize the effect using the Effect Controls panel, which appears in front of the Project panel when you apply an effect.

Applying and controlling effects

You can apply or remove an effect at any time. Once you've applied effects to a layer, you can temporarily turn off one or all of the effects in the layer to concentrate on another aspect of your composition. Effects that are turned off do not appear in the Composition panel, and typically aren't included when the layer is previewed or rendered.

By default, when you apply an effect to a layer, the effect is active for the duration of the layer. However, you can make an effect start and stop at specific times, or make the effect more or less intense over time. You'll learn more about creating animation using keyframes or expressions in Lesson 5, "Animating a Multimedia Presentation," and Lesson 6, "Animating Layers."

You can apply and edit effects on adjustment layers just as you do with other layers. Note, however, that when you apply an effect to an adjustment layer, the effect is applied to all layers below it in the Timeline panel.

Effects can also be saved, browsed, and applied as animation presets.

3 In the Effect Controls panel, reduce the drop shadow's Distance to **3** and increase its Softness to **4**. You can set each value by clicking the field and typing the number or by dragging the blue value.

The drop shadow is nice, but the logo will stand out even more if you apply an emboss effect. You can use either the Effect menu or the Effects & Presets panel to locate and apply effects.

4 Click the Effects & Presets tab to open the panel. Then click the triangle next to Stylize to expand the category.

5 With the destinations_logo layer selected in the Timeline panel, drag the Color Emboss effect into the Composition panel.

The Color Emboss effect sharpens the edges of objects in the layer without suppressing the original colors. The Effect Controls panel displays the Color Emboss effect and its settings below the Drop Shadow effect.

6 Choose File > Save to save your work.

Applying an animation preset

You've positioned thetype and applied some effects to it. It's time to add some animation! You will learn several ways to animate text in Lesson 3; for now, you'll use a simple animation preset that will fade the words *Travel Europe* onto the screen next to the logo. You'll need to work in the destinations_logo composition so that you can apply the animation to only the TRAVEL EUROPE text layer.

1 Click the destinations_logo tab in the Timeline panel, and select the TRAVEL EUROPE layer.

2 Move the current-time indicator to 1:10, which is the point at which you want the text to start fading in.

3 In the Effects & Presets panel, choose Animation Presets > Text > Blurs.

4 Drag the Bullet Train animation preset onto the TRAVEL EUROPE layer in the Timeline panel or over the words *Travel Europe* in the Composition panel. Don't worry about the text disappearing—you're looking at the first frame of the animation, which happens to be blank.

5 Click a blank area of the Timeline panel to deselect the TRAVEL EUROPE layer, and then drag the current-time indicator to 2:00 to manually preview the text animation. The text appears, letter by letter, until the words *Travel Europe* are fully onscreen at 2:00.

Precomposing layers for a new animation

The travel show ID is coming along nicely, and you're probably eager to preview the complete animation. Before you do, however, you'll add a dissolve to all of the logo elements except the words *Travel Europe*. To do this, you need to precompose the other three layers of the destinations_logo composition: rotated type, Globe logo, and crop area.

Precomposing is a way to nest layers within a composition. Precomposing moves the layers to a new composition, which takes the place of the selected layers. When you want to change the order in which layer components are rendered, precomposing is a quick way to create intermediate levels of nesting in an existing hierarchy.

1 Shift-click to select the rotated type, Globe logo, and crop area layers in the destinations_logo Timeline panel.

2 Choose Layer > Pre-compose.

3 In the Pre-compose dialog box, name the new composition **Dissolve_logo**. Make sure the Move All Attributes Into The New Composition option is selected. Then click OK.

The three layers are replaced in the destinations_logo Timeline panel with a single layer, Dissolve_logo. This new, precomposed layer contains the three layers that you selected in step 1. You can apply the dissolve effect to it without affecting the TRAVEL EUROPE text layer and its Bullet Train animation.

4 Make sure the Dissolve_logo layer is selected in the Timeline panel, and press the Home key or drag the current-time indicator to go to 0:00.

▶ **Tip:** To locate the Dissolve – Vapor preset quickly, type **vap** in the search box in the Effects & Presets panel.

5 In the Effects & Presets panel, choose Animation Presets > Transitions – Dissolves, and then drag the Dissolve – Vapor animation preset onto the Dissolve_logo layer in the Timeline panel or onto the Composition panel.

The Dissolve – Vapor animation preset includes three components—a master dissolve, a box blur, and a solid composite, all of which appear in the Effect Controls panel. The default settings are fine for this project.

6 Choose File > Save.

Previewing the effects

It's time to preview all of the effects together.

1 Click the Destinations tab in the Timeline panel to switch to the main composition. Press the Home key or drag the current-time indicator to make sure you're at the beginning of the time ruler.

2 Make sure the Video switch (●) is selected for both layers in the Destinations Timeline panel.

3 Click the Play button (▶) in the Preview panel, or press the spacebar, to watch the preview. Press the spacebar to stop playback at any time.

Adding transparency

Many TV stations display logos semitransparently in the corner of the frame to emphasize the brand. You'll reduce the opacity of the ID so that it can be used this way.

1 Still in the Destinations Timeline panel, go to 2:24.

2 Select the destinations_logo layer, and press T to display its Opacity property. By default, the Opacity is 100%—fully opaque. Click the stopwatch icon (⏱) to set an Opacity keyframe at this point in time.

3 Press the End key or drag the current-time indicator to go to the end of the time ruler (2:29), and change the Opacity to **40%**. After Effects adds a keyframe.

The logo appears, the words *Travel Europe* fly in, and it all fades to 40% opacity.

4 Click the Play button (▶) in the Preview panel, press the spacebar, or press 0 on your numeric keypad to preview your composition. Press the spacebar to stop playback when you're done.

5 Choose File > Save to save your project.

Rendering the composition

● **Note:** For more about output formats and rendering, see Lesson 14, "Rendering and Outputting."

You're ready to prepare your travel show ID for output. When you create output, the layers of a composition and each layer's masks, effects, and properties are rendered frame by frame into one or more output files or, in the case of an image sequence, into a series of consecutive files.

Making a movie from your final composition can take a few minutes or many hours, depending on the composition's frame size, quality, complexity, and compression method. When you place your composition in the Render Queue, it becomes a render item that uses the render settings assigned to it.

After Effects provides a variety of formats and compression types for rendering output; the format you choose depends on the medium from which you'll play your final output or on the requirements of your hardware, such as a video-editing system.

● **Note:** For output to final-delivery formats, you can use Adobe Media Encoder, which is installed when you install After Effects. You'll learn about Adobe Media Encoder in Lesson 14, "Rendering and Outputting."

You'll render and export the composition so that it can be broadcast on television.

1 Do one of the following to add the composition to the Render Queue:

 - Select the Destinations composition in the Project panel, and choose Composition > Add To Render Queue. The Render Queue panel opens automatically.

 - Choose Window > Render Queue to open the Render Queue panel, and then drag the Destinations composition from the Project panel onto the Render Queue panel.

▶ **Tip:** The keyboard shortcut for the Maximize Panel Group command is the accent grave character (`), which shares a key with the tilde character (~).

2 Double-click the Render Queue tab to maximize the panel so that it fills the application window.

3 Click the triangle to expand the Render Settings options. By default, After Effects renders compositions with Best Quality and Full Resolution. The default settings are fine for this project.

4 Click the triangle to expand the Output Module options. By default, After Effects uses lossless compression to encode the rendered composition into a movie file, which is fine for this project. But you need to identify where to save the file.

5 Click the blue words *Not Yet Specified* next to the Output To pop-up menu.

6 In the Output Movie To dialog box, accept the default movie name (Destinations), select the Lessons/Lesson02/Finished_Project folder for the location, and then click Save.

7 Back in the Render Queue panel, click the Render button.

After Effects displays a progress bar in the Render Queue panel as it encodes the file, and issues an audio alert when all items in the Render Queue have been rendered and encoded.

8 When the movie is complete, double-click the Render Queue tab to restore your workspace.

9 If you want to see your final product, double-click the Destinations.avi or Destinations.mov file in the Lessons/Lesson02/Finished_Project folder to open it in Windows Media Player or QuickTime, and then play the file.

10 Save and close the project file, and then quit After Effects.

Congratulations. You've created a travel show ID suitable for broadcast.

Review questions

1 How do you use Adobe Bridge to preview and import files?

2 What is *precomposing*?

3 How do you customize an effect?

4 How do you modify the transparency of a layer in a composition?

Review answers

1 Choose File > Browse In Bridge to jump from After Effects to Adobe Bridge. If Bridge isn't installed, you'll be prompted to download and install it. In Bridge, you can search for and preview image assets. When you locate the asset you want to use in an After Effects project, double-click it, or drag it to the Project panel.

2 *Precomposing* is a way to nest layers within a composition. Precomposing moves the layers to a new composition, which takes the place of the selected layers. When you want to change the order in which layer components are rendered, precomposing is a quick way to create intermediate levels of nesting in an existing hierarchy.

3 After you apply an effect to a layer in a composition, you can customize its properties in the Effect Controls panel. This panel opens automatically when you apply the effect, or you can open it at any time by selecting the layer with the effect and choosing Window > Effect Controls.

4 To modify the transparency of a layer, reduce its opacity. Select the layer in the Timeline panel, press T to reveal its Opacity property, and enter a value lower than 100%.

3 ANIMATING TEXT

Lesson overview

In this lesson, you'll learn how to do the following:

- Create and animate text layers.
- Stylize text using the Character and Paragraph panels.
- Apply and customize text animation presets.
- Preview animation presets in Adobe Bridge.
- Install fonts using Adobe Typekit.
- Animate text using keyframes.
- Animate layers using parenting.
- Edit and animate imported Adobe Photoshop text.
- Use a text animator group to animate selected characters on a layer.

 This lesson will take approximately two hours to complete. Download the project files for this lesson, following the instructions in the Getting Started section under "Accessing the lesson files and Web Edition," if you haven't already done so. As you work on this lesson, you'll preserve the start files. If you need to restore the start files, download them from your Account page.

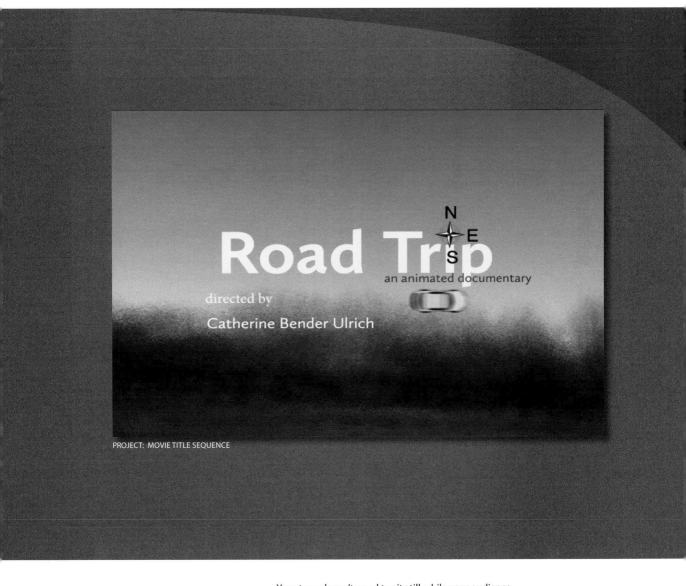

PROJECT: MOVIE TITLE SEQUENCE

Your type doesn't need to sit still while your audience is reading it. In this lesson, you'll learn several ways to animate type in After Effects, including timesaving methods unique to text layers.

Getting started

Adobe After Effects offers many ways to animate text. You can animate text layers by manually creating keyframes in the Timeline panel, using animation presets, or using expressions. You can even animate individual characters or words in a text layer. In this lesson, you'll employ several different animation techniques, including some that are unique to text, while you design the opening title credits for an animated documentary called *Road Trip*. You'll also take advantage of Adobe Typekit to install a font for use in your project.

As in other projects, you'll begin by previewing the movie you're creating, and then you'll open After Effects.

1 Make sure the following files are in the Lessons/Lesson03 folder on your hard disk, or download them from your Account page at www.peachpit.com now:

 • In the Assets folder: background_movie.mov, car.ai, compass.swf, credits.psd

 • In the Sample_Movies folder: Lesson03.mov, Lesson03.avi

2 Open and play the Lesson03.avi sample movie in Windows Media Player or the Lesson03.mov sample movie in QuickTime Player to see what you will create in this lesson. When you are done, close Windows Media Player or QuickTime Player. You may delete the sample movies from your hard disk if you have limited storage space.

As you start the application, restore the default settings for After Effects. See "Restoring default preferences" on page 2.

3 Start After Effects, and then immediately hold down Ctrl+Alt+Shift (Windows) or Command+Option+Shift (Mac OS) to restore default preferences settings. When prompted, click OK to delete your preferences.

4 Close the Start window.

After Effects opens to display a blank, untitled project.

5 Choose File > Save As > Save As, and navigate to the Lessons/Lesson03/Finished_Project folder.

6 Name the project **Lesson03_Finished.aep**, and then click Save.

Importing the footage

You need to import two footage items to begin this lesson.

1 Double-click an empty area of the Project panel to open the Import File dialog box.

2 Navigate to the Lessons/Lesson03/Assets folder on your hard disk, Ctrl-click (Windows) or Command-click (Mac OS) to select both the background_movie.mov and compass.swf files, and then click Import or Open.

After Effects can import several file formats including Adobe Photoshop and Adobe Illustrator files, as well as QuickTime and AVI movies. This makes After Effects an incredibly powerful application for compositing and motion graphics work.

Creating the composition

Now, you'll create the composition.

1 Press Ctrl+N (Windows) or Command+N (Mac OS) to create a new composition.

2 In the Composition Settings dialog box, name the composition **Title_Sequence**, choose NTSC DV from the Preset menu, and set the Duration to **10:00**, which is the length of the background movie. Then click OK.

3 Drag the background_movie.mov and compass.swf footage items from the Project panel to the Timeline panel. Arrange the layers so that compass.swf is above background_movie.mov in the layer stack.

4 Choose File > Save.

You're ready to add the title text to the composition.

About text layers

In After Effects, you can add text with flexibility and precision. The Tools, Character, and Paragraph panels contain a wide range of text controls. You can create and edit horizontal or vertical text directly on the screen in the Composition panel, and quickly change the font, style, size, and color of the text. You can apply changes to individual characters and set formatting options for entire paragraphs, including alignment, justification, and word-wrapping. In addition to all of these style features, After Effects provides tools for easily animating specific characters and properties, such as text opacity and hue.

After Effects uses two types of text: point text and paragraph text. Use *point text* to enter a single word or line of characters; use *paragraph text* to enter and format text as one or more paragraphs.

In many ways, text layers are just like any other layers in After Effects. You can apply effects and expressions to text layers, animate them, designate them as 3D layers, and edit the 3D text while viewing from multiple angles. As with layers imported from Illustrator, text layers are continuously rasterized, so when you scale the layer or resize the text, it retains crisp, resolution-independent edges. The two main differences between text layers and other layers are that you cannot open a text layer in its own Layer panel and you can animate the text in a text layer using special text-animator properties and selectors.

Installing a font using Typekit

Hundreds of fonts are available through Adobe Typekit, which is included with an Adobe Creative Cloud membership. You'll use Typekit to install a font that will work well for the title text. When you install a Typekit font on your system, it's available in any application.

1 Choose File > Add Fonts From Typekit.

After Effects opens the Adobe Typekit page in your default browser.

2 Make sure you're signed in to Creative Cloud. If not, click Sign In at the top of the screen, and then enter your Adobe ID.

You can browse fonts on the Adobe Typekit website, but because there are so many, it's often more efficient to filter them or to search for a specific font. You'll filter fonts to see those that meet your requirements.

3 Make sure the My Library tab is selected so you'll see all the fonts.

4 Choose Sort By Name from the pop-up menu in the upper right corner, and deselect Include Web Only Families. Then, on the right side of the page, click the Sans Serif button in the Classification area. In the Properties area, select the buttons for medium weight, medium width, low contrast, and standard capitalization.

● **Note:** If you haven't signed in to Creative Cloud, you'll see the Full Library and Limited Library tabs instead.

Typekit displays several fonts that meet the requirements you specified. You'll preview the fonts to see which one looks best.

5 Type **Road Trip** in the sample text field, and move the slider to decrease the sample text size so you can see the full title.

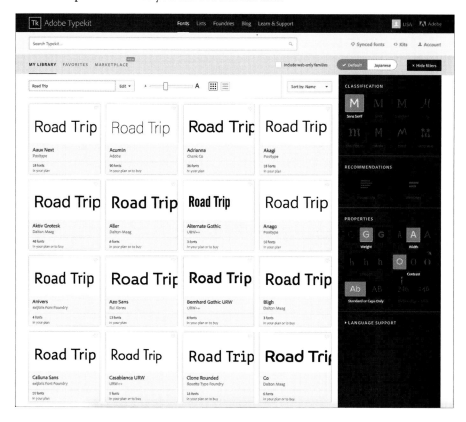

Using your own text as the sample text lets you get a feel for how a font will work in your project. Calluna Sans will work nicely.

6 Hover your mouse over Calluna Sans until you see a green overlay, and then click it. (If you don't see Calluna Sans, click Next Page until you do, or choose a different font family.)

Typekit displays sample text for all the fonts in the selected family, as well as additional information about the font.

Note: Depending on your system and your Internet connection, it may take a few minutes for Typekit to sync your fonts.

7 Click Sync next to the Regular and Bold versions of the font.

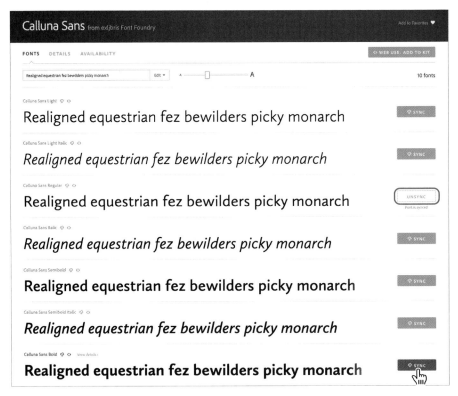

The selected fonts are automatically added to your system and are then available in any application, including After Effects. After you've synced your fonts, you can close Typekit and your browser.

Creating and formatting point text

When you enter point text, each line of text is independent—the length of a line increases or decreases as you edit the text, but it doesn't wrap to the next line. The text you enter appears in a new text layer. The small line through the I-beam marks the position of the text baseline.

1 In the Tools panel, select the Horizontal Type tool (T).

2 Click anywhere in the Composition panel, and type **Road Trip**. Then press Enter on the numeric keypad to exit text-editing mode and to select the text layer in the Composition panel. Or, you can select the layer name to exit text-editing mode.

● **Note:** If you press Enter or Return on the regular keyboard instead of on the numeric keypad, you'll begin a new paragraph.

Using the Character panel

The Character panel provides options for formatting characters. If text is highlighted, changes you make in the Character panel affect only the highlighted text. If no text is highlighted, changes you make in the Character panel affect the selected text layers and the text layers' selected Source Text keyframes, if any exist. If no text is highlighted and no text layers are selected, changes you make in the Character panel become the defaults for the next text entry.

1 Choose Window > Workspace > Text to display only those panels you need while working with text.

2 Select the Road Trip text layer in the Timeline panel.

3 In the Character panel, choose Calluna Sans from the Font Family menu.

4 Choose Bold from the Font Style menu.

5 Set the Font Size to **90** pixels.

6 Leave all other options at their default settings.

▶ **Tip:** To open the panels individually, choose Window > Character or Window > Paragraph. To open both panels, select the Horizontal Type tool, and then click the Toggle The Character And Paragraph Panels button in the Tools panel.

▶ **Tip:** To select a font quickly, begin typing its name in the Font Family box. The Font Family menu jumps to the first font on your system that matches the letters you've typed. If a type layer is selected, the text in the Composition panel takes on the newly selected font.

Using the Paragraph panel

Use the Paragraph panel to set options that apply to an entire paragraph, such as alignment, indentation, and leading. For point text, each line is a separate paragraph. You can use the Paragraph panel to set formatting options for a single paragraph, multiple paragraphs, or all paragraphs in a text layer. You just need to make one adjustment in the Paragraph panel for this composition's title text.

1 In the Paragraph panel, click the Center Text button. This aligns horizontal text to the center of the layer, not to the center of the composition.

● **Note:** Your screen may look different, depending on where you started typing.

2 Leave all other options at their default settings.

Positioning the type

To precisely position layers, such as the text layer you're working on now, you can display rulers, guides, and grids in the Composition panel. These visual reference tools don't appear in the final rendered movie.

1 Make sure the Road Trip text layer is selected in the Timeline panel.

2 Choose Layer > Transform > Fit To Comp Width. This scales the layer to fit to the width of the composition.

Now you can position the text layer using a grid.

3 Choose View > Show Grid and then View > Snap To Grid.

4 Using the Selection tool (▶), drag the text up in the Composition panel until the base of the letters sits on the horizontal gridline in the center of the composition. Press Shift after you start dragging to constrain the movement and help you position the text.

5 When the layer is in position, choose View > Show Grid again to hide the grid.

This project isn't destined for broadcast TV, so it's okay that the title extends beyond the title-safe and action-safe areas of the composition at the beginning of the animation.

6 Click Essentials in the Workspace bar at the top of the application window to return to the Essentials workspace. (Click the double arrows to see Essentials if it doesn't fit in the Workspace bar.)

7 Choose File > Save to save your project.

Using a text animation preset

Now you're ready to animate the title. The easiest way to do that is to use one of the many animation presets that come with After Effects. After applying an animation preset, you can customize it and save it to use again in other projects.

1 Press the Home key or go to 0:00 to make sure the current-time indicator is at the beginning of the time ruler.

After Effects applies animation presets from the current time.

2 Select the Road Trip text layer.

Browsing animation presets

Note: If Bridge isn't installed, you'll be prompted to install it when you choose Browse In Bridge. For more information, see page 2.

You already applied an animation preset using the Effects & Presets panel in Lesson 2, "Creating a Basic Animation Using Effects and Presets." But what if you're not sure which animation preset you want to use? To help you choose the right animation preset for your projects, you can preview them in Adobe Bridge.

1 Choose Animation > Browse Presets. Adobe Bridge opens, displaying the contents of the After Effects Presets folder.

2 In the Content panel, double-click the Text folder, and then the Blurs folder.

3 Click to select the first preset, Blur By Word. Adobe Bridge plays a sample of the animation in the Preview panel.

4 Select a few other presets, and watch them in the Preview panel.

Note: With some installations of Bridge, the effect may not be applied from Bridge. In that case, double-click the preset in the Effects & Presets panel to apply it.

5 Preview the Evaporate preset, and then double-click its thumbnail preview. Alternatively, you can right-click (Windows) or Control-click (Mac OS) the thumbnail and choose Place In Adobe After Effects CC 2017.

Note: Leave Adobe Bridge open in the background. You'll use it again later in the lesson.

After Effects applies the preset to the selected layer, which is the Road Trip layer, but nothing appears to change in the composition. This is because at 0:00, the first frame of the animation, the letters haven't yet evaporated.

Previewing a range of frames

Now, you'll preview the animation. Although the composition is 10 seconds long, you need to preview only the first few seconds, since that is where the text animation occurs.

1 In the Timeline panel, move the current-time indicator to 3:00, and press N to set the end bracket of the work area.

2 Press the spacebar to watch a preview of the animation.

The letters appear to evaporate into the background. It looks great—but you want the letters to fade in and remain onscreen, not disappear. You'll customize the preset to suit your needs.

3 Press the spacebar to stop the preview, and then press the Home key to move the current-time indicator back to 0:00.

Customizing an animation preset

After you apply an animation preset to a layer, all of its properties and keyframes are listed in the Timeline panel. You'll use those properties to customize the preset.

1 Select the Road Trip text layer in the Timeline panel, and press U.

The U key, sometimes referred to as the *Überkey*, is a valuable keyboard shortcut that reveals all the animated properties of a layer.

2 Click the Offset property name to select both of its keyframes.

▶ **Tip:** If you press U twice (UU), After Effects displays all modified properties for the layer, instead of only the animated properties. Press the U key again to hide all the layer's properties.

The Offset property specifies how much to offset the start and end of the selection.

3 Choose Animation > Keyframe Assistant > Time-Reverse Keyframes.

The Time-Reverse Keyframes command switches the order of the two Offset keyframes so that the letters are invisible at the beginning of the composition, and then emerge into view.

4 Drag the current-time indicator from 0:00 to 3:00 to manually preview the animation you edited.

The letters now fade into, rather than disappear from, the composition.

5 Press U to hide the layer's properties.

6 Press the End key to move the current-time indicator to the end of the time ruler, and then press N to set the end bracket of the work area.

7 Choose File > Save to save your project.

Animating with scale keyframes

The text layer was scaled to nearly 200% when you applied the Fit To Comp Width command to it earlier in this lesson. Now, you'll animate the layer's scale so that the type gradually shrinks down to its original size.

1 In the Timeline panel, move the current-time indicator to 3:00.

2 Select the Road Trip text layer, and press the S key to reveal its Scale property.

3 Click the stopwatch icon (🕒) to add a Scale keyframe at the current time (3:00).

4 Move the current-time indicator to 5:00.

5 Reduce the layer's Scale values to **100, 100%**. After Effects adds a new Scale keyframe at the current time.

Previewing the scale animation

Now you'll preview the change.

1 Move the current-time indicator to 5:10, and press N to set the end of the work area. The scale animation ends shortly before 5:10.

2 Press the spacebar to preview the animation from 0:00 to 5:10. The movie title fades in and then scales to a smaller size.

3 Press the spacebar to stop playback after you've viewed the animation.

Adding Easy Ease

The beginning and end of the scale animation are rather abrupt. In nature, nothing comes to an absolute stop. Instead, objects ease into and out of starting and stopping points.

1 Right-click (Windows) or Control-click (Mac OS) the Scale keyframe at 3:00, and choose Keyframe Assistant > Easy Ease Out. The keyframe becomes a left-pointing icon.

2 Right-click (Windows) or Control-click (Mac OS) the Scale keyframe at 5:00, and choose Keyframe Assistant > Easy Ease In. The keyframe becomes a right-pointing icon.

3 Watch another preview. Press the spacebar to stop it when you're done.

4 Choose File > Save.

Animating using parenting

The next task is to make it appear as if the virtual camera is zooming away from the composition. The text scale animation you just applied gets you halfway there, but you need to animate the scale of the compass as well. You could manually animate the compass layer, but it's easier to take advantage of parenting relationships in After Effects.

1 Press the Home key, or drag the current-time indicator to the beginning of the time ruler.

2 In the Timeline panel, click the Parent pop-up menu for the compass layer, and choose 1. Road Trip.

This sets the Road Trip text layer as the parent of the compass layer, which in turn becomes the child layer.

As the child layer, the compass layer inherits the Scale keyframes of its parent layer (Road Trip). Not only is this a quick way to animate the compass, but it also ensures that the compass scales at the same rate and by the same amount as the text layer.

3 In the Timeline panel, move the compass layer above the Road Trip text layer.

● **Note:** When you move the compass layer, its parent becomes 2. Road Trip, because Road Trip is now the second layer.

4 Move the current-time indicator to 9:29, so you can clearly see the compass in the Composition panel.

5 In the Composition panel, drag the compass so that its anchor point is over the dot in the letter *i* in the word *trip*. Alternatively, you can select the compass layer in the Timeline panel, press P to reveal its Position property, and then enter **124, −62**.

6 Move the current-time indicator from 3:00 to 5:00 to manually preview the scaling. Both the text and the compass scale down in size, so that it appears that the camera is moving away from the scene.

7 Press the Home key to return to 0:00, and drag the work area end bracket to the end of the time ruler.

8 Select the Road Trip layer in the Timeline panel, and press S to hide its Scale property. If you entered Position values for the compass, select the compass layer, and press P to hide the Position property, too. Then choose File > Save.

About parent and child layers

Parenting assigns one layer's transformations to another layer, called a *child layer*. Creating a parenting relationship between layers synchronizes the changes in the parent layer with the corresponding transformation values of the child layers, except opacity. For example, if a parent layer moves 5 pixels to the right of its starting position, then the child layer also moves 5 pixels to the right of its starting position. A layer can have only one parent, but a layer can be a parent to any number of 2D or 3D layers within the same composition. Parenting layers is useful for creating complex animations, such as linking the movements of a marionette or depicting the orbits of planets in the solar system.

For more on parent and child layers, see After Effects Help.

Animating imported Photoshop text

If all text animations involved just two short words, such as *road trip*, life would be easy. But in the real world, you may often have to work with longer blocks of text, and they can be tedious to enter manually. Fortunately, you can import text from Photoshop or Illustrator. You can preserve text layers, edit them, and animate them in After Effects.

Importing text

Some of the remaining text for this composition is in a layered Photoshop file, which you'll import now.

1 Click the Project tab to bring the Project panel forward, and then double-click an empty area in the Project panel to open the Import File dialog box.

2 Select the credits.psd file in the Lessons/Lesson03/Assets folder. Choose Composition – Retain Layer Sizes from the Import As menu. (In Mac OS, you may need to click Options to see the Import As menu.) Then click Import or Open.

3 In the Credits.psd dialog box, select Editable Layer Styles, and click OK.

After Effects can import Photoshop layer styles, retaining the appearance of the layers you're importing. The imported file is added as a composition to the Project panel; its layers are added in a separate folder.

4 Drag the credits composition from the Project panel into the Timeline panel, placing it at the top of the layer stack.

Because you imported the credits.psd file as a composition with layers intact, you can work on it in its own Timeline panel, editing and animating its layers independently.

Editing imported text

The text you imported isn't currently editable in After Effects. You'll change that so that you can control the type and apply animations. And if you have a sharp eye, you've noticed some typos in the imported text. So, first you'll clean up the type.

1 Double-click the credits composition in the Project panel to open it in its own Timeline panel.

2 Shift-click to select both layers in the credits Timeline panel, and choose Layer > Convert To Editable Text. (Click OK if you see a warning about missing fonts.)

Now the text layers can be edited, and you can fix the typos.

3 Deselect both layers, and then double-click layer 2 in the Timeline panel to select the text and automatically switch to the Horizontal Type tool (T).

4 Type an *e* between the *t* and *d* in the word *animated*. Then change the *k* to a *c* in *documentary*.

> ● **Note:** The layer name does not change in the Timeline panel when you correct the spelling in the layer. This is because the original layer name was created in Photoshop. To change a layer's name, select it in the Timeline panel, press Enter or Return, type the new name, and press Enter or Return again.

5 Switch to the Selection tool (▶) to exit text-editing mode.

6 Shift-click to select both layers in the Timeline panel.

7 If the Character panel isn't open, choose Window > Character to open it.

8 Choose the same typeface you used for the words *Road Trip*: Calluna Sans. Leave all other settings as they are.

9 Click an empty area of the Timeline panel to deselect both layers. Then select layer 2 again.

10 In the Character panel, click the Fill Color box. Then, in the Text Color dialog box, select a shade of green, and click OK. We used R=66, G=82, B=42.

Animating the subtitle

You want the letters of the subtitle—*an animated documentary*—to fade onscreen from left to right under the movie title. The easiest way to do this is to use another text animation preset.

1 Go to 5:00 in the timeline. At that point, the title and the compass have finished scaling to their final size.

2 Select the subtitle layer (layer 2) in the Timeline panel.

3 Press Ctrl+Alt+Shift+O (Windows) or Command+Option+Shift+O (Mac OS) to jump to Adobe Bridge.

4 Navigate to the Presets/Text/Animate In folder.

5 Select the Fade Up Characters animation preset, and watch it in the Preview panel. This effect works well to reveal the text gradually.

● **Note:** With some installations of Bridge, the effect may not be applied from Bridge. In that case, double-click the preset in the Effects & Presets panel to apply it.

6 Double-click the Fade Up Characters preset to apply it to the subtitle layer in After Effects.

7 With the subtitle layer selected in the Timeline panel, press UU to see the properties modified by the animation preset. You should see two keyframes for Range Selector 1 Start: one at 5:00, and one at 7:00.

You still have a lot of animation to do in this composition, so you will speed up the effect by 1 second.

8 Go to 6:00, and then drag the second Range Selector 1 Start keyframe to 6:00.

9 Drag the current-time indicator across the time ruler between 5:00 and 6:00 to see the letters fade in.

10 When you're done, select the subtitle layer, and press U to hide the modified properties. Then choose File > Save to save your work.

Animating type tracking

Next, you'll animate the appearance of the director's name in the composition using a text animation tracking preset. By animating tracking, you can make words seem to expand outward as they appear onscreen from a central point.

Customizing placeholder text

Currently, the director's name is simply a layer with placeholder text—*Your Name Here*. Before you animate it, change it to your own name.

● **Note:** It doesn't matter where the current-time indicator is located when you edit the text of this layer. Currently, the text is onscreen for the duration of the composition. That will change once you animate it.

1 Still working in the credits timeline in the Timeline panel, select the Your Name Here layer.

2 Select the Horizontal Type tool (T), and then replace *Your Name Here* in the Composition panel with your own name. Use a first, middle, and last name so that you have a nice long string of text to animate. Click the layer name when you're done. The layer name doesn't change, because it was named in Photoshop.

Applying a tracking preset

Now you will animate the director's name with a tracking preset so that it starts to appear onscreen shortly after the words *an animated documentary* are fully visible in the composition.

1 Go to 7:10.

2 Select the Your Name Here layer in the Timeline panel.

3 Typee Increase Tracking in the search box of the Effects & Presets panel. Then double-click the preset to apply it to the Your Name Here layer.

4 Drag the current-time indicator across the time ruler between 7:10 and 9:10 to manually preview the tracking animation.

Customizing the tracking animation preset

The text expands, but you want the letters to be so close initially that they're on top of each other, and then to expand to a reasonable, readable distance apart. The animation should also occur more quickly. You'll adjust the Tracking Amount to achieve both goals.

1 Select the Your Name Here layer in the Timeline panel, and press UU to reveal the properties that were modified.

2 Go to 7:10.

3 Under Animator 1, change the Tracking Amount to **−5** so that the letters are squeezed together.

4 Click the Go To Next Keyframe arrow (▶) for the Tracking Amount property, and then change the value to **0**.

5 Drag the current-time indicator across the time ruler between 7:10 and 8:10. The letters expand as they appear onscreen, and stop animating at the last keyframe.

Animating text opacity

You'll take the animation of the director's name a little further by having it fade onscreen as the letters expand. To do this, you'll animate the layer's Opacity property.

1 Make sure the Your Name Here layer is selected in the credits timeline.

2 Press T to reveal only the layer's Opacity property.

3 Go to 7:10, and set the Opacity to **0%**. Then click the stopwatch icon (⏱) to set an Opacity keyframe.

4 Go to 7:20, and set the Opacity to **100%**. After Effects adds a second keyframe.

Now the letters of the director's name will fade in as they expand onscreen.

5 Drag the current-time indicator across the time ruler between 7:10 and 8:10 to see the letters of the director's name fade in as they spread out.

6 Right-click (Windows) or Control-click (Mac OS) the ending Opacity keyframe, and choose Keyframe Assistant > Easy Ease In.

7 Choose File > Save.

Using a text animator group

Text animator groups let you animate individual letters within a block of text in a layer. You'll use a text animator group to animate only the characters in your middle name without affecting the tracking and opacity animation of the other names in the layer.

1 In the Timeline panel, go to 8:10.

2 Hide the Opacity property for the Your Name Here layer. Then expand the layer to see its Text property group name.

3 Next to the Text property name, click the Animate pop-up menu, and choose Skew.

A property group named Animator 2 appears in the layer's Text properties.

4 Select Animator 2, press Enter or Return, and rename it **Skew Animator**. Then press Enter or Return again to accept the new name.

Now you're ready to define the range of letters that you want to skew.

5 Expand the Skew Animator's Range Selector 1 properties.

Each animator group includes a default range selector. Range selectors constrain the animation to particular letters in the text layer. You can add additional selectors to an animator group, or apply multiple animator properties to the same range selector.

6 While watching the Composition panel, drag the Skew Animator's Range Selector 1 Start value up (to the right) until the left selector indicator (▸) is just before the first letter of your middle name (the *B* in *Bender*, in this example).

7 Drag the Skew Animator's Range Selector 1 End value down (to the left) until its indicator (◂) is just after the last letter of your middle name (the *r* in *Bender*, in this example) in the Composition panel.

Now, any properties that you animate with the Skew Animator will affect only the middle name that you selected.

About text animator groups

A text animator group includes one or more *selectors* and one or more *animator properties*. A selector is like a mask—it specifies which characters or section of a text layer you want an animator property to affect. Using a selector, you can define a percentage of the text, specific characters in the text, or a specific range of text.

Using a combination of animator properties and selectors, you can create complex text animations that would otherwise require painstaking keyframing. Most text animations require you to animate only the selector values—not the property values. Consequently, text animators use a small number of keyframes even for complex animations.

For more about text animator groups, see After Effects Help.

Skewing the range of text

Now, make that middle name shake and shimmy by setting Skew keyframes.

1 Drag the Skew Animator's Skew value left and right, and notice that only the middle name sways. The other names in the line of text remain steady.

2 Set the Skew Animator's Skew value to **0**.

3 Go to 8:05, and click the stopwatch icon (⏱) for Skew to add a keyframe to the property.

4 Go to 8:08, and set the Skew value to **50**. After Effects adds a keyframe.

5 Go to 8:15, and change the Skew value to **−50**. After Effects adds another keyframe.

6 Go to 8:20, and change the Skew value to **0** to set the final keyframe.

 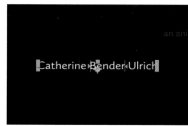

7 Click the Skew property name to select all of the Skew keyframes. Then choose Animation > Keyframe Assistant > Easy Ease to add an Easy Ease to all keyframes.

8 Drag the current-time indicator across the time ruler from 7:10 to 8:20 to see how the director's name fades in and expands onscreen, and the middle name rocks side to side while the other names are unaffected.

9 Hide the properties for the Your Name Here layer in the Timeline panel.

10 Select the Title_Sequence tab to open its timeline.

11 Press Home, or go to 0:00, and then preview the entire composition.

12 Press the spacebar to stop playback, and then choose File > Save to save your work.

▶ **Tip:** To quickly remove all text animators from a text layer, select the layer in the Timeline panel, and choose Animation > Remove All Text Animators. To remove only one animator, select its name in the Timeline panel, and press Delete.

Animating a layer's position

You've used several text animation presets to dazzle your audience. But for a simpler effect, you can animate the Transform properties for a text layer, just as you can any other layer.

Currently, your name appears onscreen, but there's no context for it. You'll add the words "directed by," animating them so that they move into position as your name is appearing onscreen.

1 In the Title_Sequence Timeline panel, go to 9:29, the end of the project.

At this point, all the other text is onscreen, so you can position the "directed by" line accurately.

2 Select the Horizontal Type tool.

3 Make sure no layers are selected, and then click in the Composition panel. Make sure you're clicking in an area that doesn't overlap an existing text layer.

▶ **Tip:** To make sure no layers are deselected, click an empty area in the Timeline panel, press F2, or choose Edit > Deselect All.

4 Type **directed by**.

5 Select the directed by layer. Then, in the Character panel, choose Minion Pro from the Font Family menu.

6 Choose Regular for the Font Style, and set the Font Size to 20 pixels.

7 In the Character panel, click the Fill Color box. Then, in the Text Color dialog box, select white, and click OK. Leave all other options at their default settings.

8 Select the Selection tool, and then drag the directed by layer so that the text is centered over your name.

9 Press P to display the layer's Position property. Click the stopwatch icon to create an initial keyframe for the layer.

10 Go to 7:00, the point where "documentary" has just finished appearing and your name hasn't yet started to appear.

11 Drag the directed by layer off the left edge of the Composition window. Press the Shift key as you drag to create a straight path.

12 Preview the animation, and then hide the Position property.

It's simple, but effective. The text moves in from the left side and stops in its final position above your name. To make the text's entrance a little more interesting, you'll add a car graphic that will appear to be dragging the text onscreen.

Timing layer animations

You'll animate a simple car graphic so that the text appears to trail behind the car onscreen. The words should follow the car and come to rest above your name, while the car continues to fly off screen. The timing will require some adjustment, in order to keep the text and the car in sync.

First, you'll import the car graphic and add it to your composition.

1 Double-click an empty area in the Project panel to open the Import File dialog box.

2 In the Lessons/Lesson03/Assets folder, select the car.ai file, choose Composition – Retain Layer Sizes from the Import As menu, and then click Import or Open.

3 Drag the car composition from the Project panel to the top of the layer stack in the Title_Sequence Timeline panel.

4 Go to 6:25, just before the directed by text begins moving.

5 Select the car layer, and press P to reveal its Position property.

6 Drag the car off the left of the Composition window, so that it overlaps the directed by text.

7 Click the stopwatch icon for the layer's Position property to create an initial keyframe.

8 Go to 9:29, the end of the composition.

9 Drag the car off the right side of the Composition window. The car shouldn't be visible on the screen. Hold down the Shift key as you drag to create a straight path.

10 Manually preview the animation from 6:25 to 9:29.

The text trails the car, but the car picks up speed too quickly so it's not obvious that it's dragging the text. You'll need to make an adjustment to its timing to slow the car down until the text is in place.

11 Go to 8:29.

12 Move the car immediately to the right of the text.

13 Preview the animation again.

The timing is better, but now the car overlaps the text at the beginning. One more adjustment should do the trick.

14 Go to 7:19.

15 Pull the car forward, just ahead of the text.

16 Preview the animation again.

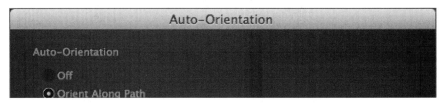

Now the car is clearly pulling the text, and it speeds up to roll off the screen before the composition finishes. If you'd like to more precisely control the animation, you can add more keyframes.

17 Hide the properties for all layers, and then choose File > Save to save your work.

Adding motion blur

Motion blur is the blur that occurs as an object moves. You'll apply motion blur to finesse the composition and make the movement look more natural.

1 In the Timeline panel, click the Motion Blur switch (⬤) for each layer *except* the background_movie and credits layers.

Now you'll apply motion blur to the layers in the credits composition.

2 Switch to the credits Timeline panel, and enable motion blur for both layers.

3 Switch back to the Title_Sequence Timeline panel, and select the Motion Blur switch for the credits layer. Then click the Enable Motion Blur button (⬤) at the top of the Timeline panel so that you can see the motion blur in the Composition panel.

4 Preview the entire, completed animation.

5 Choose File > Save.

Give yourself a pat on the back. You just completed some hard-core text animations. If you'd like to export the composition as a movie file, see Lesson 14, "Rendering and Outputting," for instructions.

Review questions

1 What are some similarities and differences between text layers and other types of layers in After Effects?

2 How can you preview a text animation preset?

3 How can you assign one layer's transformations to another layer?

4 What are text animator groups?

Review answers

1 In many ways, a text layer is just like any other layer in After Effects. You can apply effects and expressions to text layers, animate them, designate them as 3D layers, and edit the 3D text while viewing it in multiple views. However, text layers are like shape layers in that you can't open them in their own Layer panels, and in that they are synthetic layers that consist entirely of vector graphics. You can animate the text in a text layer using special text animator properties and selectors.

2 You can preview text animation presets in Adobe Bridge by choosing Animation > Browse Presets. Adobe Bridge opens and displays the contents of the After Effects Presets folder. Navigate to folders containing categories of text animation presets, such as Blurs or Paths, and watch samples in the Preview panel.

3 You can use parenting relationships in After Effects to assign one layer's transformations to another layer (except opacity transformations). When a layer is made a parent to another layer, the other layer is called the *child layer*. Creating a parenting relationship between layers synchronizes the changes in the parent layer with corresponding transformation values of the child layers.

4 Text animator groups enable you to animate the properties of individual characters in a text layer over time. Text animator groups contain one or more *selectors*, which are like masks: They let you specify which characters or section of a text layer you want an animator property to affect. Using a selector, you can define a percentage of the text, specific characters in the text, or a specific range of text.

4 WORKING WITH SHAPE LAYERS

Lesson overview

In this lesson, you'll learn how to do the following:

- Create custom shapes.
- Customize a shape's fill and stroke.
- Use path operations to transform shapes.
- Animate shapes.
- Repeat shapes.
- Snap layers into alignment.
- Use an expression to animate properties in time with audio.

 This lesson will take approximately an hour to complete. Download the project files for this lesson, following the instructions in the Getting Started section under "Accessing the lesson files and Web Edition," if you haven't already done so. As you work on this lesson, you'll preserve the start files. If you need to restore the start files, download them from your Account page.

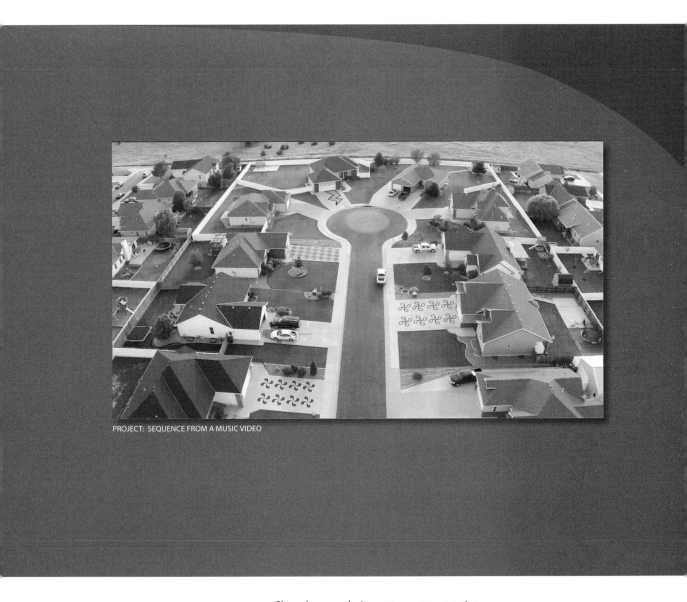

PROJECT: SEQUENCE FROM A MUSIC VIDEO

Shape layers make it easy to create expressive backgrounds and intriguing results. You can animate shapes, apply animation presets, and add Repeaters to intensify their impact.

Getting started

Shape layers are created automatically when you draw a shape with any of the drawing tools. You can customize and transform an individual shape or its entire layer to create interesting results. In this lesson, you will use shape layers to build dynamic and whimsical designs on the street and driveways of a neighborhood.

First, you'll preview the final movie and set up the project.

1 Make sure the following files are in the Lessons/Lesson04 folder on your hard disk, or download them from your Account page at www.peachpit.com now:

 • In the Assets folder: Beat.aif, drop.aep, Melody.aif, tracking.aep, Tracking.mp4

 • In the Sample_Movies folder: Lesson04.avi, Lesson04.mov

2 Open and play the Lesson04.avi sample movie in Windows Media Player or the Lesson04.mov sample movie in QuickTime Player to see what you will create in this lesson. When you are done, close Windows Media Player or QuickTime Player. You may delete the sample movies from your hard disk if you have limited storage space.

As you start After Effects, restore the default application settings. See "Restoring default preferences" on page 2.

3 Start After Effects, and then immediately hold down Ctrl+Alt+Shift (Windows) or Command+Option+Shift (Mac OS) to restore default preferences settings. When prompted, click OK to delete your preferences.

4 Close the Start window.

After Effects opens to display a blank, untitled project.

5 Choose File > Save As > Save As, and then navigate to the Lessons/Lesson04/Finished_Project folder.

6 Name the project **Lesson04_Finished.aep**, and then click Save.

Creating the composition

Next, you'll import the files you need and create the composition. You'll import two footage items and two saved project files.

1 Double-click an empty area of the Project panel to open the Import File dialog box.

2 Navigate to the Lessons/Lesson04/Assets folder on your hard disk, Ctrl-click (Windows) or Command-click (Mac OS) to select the Beat.aif and Melody.aif files, and then click Import or Open.

3 Choose File > New > New Folder to create a new folder in the Project panel.

4 Name the folder **Audio**, press Enter or Return to accept the name, and then drag the two audio files you imported into the Audio folder. Then expand the folder so you can see its contents.

5 Double-click an empty area of the Project panel to open the Import File dialog box again.

6 Navigate to the Lessons/Lesson04/ Assets folder. Ctrl-click (Windows) or Command-click (Mac OS) to select the drop.aep and tracking. aep project files, and then click Import or Open. The video files and other elements you will need later are imported with the projects.

Now you're ready to create the composition.

7 Press Ctrl+N (Windows) or Command+N (Mac OS) to create a new composition.

8 In the Composition Settings dialog box, name the composition **Spiral**, select the HDTV 1080 24 preset, and set the Duration to **10:00**. Then click OK.

After Effects opens the new composition in both the Timeline and Composition panels.

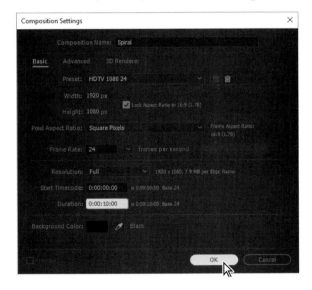

▶ **Tip:** To specify 10 seconds, type **10.** in the Duration box. The period indicates that there are no units in that position. To specify 10 minutes, type **10..** in the box.

Adding a shape layer

After Effects includes five shape tools: Rectangle, Rounded Rectangle, Ellipse, Polygon, and Star. When you draw a shape directly in the Composition panel, After Effects adds a new shape layer to the composition. You can apply stroke and fill settings to a shape, modify its path, and apply animation presets. Shape attributes are all represented in the Timeline panel, and you can animate each setting over time.

The same drawing tools can create both shapes and masks. Masks are applied to layers to hide or reveal areas or as input into effects; shapes have their own layers. When you select a drawing tool, you can specify whether the tool draws a shape or a mask.

Drawing a shape

You'll begin by drawing a rectangle with a fill and stroke.

1 Select the Rectangle tool (▢).

2 Choose Fit from the Magnification Ratio pop-up menu at the bottom of the Composition panel so that you can see the entire composition.

3 Click the Info panel's title bar to open it. Using the values in the Info panel to guide you, position the cursor at approximately 950, 540, which is near the center of the Composition panel. (You may need to widen the Info panel to see the X and Y coordinates.)

4 Drag down and to the right to create a rectangle. Again, watch the Info panel. The bottom (B) value should be approximately 40 pixels and the right side (R) value should be about 400 pixels. The shape appears in the Composition panel, and After Effects adds a shape layer named Shape Layer 1 to the Timeline panel.

5 Select the Shape Layer 1 layer name, press Enter or Return, change the layer
 name to **Spiral**, and press Enter or Return to accept the change.

Applying a fill and stroke

You can change the color of a shape by modifying its Fill settings in the Tools panel.
Clicking the word *Fill* opens the Fill Options dialog box, where you can select the kind
of fill, its blending mode, and its opacity. Clicking the Fill Color box opens the Adobe
Color Picker if the fill is solid, or the Gradient Editor if the fill is a gradient.

Similarly, you can change the stroke color and width of a shape by modifying its
Stroke settings in the Tools panel. Click the word *Stroke* to open the Stroke Options
dialog box; click the Stroke Color box to select a color.

1 Select Rectangle 1 in the Timeline panel.

2 Click the Fill Color box (next to *Fill*)
 to open the Shape Fill Color dialog box.

3 Change the color to a light blue (we used
 R=0, G=170, B=255), and click OK.

4 Click the Stroke Color box in the Tools
 panel, change the stroke color to the same
 light blue color, and then click OK.

5 Choose File > Save to save your work so far.

Twisting a shape

The rectangle is fine, but it isn't very exciting. In After Effects, you can easily modify a basic shape into something more complex and interesting. You'll use the Twist path operation to transform this rectangle into a spiral shape.

As you work with the Twist path operation, keep in mind that it rotates a path more sharply in the center than at the edges. Positive values twist clockwise; negative values twist counterclockwise.

1 In the Timeline panel, open the Add pop-up menu next to Contents in the Spiral layer, and choose Twist.

2 Expand Twist 1.

3 Change the Angle to **220**.

The rectangle changes dramatically. Next, you'll change the center point of the twist to create a larger spiral.

4 In the Timeline panel, change the x-axis value for Center to **−220**.

Note: If the center of your spiral looks different from ours, you probably drew a slightly larger or smaller rectangle. You can delete what you have and start over with a fresh composition or try adjusting the x-axis value for Center.

The spiral is a bit thin. You'll change the stroke width to thicken it.

5 Select the Spiral layer in the Timeline panel, and then change the Stroke Width value in the Tools panel to **20** px.

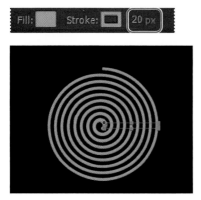

The center of the spiral has a rounded cap, but the end is square. You'll change the end so that they match.

6 Expand Stroke 1 to see its properties.

7 Choose Round Join from the Line Join menu.

The spiral looks great. Now you just need to center it, so that it looks natural when it rotates, and then you'll set up its rotation and add motion blur.

8 Press A to reveal the Anchor Point property for the layer. Then adjust the x-axis and y-axis values until the anchor point is centered in the black center (negative space) of the spiral, just above the center end cap. (The exact values will vary depending on how you created the initial shape.)

9 Make sure the current-time indicator is at the beginning of the timeline. Then press R to reveal the Rotation property for the layer. Click the stopwatch icon (⏱) to create an initial keyframe.

10 Press the End key, or move the current-time indicator to the end of the timeline. Change the Rotation value to **1x+0.0°**. With this setting, the shape will rotate once during its ten-second cycle.

11 Click the Motion Blur switch for the layer, and then click the Enable Motion Blur button (◑) at the top of the Timeline panel.

12 Press the spacebar to preview your animation, and press the spacebar again to stop the preview. Choose File > Save to save your work so far.

Creating custom shapes

You can use the five shape tools to create a wide variety of shapes. However, the real power in using shape layers is that you can draw any shape and manipulate it in a myriad of ways.

Drawing a shape with the Pen tool

You'll use the Pen tool to draw a shape that resembles a lightning bolt. In order to position it properly in the final project, you'll create a separate composition for this shape.

1 Press Ctrl+N (Windows) or Command+N (Mac OS) to create a new composition.

2 In the Composition Settings dialog box, name the composition **Bolt**, select the HDTV 1080 24 preset, set the duration to **10:00**, and then click OK.

3 Select the Pen tool (✒) in the Tools panel.

4 In the Composition panel, draw a shape that resembles a lightning bolt, as in the illustration. When you create the first vertex, After Effects automatically adds a shape layer to the Timeline panel.

▶ **Tip:** Your lightning bolt doesn't need to look exactly like ours, but you can use the one in the illustration as a guide. Click an initial vertex at the bottom of the shape, and then click to create each additional point. If you're not familiar with the Pen tool, you may find the display distracting, as the fill seems to jump around as you draw; ignore the preview until you've clicked each vertex and completed the shape.

5 Select Shape Layer 1, press Enter or Return, and change the layer's name to **Bolt**. Press Enter or Return to accept the new name.

6 With the Bolt layer selected, click the Fill Color box in the Tools panel, and select a yellow color (we used R=255, G=237, B=0). Then click the Stroke Color box in the Tools panel, and select black (R=0, G=0, B=0).

7 Change the Stroke Width to **10** px.

Creating a self-animating shape

Wiggle Paths turns a smooth shape into a series of jagged peaks and valleys. You'll use it to make the lightning bolt more electrifying. Because the operation is self-animating, you need to change only a few properties for the entire shape to move on its own.

1 Expand the Bolt layer in the Timeline panel, and choose Wiggle Paths from the Add pop-up menu.

2 Expand Wiggle Paths 1. Then change the Size to **15** and the Detail to **30**.

3 Change Wiggles/Second to **24** to speed up the movement.

4 Click the Motion Blur switch for the layer, and then click the Enable Motion Blur button at the top of the Timeline panel. Then hide the layer properties.

5 Move the current-time indicator across the time ruler to see the shape move.

Duplicating shapes

You could draw a shape multiple times, but it's easier to duplicate the shape automatically. The Repeater path operation lets you multiply a shape and transform its properties to achieve different results.

You'll use the Repeater path operation to duplicate a shape that was created in Adobe Illustrator and then pasted into the Path property of a shape layer in the Drop.aep project file.

1 In the Project panel, expand the drop.aep folder, and then double-click the Drop composition to open it.

The Drop composition opens in the Timeline panel and the Composition panel.

2 Expand the Drop layer and its Contents folder if its properties aren't visible. Then select Shape 1, and choose Repeater from the Add pop-up menu.

Note: Choose Fit from the Magnification Ratio pop-up menu in the Composition window if you don't see the full shape.

You're selecting Shape 1 because you want to add the Repeater to the individual shape, not the entire layer.

3 Expand Repeater 1.

4 Change the number of copies to **4**.

The Repeater creates three copies of the shape, for a total of four. You'll rotate the shapes and then reposition them to create a pinwheel.

● **Note:** There are multiple Transform properties in the Timeline panel, applying to different path operators. Make sure you're selecting the appropriate Transform property for the object or layer you want to affect. In this case, you want to affect only the Repeater.

5 Expand Transform: Repeater 1.

6 Change the Rotation to **90°**.

Because you applied the rotation to the Repeater rather than to the shape, each drop rotates around the layer's anchor point to a different degree. When you change the Transform properties for the Repeater, the change is multiplied by the number of copies created. In this case, the first shape retains the original value of 0, the second shape rotates 90 degrees, the third shape rotates 180 degrees, and the fourth shape rotates 270 degrees. The same concept applies to each of the Transform properties.

7 In the Transform: Repeater 1 properties, change the Position to **0, 0**.

The shapes overlap because the anchor point is located in the center of each shape.

8 Change the Anchor Point value to **15, 45**.

The shapes align to form a pinwheel. Now you'll make the pinwheel rotate.

9 Make sure the current-time indicator is at the beginning of the time ruler. Then, expand the Transform: Shape 1 category, and click the stopwatch icon (⏱) next to the Rotation value to create an initial keyframe.

10 Press the End key or move the current-time indicator to the end of the time ruler, and change the Rotation value to **2x+0.0°**.

11 Drag the current-time indicator across the time ruler to see the pinwheel rotate.

You used the Repeater path operation to duplicate an individual shape. Now you'll use it to copy all the contents of the layer, turning one pinwheel into eight.

12 In the Timeline panel, hide all the properties under Shape 1. Then select the Drop layer, and choose Repeater from the Add pop-up menu.

13 Expand the new Repeater 1 category, and change the number of copies to **4**.

Because you applied the Repeater to the entire layer, the full pinwheel was copied.

14 Expand the Transform: Repeater 1 category, and change the Position values to **450, 0**.

There are now four pinwheels across the top of the Composition window.

15 Select the Drop layer, and choose Repeater from the Add pop-up menu again to create the Repeater 2 category.

16 Expand the Repeater 2 category, and change the number of copies to **2**. Then expand the Transform: Repeater 2 category, and change the Position values to **0, 575**.

By applying another Repeater to the entire layer, you copied the full row of pinwheels.

17 Hide all the properties for the layer.

18 Click the Motion Blur switch for the layer, and then click the Enable Motion Blur button (⚫) at the top of the Timeline panel.

19 Press the spacebar to preview eight pinwheels rotating in unison; press the spacebar again to stop the preview. Then choose File > Save to save your work so far.

Duplicating and modifying a composition

You'll use the Drop composition as a starting point for a similar composition that uses different fill and stroke options.

1 In the Project panel, select the Drop composition, and choose Edit > Duplicate to create a copy of the composition.

2 Double-click the Drop 2 composition in the Project panel to open it. Then, in the Timeline panel, expand the Drop layer, and then the Contents category.

3 Select Shape 1, and then choose Fill from the Add pop-up menu.

4 Expand Fill 1, click the Color box, and choose any fill color you like.

5 Expand Stroke 1, click the Color box, and choose the stroke color you like.

6 Move the current-time indicator across the time ruler to preview the rotating pinwheels.

7 Hide all the properties for the layer.

8 Choose File > Save to save your work so far.

Positioning layers with snapping

You've created and manipulated shapes in a variety of ways. Now you'll create a checkerboard pattern. Positioning the layers will be easy with the snapping feature in After Effects.

Creating a new composition

This checkerboard background includes multiple layers, so you'll create a new composition for it.

1 Press Ctrl+N (Windows) or Command+N (Mac OS) to create a new composition.

2 In the Composition Settings dialog box, name the composition **Checkerboard**, choose HDTV 1080 24 from the Preset menu, and type **10:00** for Duration. Then click OK.

After Effects opens the new Checkerboard composition in the Timeline and Composition panels. You'll start by adding two solid layers—the building blocks of the checkerboard background.

3 Choose Layer > New > Solid to create a solid layer.

4 In the Solid Settings dialog box, do the following, and then click OK:

- Name the layer **Dark Red**.

- Change both the Width and Height to **200** px.

- Choose Square Pixels from the Pixel Aspect Ratio menu.

- Select a dark red color. (We used R=145, G=0, B=0.)

5 With the Dark Red layer selected in the Timeline panel, press R to display the Rotation property for the layer. Then change the Rotation to **45** degrees.

6 Select the Selection tool (▶). Then, in the Composition panel, drag the layer up so that only the bottom half of the diamond appears in the composition.

7 Press Ctrl+Y (Windows) or Command+Y (Mac OS) to create another solid layer.

8 In the Solid Settings dialog box, name the layer **Light Red**, and change the color to a light red (we used R=180, G=75, B=75). Then click OK.

The default width and height for the new solid layer match the settings you used previously, so the Light Red layer has the same dimensions as the Dark Red layer.

9 With the Light Red layer selected in the Timeline panel, press R to display the Rotation property. Then change the Rotation to **45** degrees.

Snapping layers into position

● **Note:** You can snap two shape layers together, but not two shapes within a single layer. Also, a layer must be visible to snap to it. 2D layers can snap to 2D layers, and 3D layers can snap to 3D layers.

You've created two layers, but they have no relationship to each other in the composition. You'll use the Snapping option in After Effects to quickly align the layers. When the Snapping option is enabled, the layer feature that is closest to your pointer when you click becomes the snapping feature. As you drag the layer near other layers, features on other layers are highlighted, showing you where the snapping feature would snap if you released the mouse button.

1 Select Snapping in the options section of the Tools panel, if it's not already selected.

Tip: If the Snapping option isn't selected, you can temporarily enable it: Click a layer and start dragging, and then press Ctrl (Windows) or Command (Mac OS) as you drag the layer.

2 Using the Selection tool, select the Light Red layer in the Composition panel.

When you select a layer in the Composition panel, After Effects displays the layer handles and anchor point. You can use any of these points as the snapping feature for a layer.

3 Click near the corner handle on the left side of the Light Red layer, and drag it near the lower right edge of the Dark Red layer until it snaps into place, with the sides abutted. Be careful not to drag the corner itself, or you'll resize the layer.

As you drag the layer, a box appears around the left corner handle you selected, indicating that it is the snapping feature.

4 In the Timeline panel, select both of the layers, and press R to hide the Rotation property for both layers.

5 With both layers still selected, choose Edit > Duplicate to copy them.

6 In the Composition panel, drag the two new layers down to the left, and then down to the right, so that the new Dark Red layer abuts the original Light Red layer. Remember that the snapping feature is determined by where you initially click when you begin to drag.

Tip: Instead of choosing Edit > Duplicate, you can press Ctrl+D (Windows) or Command+D (Mac OS) to duplicate layers.

7 Repeat steps 5–6 until you have a column of diamonds filling the screen.

8 Choose Edit > Select All to select the layers in the Timeline panel.

9 Press Ctrl+D (Windows) or Command+D (Mac OS) to duplicate the layers. Then move them to the left in the Composition panel until they snap into place.

▶ **Tip:** If you need to generate a checkerboard more quickly, use the Checkerboard effect. For more information, see After Effects Help.

10 Repeat step 9 until the Composition panel is full. Pull the duplicate layers to the left or right as necessary. Remember to click near an appropriate snapping feature as you begin dragging each time.

11 Choose File > Save to save your work.

Adding compositions to a 3D project

You've created several compositions, all of which need to stay in position as the camera moves through the scene. You'll integrate the compositions using the 3D Camera Tracker effect, which lets you add 3D layers to a clip with the same movement and perspective changes as the original.

You'll work extensively with the 3D Camera Tracker effect in Lesson 12. For this project, we've set up the effect so that all you need to do is to position layers and parent them to a null object to attach them to the 3D scene. A null object is an invisible layer that has all the properties of a visible layer, so that it can be a parent to any layer in the composition. In this case, the null object tracks the camera movement.

1 In the Project panel, expand the tracking.aep folder, and then double-click the Tracking composition to open it. Choose Fit from the Magnification Ratio pop-up menu at the bottom of the Composition panel so that you can see the entire composition.

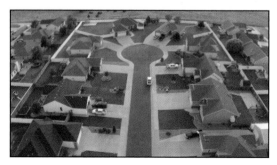

The Tracking composition includes the background video you'll use to place the shapes you've created.

2 Select the Spiral composition in the Timeline panel, and then select the 3D switch (⊕) for the Spiral layer.

3 Select the Tracking composition in the Timeline panel again. Then drag the Spiral composition from the Project panel to the Timeline panel, placing it at the top of the layer stack.

4 Select the 3D switch for the Spiral layer, and then select the Collapse Transformations switch (✱) for the layer, too.

The Collapse Transformations switch ensures that transformations in a nested composition aren't flattened; instead, when the project is rendered, transformations in the nested composition will be performed at the same time transformations are performed for the containing composition.

5 In the Timeline panel, click the Parent pop-up menu for the Spiral layer, and choose 2. Track Null 1. This sets the Track Null 1 layer as the parent of the Spiral layer, which in turn becomes the child layer.

6 With the Spiral layer selected, press P to reveal its Position property. Change the value to **0, 0, 0**. This moves the spiral to the same location as the Null object.

7 Move the current-time indicator to 5:00 so you can clearly see the Spiral layer's position in the image. Then press Shift+R to reveal the Rotation properties, and change the Orientation values to **0, 0, 0**.

The spiral is almost in the right place, but you want to position it perfectly in the cul-de-sac. You'll tweak its position.

8 Change the Position for the layer to **−35, −225, 0**.

9 Press the spacebar to preview the spiral rotating in the cul-de-sac. Press the spacebar again to stop the preview. Hide the Spiral layer's properties to keep the Timeline panel tidy.

You've placed the first composition. You'll repeat the process to place the others.

10 Drag the Bolt composition from the Project panel to the top of the Timeline panel, and select the 3D switch (⊕) for the Bolt layer.

11 Select 3. Track Null 1 from the Parent menu for the Bolt layer. Then press the P key, press Shift+R, and press Shift+S to reveal the Position, Rotation, and Scale properties for the layer.

Pressing the Shift key as you press keyboard shortcuts lets you view multiple layer properties at the same time.

● **Note:** You may need to adjust the Position, Orientation, and Scale values, depending on how you drew the lightning bolt.

12 Change the Position values to **−650, −1200, 0**. Change the Orientation to **0, 0, 345**. Change the Scale to **85%**. Finally, select the Motion Blur switch for the Bolt layer, and then hide the layer's properties.

Next, you'll use the same process to integrate the Drop composition.

13 Go to 2:00 so you can see the driveway where this composition will be placed. Drag the Drop composition from the Project panel to the top of the stack in the Timeline panel, and select the 3D switch for the layer.

14 Select 4. Track Null 1 from the Parent menu for the Drop layer. Then press P, Shift+R, and Shift+S to reveal the Position, Rotation, and Scale properties.

15 Change the Position values to **730, 2275, 0**; the Orientation values to **5, 8, 2**; and the Scale to **45%**. Then select the Motion Blur switch for the layer, and hide the layer's properties.

You'll place the Drop2 composition in the lower left driveway, visible as the camera begins to pan.

16 Go to the beginning of the time ruler. Drag the Drop2 composition from the Project panel to the top of the Timeline panel, select the 3D switch, and select 5. Track Null 1 from the Parent menu.

17 Press P, Shift+R, and Shift+S. Change the Position values to **−1025, 3575, 0**; the Orientation to **0, 352, 0**; and the Scale to **35%**. Select the Motion Blur switch for the layer, and hide the layer's properties.

Finally, you'll add the Checkerboard composition. You'll need to scale it a little differently so that it fits into the driveway.

18 Go to 4:00 in the time ruler. Drag the Checkerboard composition from the Project panel to the top of the Timeline panel, select its 3D switch, and choose 6. Track Null 1 from the Parent menu.

19 Press P, Shift+R, and Shift+S. Change the Position values to **−922, 814, 10** and the Orientation to **1, 355, 2**. Then click the link icon for the Scale property to unlink the values, and change the values to **42%, 35%, 42%**. Select the Motion Blur switch for the layer, and hide the layer's properties.

Adding the finishing touches

The layers work pretty well with the underlying video, but they'll blend more convincingly if you change the blending modes. You'll also add the audio file.

1 Click the Toggle Switches/Modes button at the bottom of the Timeline panel.

2 Choose Multiply from the Mode menu for all the layers except the Checkerboard layer; choose Overlay for the Checkerboard layer. (You won't be able to change the mode for the Spiral layer, because Collapse Transformations is selected.)

3 Drag the Melody.aif clip from the Project panel to the bottom of the layer stack in the Timeline panel.

4 Press the spacebar to preview your creation! When you're done previewing the project, save your work.

● **Note:** Sound may not play back in realtime the first time through the preview. After all the frames have been buffered, it should play more smoothly.

Extra credit

Animating layers to match audio

Currently, the spiral shape turns in a slow circle. The movie will be more compelling if the size of the spiral is animated to match the beat of the music. You can scale the spiral in time with the amplitude of an audio file. First, you need to create keyframes from the audio information.

1 Select the Spiral composition in the Timeline panel. Drag the Beat.aif file from the Project panel into the Timeline panel, and place it beneath the Spiral layer.

2 Right-click or Control-click the Beat.aif layer, and choose Keyframe Assistant > Convert Audio To Keyframes.

After Effects adds the Audio Amplitude layer. The new layer is a null object layer, meaning it has no size or shape and won't appear in a final render. Null objects let you parent layers or drive effects.

3 Select the Audio Amplitude layer, and press E to display the effects properties for the layer.

Three categories of effects properties are available for the layer: Left Channel, Right Channel, and Both Channels. You'll work with the Both Channels category.

4 Expand the Both Channels category.

When you converted the audio to keyframes, After Effects created keyframes that specify the amplitude of the audio file in each frame of the layer. You'll sync the scale of the spiral to those values.

5 Select the Spiral layer, and press S to reveal the Scale property for the layer.

6 Alt-click (Windows) or Option-click (Mac OS) the Scale stopwatch to add an expression. The words *transform.scale* appear in the time ruler for the layer.

7 With the transform.scale expression selected in the time ruler, click the pick whip icon (◉) on the Expression:Scale line, and drag it to the Slider property name in the Audio Amplitude layer.

When you release the mouse, the pick whip snaps, and the expression in the shape layer time ruler now reads *temp = thisComp.layer("Audio Amplitude").effect("Both Channels")("Slider"); [temp, temp, temp].* (You may need to click the expression to see the full thing.) This expression means that the Scale values for the shape layer will depend on the Slider values of the Audio Amplitude layer.

Note: *You'll learn more about expressions in Lesson 6.*

8 Choose Edit > Deselect All to deselect the layers. Then move the current-time indicator through the time ruler to see the spiral resize with the audio's amplitude.

The scale definitely changes, but sometimes the spiral disappears. You'll modify the expression so that the spiral remains visible.

9 In the time ruler, click the expression to make it active. Click an insertion point at the end of the first line, between the closing parentheses and the semicolon. Type **+90**, and then click an empty area of the Timeline panel to accept the change.

10 Preview the composition, and watch the spiral pulse to the beat of the audio file.

11 Return to the Tracking composition in the Timeline panel. Then press the spacebar, and watch the spiral pulse as the camera moves through the scene. Save your work.

Review questions

1 What is a shape layer, and how do you create one?

2 How can you quickly create multiple copies of a shape?

3 How can you snap one layer to another?

4 What does the Twist path operation do?

Review answers

1 A shape layer is simply a layer that contains a vector graphic called a shape. To create a shape layer, draw a shape directly in the Composition panel using any of the drawing tools or the Pen tool.

2 To quickly duplicate a shape multiple times, apply a Repeater operation to the shape layer. The Repeater path operation creates copies of all paths, strokes, and fills included in the layer.

3 To snap one layer to another in the Composition panel, select Snapping in the options section of the Tools panel. Then click next to the handle or point you want to use as a snapping feature, and drag the layer close to the point to which you want to align it. After Effects highlights the points to which it will align when you release the mouse button. Note that you cannot snap shape layers.

4 The Twist path operation rotates a path more sharply in the center than it does at the edges. Entering a positive value twists clockwise; entering a negative value twists counterclockwise.

5 ANIMATING A MULTIMEDIA PRESENTATION

Lesson overview

In this lesson, you'll learn how to do the following:

- Create a complex animation with multiple layers.

- Adjust the duration of a layer.

- Animate with Position, Scale, and Rotation keyframes.

- Use parenting to sync the animation of layers.

- Use Bezier curves to smooth a motion path.

- Animate a precomposed layer.

- Apply effects to a solid layer.

- Fade out audio.

 This lesson will take about an hour to complete. Download the project files for this lesson, following the instructions in the Getting Started section under "Accessing the lesson files and Web Edition," if you haven't already done so. As you work on this lesson, you'll preserve the start files. If you need to restore the start files, download them from your Account page.

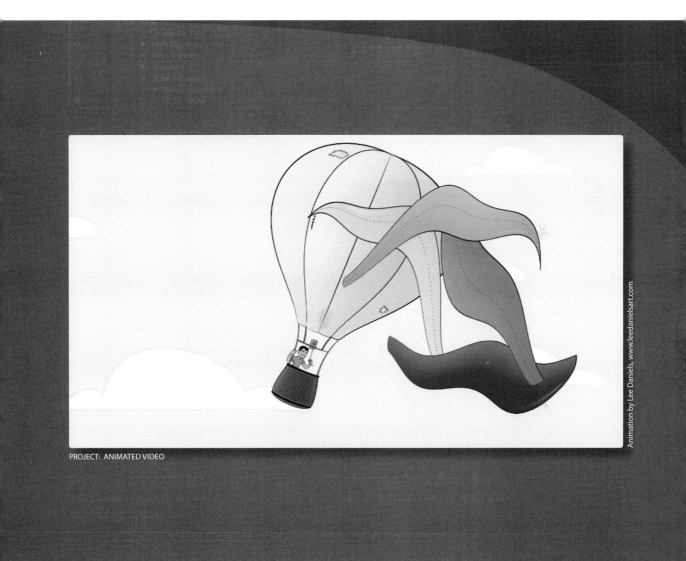

PROJECT: ANIMATED VIDEO

Adobe After Effects projects typically use a variety of imported footage, arranged in a composition, that is edited and animated using the Timeline panel. In this lesson, you'll become more familiar with animation fundamentals as you build a multi-media presentation.

115

Getting started

In this project, you will animate a hot air balloon floating through the sky. All seems peaceful until a gust of wind blows the balloon's colorful canvas off to cover the clouds.

1 Make sure the following files are in the Lessons/Lesson05 folder on your hard disk, or download them from your Account page at www.peachpit.com now:

 • In the Assets folder: Balloon.ai, Fire.mov, Sky.ai, Soundtrack.wav

 • In the Sample_Movies folder: Lesson05.mov, Lesson05.avi

2 Open and play the Lesson05.avi sample movie in Windows Media Player or the Lesson05.mov sample movie in QuickTime Player to see what you will create in this lesson. When you are done, close Windows Media Player or QuickTime Player. You may delete the sample movies from your hard disk if you have limited storage space.

As you start After Effects, restore the default application settings. See "Restoring default preferences" on page 2.

3 Start After Effects, and then immediately hold down Ctrl+Alt+Shift (Windows) or Command+Option+Shift (Mac OS) to restore default preferences settings. When prompted, click OK to delete your preferences.

4 Close the Start window.

5 Choose File > Save As > Save As.

6 In the Save As dialog box, navigate to the Lessons/Lesson05/Finished_Project folder. Name the project **Lesson05_Finished.aep**, and then click Save.

Importing the footage

Next, you'll import the footage you need for the project, including the balloon.ai composition.

1 Double-click an empty area of the Project panel to open the Import File dialog box.

2 Navigate to the Lessons/Lesson05/Assets folder on your hard disk, and select the Sky.ai file.

3 Choose Footage from the Import As menu, and then click Import or Open.

4 In the Sky.ai dialog box, make sure Merged Layers is selected, and then click OK.

5 Double-click an empty area of the Project panel, navigate to the Lessons/Lesson05 /Assets folder, and select the Balloon.ai file.

6 Choose Composition – Retain Layer Sizes from the Import As menu, and click Import or Open.

7 Press Ctrl+I (Windows) or Command+I (Mac OS) to open the Import File dialog box again.

8 Navigate to the Lessons/Lesson05/Assets folder, and select the Fire.mov file.

9 Make sure Footage is chosen in the Import As menu, and click Import or Open.

Using Creative Cloud Libraries in After Effects

Easily access images, videos, colors, and other assets you've created in After Effects and other Adobe applications. Through Creative Cloud Libraries, you can also use Looks, shapes, and other assets you create with Adobe Capture CC and other mobile apps.

Even Adobe Stock images and videos are available in the Libraries panel: Search and browse assets within the panel, download watermarked versions to see how they work with your projects, and license the ones you want to keep—all without leaving After Effects.

The same search bar you use to search Adobe Stock makes it easier to find specific items in your Creative Cloud Libraries, too.

To learn more about all the ways you can use Creative Cloud Libraries, see After Effects Help.

Creating the composition

You'll create the composition and add the sky.

1 Choose Composition > New Composition.

● **Note:** If you change Pixel Aspect Ratio or Width settings, the Preset name may change to Custom in the Composition Settings panel.

2 In the Composition Settings dialog box, do the following:

- Name the composition **Balloon Scene**.
- Choose HDTV 1080 25 from the Preset menu.
- Make sure Square Pixels is chosen from the Pixel Aspect Ratio menu.
- Make sure the Width is **1920** px.
- Choose Quarter for the Resolution.
- Set Duration to **20** seconds.
- Click OK.

3 Drag the Sky.ai footage item from the Project panel into the Timeline panel.

The balloon will float across the Sky.ai image. The far right of the image contains the canvas-wrapped clouds that appear at the end of the scene. The wrapped clouds shouldn't be visible earlier in the movie.

4 In the Composition window, drag the Sky layer so that its lower left corner is even with the lower left corner of the composition.

Adjusting anchor points

The anchor point is the point about which transformations, such as scaling or rotation, are performed. By default, a layer's anchor point is at the center of the layer.

You'll change the anchor points for the character's arm and head so that you can better control the character's movements as he tugs on the cord to ignite the fire, and as he looks up and down.

1 Double-click the Balloon composition in the Project panel to open it in the Composition panel and the Timeline panel.

The Balloon composition includes layers for the canvas colors, the balloon itself, and the character's eyes, head, forearm, and upper arm.

2 Choose 50% from the Magnification Ratio pop-up menu at the bottom of the Composition panel so you can see the balloon's detail more clearly.

3 Select the Hand tool (✋) in the Tools panel, and then pan so that the character is centered in the Composition panel.

4 Select the Selection tool (▶) in the Tools panel.

5 Select the Upper arm layer in the Timeline panel.

6 Select the Pan Behind tool (🔲) in the Tools panel (or press Y to activate it).

With the Pan Behind tool, you can move the anchor point without moving the entire layer in the Composition window.

7 Move the anchor point to the character's shoulder.

8 Select the Forearm layer in the Timeline panel, and then move its anchor point to the elbow.

9 Select the Head layer in the Timeline panel, and move its anchor point to the character's neck.

10 Select the Selection tool in the Tools panel.

11 Choose File > Save to save your work so far.

Parenting layers

This composition includes several layers that need to move together. For example, as the balloon floats, the character's arm and head should move along with it. As you've seen in previous lessons, a parenting relationship synchronizes changes in the parent layer with corresponding changes in the child layer. You'll establish parenting relationships among the layers in this composition, and you'll add the fire video as well.

1 Deselect all layers in the Timeline panel, and then press Ctrl (Windows) or Command (Mac OS) as you select the Head and Upper arm layers.

2 In the Parent column for either of the selected layers, choose 7. Balloon from the pop-up menu.

This establishes both the Head and Upper arm layers as child layers of the Balloon layer. When the Balloon layer moves, the other two layers will move with it.

The eyes not only need to move with the balloon, they need to move with the head, so you'll create that parenting relationship next.

3 In the Parent column for the Eyes layer, choose 6. Head from the pop-up menu.

The forearm should move with the upper arm as well.

4 In the Parent column for the Forearm layer, choose 9. Upper arm from the pop-up menu.

Now you need to ensure that the fire video travels with the balloon.

5 Drag the Fire.mov file from the Project panel to the Timeline panel, positioning it directly below the canvas layers so that the fire will appear to go inside the balloon, rather than outside it. (The Fire layer should be between the Yellow Canvas layer and the Eyes layer.)

The fire video is positioned in the center of the composition, so you'll need to zoom out a bit to see it.

6 Choose 25% from the Magnification Ratio pop-up menu so that you can see the outline of the selected video.

7 In the Composition window, drag the fire video over the burner. To see the flame in action so you can position it correctly, drag the current-time marker across the first second of the time ruler.

8 When you're satisfied with the Fire layer's position, choose 8. Balloon from the pop-up menu in the Fire layer's Parent column.

9 Choose File > Save to save your work so far.

Precomposing layers

Sometimes it's easier to work with a set of layers in a composition. Precomposing layers moves them to a new composition, nested inside the original composition. You'll precompose the canvas layers so that you can work with them separately when you animate them sailing off the balloon.

1 In the Balloon Timeline panel, Shift-click the Green Canvas and Yellow Canvas layers to select all four canvas layers.

2 Choose Layer > Pre-compose.

3 In the Pre-compose dialog box, name the composition **Canvas**, select Move All Attributes Into The New Composition, and click OK.

The four layers you selected in the Timeline panel are replaced by a single Canvas composition layer.

4 Double-click the Canvas layer in the Timeline panel to edit the composition.

5 Choose Composition > Composition Settings.

6 In the Composition Settings dialog box, deselect Lock Aspect Ratio, change the Width value to **5000** px, and click OK.

7 Shift-select all four layers in the Timeline panel, and then drag them to the far left side of the Composition panel. You may need to change the magnification.

Increasing the width of the composition and then moving the canvas to the far left side will give you room to animate the canvas layers later.

8 Switch to the Balloon Timeline panel.

You moved the canvas to the far left side of the Canvas composition, revealing the uncovered balloon in the Balloon composition. At the beginning of the animation, though, the canvas should be *on* the balloon. You'll reposition the Canvas layer.

9 Choose Fit from the Magnification Ratio pop-up menu in the Composition panel so you can see the full balloon.

10 Select the Canvas layer in the Timeline panel, and then drag the layer so that it covers the bare balloon in the Composition panel.

11 In the Parent column of the Canvas layer, choose 5. Balloon from the pop-up menu so that the canvas will follow the balloon.

Keyframing a motion path

Now that all the initial pieces are set up, you're ready to animate the balloon and the character using position and rotation keyframes.

Copying layers into a composition

You've worked with the balloon, character, and fire layers in the Balloon composition. Now, you'll copy those layers into the Balloon Scene composition.

1 In the Balloon Timeline panel, Shift-click the Canvas and Upper arm layers to select all the layers in the composition.

2 Press Ctrl+C (Windows) or Command+C (Mac OS) to copy all the layers.

3 Switch to the Balloon Scene Timeline panel.

4 Press Ctrl+V (Windows) or Command+V (Mac OS) to paste the layers.

5 Click an empty area in the Timeline panel to deselect all layers.

The layers appear in the same order they were when you copied them, and they retain all the properties they had in the Balloon composition, including parenting relationships.

Placing initial keyframes

The balloon will enter the scene from the bottom, drift through the sky, and eventually depart from the upper right corner of the frame. You'll keyframe the balloon's starting and ending points first.

1 Select the Balloon/Balloon.ai layer, and press S to reveal its Scale property.

2 Press Shift+P to display its Position property, and then press Shift+R to display the Rotation property.

3 Change the Scale property to **60%**.

The balloon and all of its child layers scale to 60%.

4 Choose 12.5% from the Magnification Ratio pop-up menu in the Composition panel so that you can see the pasteboard around the composition.

5 In the Composition panel, drag the balloon and its child layers offscreen, below the scene. (We used Position values 844.5, 2250.2.)

6 Drag the Rotation value to rotate the balloon so it tilts to the right. (We used 19 degrees.)

7 Click the stopwatch icons (⏱) for the Position, Scale, and Rotation properties to create initial keyframes.

8 Go to 14:20.

9 Scale the balloon to about one-third its original size. We used 39.4%.

10 Drag the balloon off the upper right corner of the frame, tilted slightly to the left. We used the following values: Position 2976.5, −185.8; Rotation −8.1 degrees.

11 Move the current-time indicator across the timeline to see the animation so far.

Customizing a motion path

The balloon moves through the scene, but its path isn't very interesting, and it isn't onscreen long. You'll customize the path between its starting point and end point. You can use the values we used or create your own path, as long as the balloon stays fully visible on the screen until a little after 11 seconds, and then slowly makes its way offscreen.

1 Go to 3:00.

2 Drag the balloon straight up so that the character and the basket are fully visible, and then rotate it slightly to the left. (We used Position: 952.5, 402.2; Rotation: −11.1 degrees.)

3 Go to 6:16.

4 Shift the balloon's rotation the other direction. (We used 9.9 degrees.)

5 Move the balloon to the left side of the scene. (We used Position: 531.7, 404.)

6 Go to 7:20.

7 Change the scale to 39.4%.

8 Set additional Rotation keyframes to create swirling motions. If you're using our values, do the following:

 • At 8:23, change the Rotation value to **−6.1**.

 • At 9:16, change the Rotation value to **22.1**.

 • At 10:16, change the Rotation value to **−18.3**.

 • At 11:24, change the Rotation value to **11.9**.

 • At 14:19, change the Rotation value to **−8.1**.

9 Set additional Position keyframes to move the balloon. If you're using our values, do the following:

 • At 9:04, change the Position to **726.5**, **356.2**.

 • At 10:12, change the Position to **1396.7**, **537.1**.

10 Press the spacebar key to preview the balloon's current path, and then press the spacebar to stop the preview. Save your work so far.

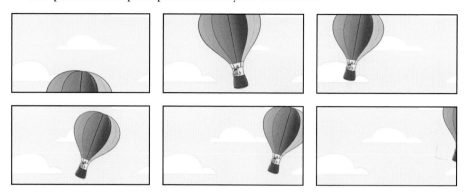

Using Bezier handles to smooth a motion path

The basic path is in place, but you can smooth it out a bit. Each keyframe includes Bezier handles that you can adjust to change the angle of the curve. You'll learn more about Bezier curves in Lesson 7.

1 Choose 50% from the Magnification Ratio pop-up menu in the Composition panel.

2 Make sure the Balloon/Balloon.ai layer is selected in the Timeline panel. Then move the current-time indicator to a position where you can clearly see the motion path in the Composition panel. (Between 4 and 6 seconds is probably good.)

3 Click a keyframe point in the Composition panel to reveal its Bezier handles, if they aren't already shown.

4 Drag a Bezier handle to change the curve for that keyframe.

5 Continue to drag Bezier handles for the keyframe points until you achieve the path you want. Our final path is shown below in the image on the right.

6 Preview the balloon on the path by moving the current-time indicator across the time ruler. Make any adjustments you want. You can also make adjustments later, after you've animated the canvas and sky.

7 Hide the properties for the Balloon layer, and save your work so far.

Animating additional elements

The balloon swoops and swirls through the sky, and its child layers go with it. But the character is currently static in his balloon. You'll animate his arm tugging on the cord to ignite the burner.

1 Go to 3:08.

2 Choose 100% from the Magnification Ratio pop-up menu in the Composition window so that you can see the character clearly. Use the Hand tool to adjust the image in the Composition window if you need to.

3 Shift-select the Forearm/Balloon.ai layer and the Upper arm/Balloon.ai layer.

4 Press R to reveal the Rotation property for both layers.

5 Click the stopwatch icon next to one of the Rotation properties to create an initial keyframe for each.

6 Go to 3:17, the point at which the character will tug the cord to ignite the burner.

7 Deselect the layers.

8 Change the Rotation property for the Forearm layer to **−35** and the Rotation property for the Upper arm layer to **46**.

The character tugs the cord down. You may need to deselect the layers so you can see the action clearly in the Composition window.

9 Go to 4:23.

10 Change the Rotation property for the Forearm layer to −**32.8**.

11 Click the Add Or Remove Keyframe At Current Time button (◆) to the left of the Rotation property for the Upper arm layer.

12 Go to 5:06.

13 Change the Rotation value for both layers to **0**.

14 Deselect both layers, and then manually preview from 3:00 to 5:07 to see the character tug the cord. You may need to zoom out to see the animation.

Duplicating keyframes to repeat an animation

Now that you've created the initial movements, you can easily repeat them at different times in the timeline. You'll duplicate the tugging arm, and then create corresponding head and eye movements.

1 Select the Rotation property for the Forearm layer to select all its keyframes.

2 Press Ctrl+C (Windows) or Command+C (Mac OS) to copy the keyframes.

3 Go to 7:10, the point at which the character tugs the cord again.

4 Press Ctrl+V (Windows) or Command+V (Mac OS) to paste the keyframes.

5 Repeat steps 1–4 to copy the Upper arm Rotation property keyframes.

6 Hide the properties for all layers.

7 Select the Head layer, and press R to reveal its Rotation property.

8 Go to 3:08, and click the stopwatch icon to create an initial keyframe.

9 Go to 3:17, and change the Rotation property to **–10.3**.

10 Go to 4:23, and click the Add Or Remove Keyframe At Current Time icon
 to add a keyframe at the current value.

11 Go to 5:06, and change the Rotation property to **0**.

12 Select the Rotation property to select all of its keyframes, and press Ctrl+C
 (Windows) or Command+C (Mac OS) to copy them.

13 Go to 7:10, and press Ctrl+V (Windows) or Command+V (Mac OS) to paste them.

14 Press R to hide the Rotation property for the Head layer.

Now the character tilts his head up each time he tugs the cord. You'll also animate
the position of his eyes to create a subtle change each time he tilts his head.

15 Select the Eyes layer, and press P to reveal the Position property.

16 Go to 3:08, and click the stopwatch icon to create an initial keyframe
 at the current value (62, 55).

17 Go to 3:17, and change the Position value to **62.4**, **53**.

18 Go to 4:23, and create a keyframe at the current value.

19 Go to 5:06, and change the Position value to **62**, **55**.

20 Select the Position property to select all its keyframes, and then copy them.

21 Go to 7:10, and paste the keyframes.

22 Hide all layer properties, and then deselect all layers.

23 Choose Fit from the Magnification Ratio pop-up menu in the Composition window so that you can see the entire scene. Then preview the animation.

24 Save your work.

Positioning and duplicating a video

When the character tugs the cord, flame should emerge from the burner. You'll use the four-second Fire.mov video to represent the flame each time the cord is tugged.

1 Go to 3:10.

2 Drag the Fire.mov video in the Timeline panel so that it starts at 3:10.

3 Select the Fire.mov layer, and choose Edit > Duplicate.

4 Go to 7:10.

5 Press the left bracket key ([) on your keyboard to move the In point of the duplicate Fire.mov layer to 7:10.

Applying an effect

Now that the balloon and character are taken care of, you'll create the gust of wind that blows the canvas off the balloon. The Fractal Noise and Directional Blur effects will work well.

Adding a solid-color layer

You need to apply the effects on their own layer, which will be a solid-color layer. You'll create a new composition for the layer.

1 Press Ctrl+N (Windows) or Command+N (Mac OS) to create a new composition.

2 In the Composition Settings dialog box, do the following:

 • Name the composition **Wind**.

 • Make sure the width is **1920** px.

 • Make sure the height is **1080** px.

 • Make sure the duration is **20** seconds.

 • Make sure the Frame Rate is 25 fps to match the Balloon Scene composition.

 • Click OK.

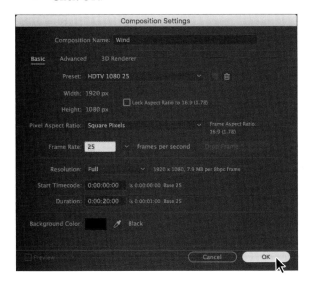

3 Right-click in the Timeline panel, and choose New > Solid.

4 In the Solid Settings dialog box, do the following:

- Name the layer **Wind**.

- Select black for the color.

- Click the Make Comp Size button.

- Click OK.

About solid-color layers

You can create solid images of any color or size (up to 30,000 x 30,000 pixels) in After Effects. After Effects treats solids as it does any other footage item: You can modify the mask, transform properties, and apply effects to a solid layer. If you change settings for a solid that is used by more than one layer, you can apply the changes to all layers that use the solid or to only the single occurrence of the solid. Use solid layers to color a background or to create simple graphic images.

Applying the effects

You're ready to apply the effects to the solid layer. The Fractal Noise effect will create the gust of wind. The Directional Blur effect will create a blur in the direction the canvas flies.

1 In the Effects & Presets panel, search for the Fractal Noise effect; it's in the Noise & Grain category. Double-click the Fractal Noise effect to apply it.

2 In the Effect Controls panel, do the following:

- Choose Smeary for the Fractal Type.

- Choose Soft Linear for the Noise Type.

- Set the Contrast to **700**.

- Set the Brightness to **59**.

- Expand the Transform properties, and set the Scale to **800**.

3 Click the stopwatch next to Offset Turbulence to create an initial keyframe at the beginning of the time ruler.

4 Go to 2:00, and change the x value for Offset Turbulence to **20,000** px.

5 Hide the Fractal Noise properties in the Effect Controls panel.

6 In the Effects & Presets panel, search for the Directional Blur effect, and then double-click it to apply it.

7 In the Effect Controls panel, set the Direction to **90** degrees and the Blur Length to **236**.

You've created a sense of motion. Now you need to add the Wind composition to the Balloon Scene composition.

8 Switch to the Balloon Scene Timeline panel.

9 Click the Project tab, and then drag the Wind composition from the Project window into the Balloon Scene Timeline above all the other layers.

10 Go to 8:10, and then press the left bracket key ([) so that the Wind layer starts at 8:10.

Finally, you'll apply a blending mode and adjust the opacity to make the effect of the wind more subtle.

11 Click Toggle Switches/Modes at the bottom of the Timeline panel to view the Mode column.

12 Choose Screen from the Wind layer's Mode pop-up menu.

13 Press T to reveal the Opacity property for the Wind layer, and then click the stopwatch to create an initial keyframe at the beginning of the layer (8:10).

14 Go to 8:20, and change the opacity to **35**%.

15 Go to 10:20, and change the opacity to **0**%.

16 Press T to hide the Opacity property, and then save your work so far.

Animating precomposed layers

Earlier, you precomposed the four canvas layers, creating a composition called Canvas. You then positioned the Canvas composition layer to match the balloon, and parented the two. Now, you'll animate the canvas layers so that they blow off the balloon when the gust of wind occurs.

1 Double-click the Canvas layer to open the Canvas composition in the Composition panel and the Timeline panel.

2 Go to 9:10, which is about a second after the wind effect begins.

3 Shift-select all four layers, and then press R to display their Rotation properties; press Shift+P to display the Position properties, too.

4 With all layers still selected, click the stopwatch icons for the Position and Rotation properties in one of the layers to create initial keyframes for all of them.

5 Go to 9:24.

6 With all layers still selected, drag a Rotation value until the canvas is nearly horizontal (about 81 degrees). All four canvas layers become nearly horizontal.

7 Press F2 or click an empty area in the Timeline panel to deselect all areas so you can adjust their Rotation values separately.

8 Adjust each Rotation value, using positive and negative numbers so that there is some variation in their appearance. (We used these values: Green: +100, Red: −74, Blue: +113, Yellow: −103.)

9 Go to 10:12.

10 Move all the canvas layers off the screen to the right. Vary their motion paths to make them more interesting. You can add intermediate rotation and position keyframes (between 10:06 and 10:12), edit Bezier curves, or just drag the canvas layers off the edge. If you edit the Bezier curves, make changes only to the keyframes on the right side of the motion path (at 10:12) so you don't disturb the original balloon formation.

11 Move the current-time indicator across the time ruler to preview the animation, and then make any adjustments you want.

12 Hide the properties for all layers, and save your work.

Adding an adjustment layer

You'll add a warp effect to the canvas. You can use an adjustment layer to apply an effect to all the layers beneath it at once.

1 Click an empty area in the Timeline panel to deselect all layers.

2 Choose Layer > New > Adjustment Layer.

A new adjustment layer is automatically added to the top of the layer stack.

3 In the Effects & Presets panel, navigate to the Wave Warp effect in the Distort category, and then double-click the effect.

4 Go to 9:12.

5 In the Effect Controls panel, change Wave Height to **0** and Wave Width to **1**. Then click the stopwatch icons to create initial keyframes for each of them.

6 Go to 9:16.

7 Change the Wave Height value to **90** and the Wave Width value to **478**.

Trimming a layer

You don't need the Wave Warp effect until the canvas flies off the balloon, but even if the values are 0, After Effects will have to calculate the effect for the entire layer. So you'll trim the layer to speed up the time it takes to render the file.

1 Go to 9:12.

2 Press Alt+[(Windows) or Option+[(Mac OS) to set the In point to **9:12**.

3 Return to the Balloon Scene Timeline panel.

4 Press the spacebar to preview the movie. Press the spacebar again to stop the preview.

5 Save your work so far.

● **Note:** Press [to move the In point of a clip without changing its duration. Press Alt+[or Option+[to trim a clip to a new In point, shortening its duration.

Animating the background

The movie should end with the revelation that the canvas from the balloons has been draped on the clouds. But right now, the canvas flies off and the balloon floats away. You need to animate the sky so that the canvas-covered clouds are centered at the end of the scene.

1 In the Balloon Scene Timeline panel, go to the beginning of the time ruler (0:00).

2 Select the Sky layer, and press P to display its Position property.

3 Click the stopwatch icon to create an initial keyframe.

4 Go to 16:00, and drag the Sky layer to the left until the wrapped clouds are in the center of the frame. (Our values are −236.4, 566.7.)

5 Go to 8:00, and move the wrapped clouds completely off the screen, far off to the right.

6 Right-click the first keyframe, and choose Keyframe Assistant > Easy Ease Out.

7 Right-click the middle keyframe, and choose Keyframe Assistant > Easy Ease, and then right-click the last keyframe, and choose Keyframe Assistant > Easy Ease In.

8 Move the current-time indicator through the time ruler to see how the departure of the canvas matches up with the appearance of the canvas-colored clouds. The canvas should be completely offscreen before the canvas-colored clouds appear.

9 Move the middle keyframe forward and backward in the time ruler to adjust the sky animation so that it matches the progress of the canvas and the balloon. The bare balloon should float in front of at least a few of the canvas-colored clouds before it disappears.

10 Press the spacebar to preview the entire video. Press the spacebar again to stop the preview.

11 Adjust the motion paths and rotations for the balloon, canvas pieces, or the sky as necessary.

12 Hide the properties for all layers, and save the project.

Adding an audio track

Give yourself a hand—you've done a lot of animating in this project. But you're not quite done. You'll add a soundtrack that matches the lighthearted mood of the video, and fade it out. You'll also shorten the composition, since the last few seconds are static.

1 Click the Project tab to bring the Project panel forward. Then, double-click an empty area of the Project panel to open the Import File dialog box.

2 Navigate to the Lessons/Lesson05/Assets folder, and double-click the Soundtrack.wav file.

3 Drag the Soundtrack.wav item from the Project panel into the Balloon Scene Timeline panel, placing it at the bottom of the layer stack.

4 Preview the movie. The music changes just as the canvas flies off the balloon.

5 Go to 18:00, and press N to move the work area end point to the current time.

6 Choose Composition > Trim Comp to Work Area.

7 Go to 16:00. Expand the Soundtrack.wav layer and the Audio properties.

8 Click the stopwatch icon to create an initial keyframe for the Audio Levels value.

9 Go to 18:00, and change the Audio Levels value to **−40** dB.

10 Preview the animation, and then save it.

Congratulations. You've just created a complex animation, practicing all kinds of After Effects techniques and capabilities along the way.

Supported audio file formats

You can import any of the following types of audio files into After Effects:

- Advanced Audio Coding (AAC, M4A)
- Audio Interchange File Format (AIF, AIFF)
- MP3 (MP3, MPEG, MPG, MPA, MPE)
- Waveform (WAV)

Editing audio files in Adobe Audition

You can make some very simple changes to audio in After Effects. For more substantial edits, use Adobe Audition. Audition is available with a full Adobe Creative Cloud membership.

You can use Audition to change the length of an audio file, alter its pitch, or change its tempo. You can apply effects, record new audio, mix multitrack sessions, and more.

To edit an audio clip you've used in After Effects, select the file in the Project panel, and choose Edit > Edit In Adobe Audition. Then, make your changes in Audition, and save the file. The changes you made are automatically reflected in your After Effects project.

Review questions

1 How does After Effects display an animation of the Position property?

2 What is a solid-color layer, and what can you do with it?

3 What types of audio can you import into an After Effects project?

Review answers

1 When you animate the Position property, After Effects displays the movement as a motion path. You can create a motion path for the position of the layer or for the anchor point of a layer. A position motion path appears in the Composition panel; an anchor-point motion path appears in the Layer panel. The motion path appears as a sequence of dots, where each dot marks the position of the layer at each frame. A box in the path marks the position of a keyframe.

2 You can create solid images of any color or size (up to 30,000 x 30,000 pixels) in After Effects. After Effects treats solids as it does any other footage item: You can modify the mask, transform properties, and apply effects to the solid layer. If you change settings for a solid that is used by more than one layer, you can apply the changes to all layers that use the solid or to only the single occurrence of the solid. Use solid layers to color a background or create simple graphic images.

3 You can import any of the following types of audio files into After Effects: Adobe Sound Document (ASND; multitrack files import as merged single track), Advanced Audio Coding (AAC, M4A), Audio Interchange File Format (AIF, AIFF), MP3 (MP3, MPEG, MPG, MPA, MPE), Video for Windows (AVI, WAV; requires QuickTime on Mac OS), and Waveform (WAV).

6 ANIMATING LAYERS

Lesson overview

In this lesson, you'll learn how to do the following:

- Animate a layered Adobe Photoshop file.

- Duplicate an animation using the pick whip.

- Work with imported Photoshop layer styles.

- Apply a track matte to control the visibility of layers.

- Animate a layer using the Corner Pin effect.

- Apply the Lens Flare effect to a solid layer.

- Use time remapping and the Layer panel to dynamically retime footage.

- Edit Time Remap keyframes in the Graph Editor.

This lesson will take approximately an hour to complete. Download the project files for this lesson, following the instructions in the Getting Started section under "Accessing the lesson files and Web Edition," if you haven't already done so. As you work on this lesson, you'll preserve the start files. If you need to restore the start files, download them from your Account page.

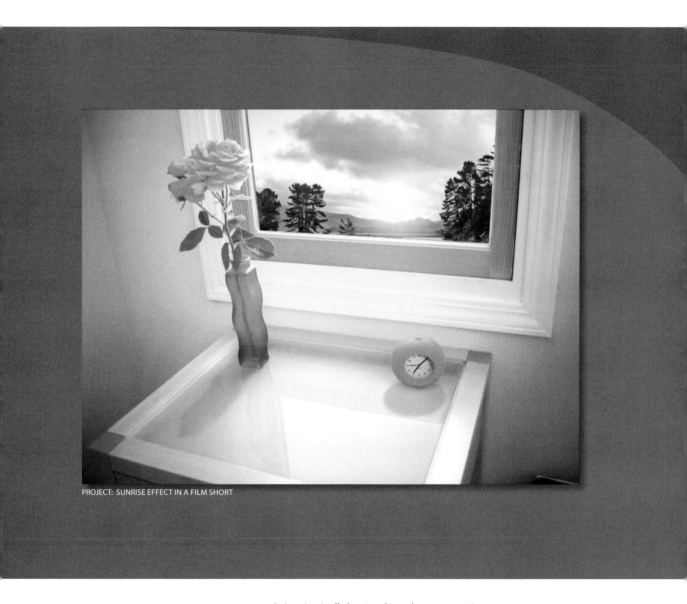

PROJECT: SUNRISE EFFECT IN A FILM SHORT

Animation is all about making changes over time—
changes to an object or image's position, opacity, scale,
and other properties. This lesson provides more practice
animating the layers of a Photoshop file, including
dynamically remapping time.

Getting started

Adobe After Effects provides several tools and effects that let you simulate motion video using a layered Photoshop file. In this lesson, you will import a layered Photoshop file of the sun appearing through a window, and then animate it to simulate the motion of the sun rising behind the panes of glass. This is a stylized animation in which the motion is first accelerated, and then slows down as clouds and birds move through the window frame at the end.

First, you'll preview the final movie and set up the project.

1 Make sure the following files are in the Lessons/Lesson06 folder on your hard disk, or download them from your Account page at www.peachpit.com now:

 • In the Assets folder: clock.mov, sunrise.psd

 • In the Sample_Movies folder: Lesson06_regular.avi, Lesson06_regular.mov, Lesson06_retimed.avi, Lesson06_retimed.mov

2 Open and play the Lesson06_regular.avi file in Windows Media Player or the Lesson06_regular.mov file in QuickTime Player to see the straightforward time-lapse animation you will create in this lesson.

3 Open and play the Lesson06_retimed.avi file or Lesson06_retimed.mov file to see the same animation after time has been remapped, later in the lesson.

4 When you're done, quit Windows Media Player or QuickTime Player. You may delete the sample movies from your hard disk if you have limited storage space.

When you begin the lesson, restore the default application settings for After Effects. See "Restoring default preferences" on page 2.

5 Start After Effects, and then immediately hold down Ctrl+Alt+Shift (Windows) or Command+Option+Shift (Mac OS) to restore default preferences settings. When prompted, click OK to delete your preferences file. Then, close the Start window.

After Effects opens to display an empty, untitled project.

6 Choose File > Save As > Save As.

7 In the Save As dialog box, navigate to the Lessons/Lesson06/Finished_ Project folder.

8 Name the project **Lesson06_Finished.aep**, and then click Save.

Importing the footage

You need to import one source item for this lesson.

1 Double-click an empty area of the Project panel to open the Import File dialog box.

2 Navigate to the Lessons/Lesson06/Assets folder on your hard disk, and select the sunrise.psd file.

3 Choose Composition – Retain Layer Sizes from the Import As menu, so the dimensions of each layer will match the layer's content. (In Mac OS, you may need to click Options to see the Import As menu.)

4 Click Import or Open.

5 In the Sunrise.psd dialog box, make sure Composition – Retain Layer Sizes is selected in the Import Kind menu, and click OK.

Before continuing, take a moment to study the layers of the file you just imported.

6 In the Project panel, expand the sunrise Layers folder to see the Photoshop layers. Resize the Name column to make it wider and easier to read, if necessary.

Each of the elements you'll animate in After Effects—the shadows, birds, clouds, and sun—is on a separate layer. In addition, there is one layer representing the initial, predawn lighting conditions in the room (Background), and a second layer that represents the final, bright daylight conditions in the room (Background Lit). Similarly, there are two layers for the two lighting conditions outside the window: Window and Window Lit. The Window Pane layer includes a Photoshop layer style that simulates a pane of glass.

After Effects preserves the layer order, transparency data, and layer styles from the source Photoshop document. It also preserves other features, such as adjustment layers and type, which you don't happen to be using in this project.

Creating the composition

For this lesson, you'll use the imported Photoshop file as the basis of the composition.

1 Double-click the sunrise composition in the Project panel to open it in the Composition panel and in the Timeline panel.

2 Choose Composition > Composition Settings.

3 In the Composition Settings dialog box, change the Duration to **10:00** to make the composition 10 seconds long, and then click OK.

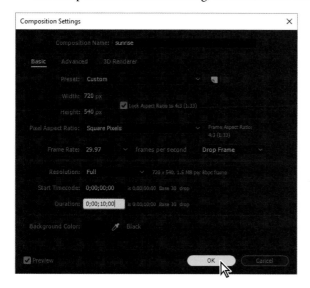

About Photoshop layer styles

Adobe Photoshop provides a variety of layer styles—such as shadows, glows, and bevels—that change the appearance of a layer. After Effects can preserve these layer styles when you import Photoshop layers. You can also apply layer styles in After Effects.

Though layer styles are referred to as *effects* in Photoshop, they behave more like blending modes in After Effects. Layer styles follow transformations in the standard render order, whereas effects precede transformations. Another difference is that each layer style blends directly with the underlying layers in the composition, whereas an effect is rendered on the layer to which it's applied, the result of which then interacts with the underlying layers as a whole.

The layer style properties are available for the layer in the Timeline panel.

To learn more about working with layer styles in After Effects, see After Effects Help.

Simulating lighting changes

The first part of the animation involves lightening the dark room. You'll use Opacity keyframes to animate the light.

1 In the Timeline panel, click the Solo switch (●) for both the Background Lit and Background layers.

Soloing the layers isolates them to speed animating, previewing, and rendering.

Currently, the lit background is on top of the regular (darker) background, obscuring it and making the initial frame of the animation light. However, you want the animation to start dark, and then lighten. To accomplish this, you will make the Background Lit layer initially transparent, and then animate its opacity so that it appears to lighten the background over time.

2 Go to 5:00.

3 Select the Background Lit layer in the Timeline panel, and press T to reveal its Opacity property.

4 Click the stopwatch icon (◔) to set an Opacity keyframe. Note that the Opacity value is 100%.

5 Press the Home key, or drag the current-time indicator to 0:00. Then set the
 Opacity for the Background Lit layer to **0%**. After Effects adds a keyframe.

Now, when the animation begins, the Background Lit layer is transparent, which
allows the dark Background layer to show through.

6 Click the Solo switches (●) for the Background Lit and Background layers to
 restore the view of the other layers, including Window and Window Lit. Make
 sure to leave the Opacity property for the Background Lit layer visible.

7 Expand the Window Pane layer's Transform properties. The Window Pane layer
 has a Photoshop layer style that creates a bevel on the window.

8 Go to 2:00, and click the stopwatch next to the Opacity property for the Window
 Pane layer to create a keyframe at the current value, 30%.

9 Press the Home key or drag the current-time indicator to the beginning
 of the time ruler, and change the Opacity property to **0%**.

10 Hide the Window Pane properties.

11 Click the Play/Pause button (▶) in the Preview panel, or press the spacebar, to preview the animation.

The interior of the room transitions gently from dimly to brightly lit.

12 Press the spacebar to stop playback at any time after 5:00.

13 Choose File > Save.

About expressions

When you want to create and link complex animations, such as multiple car wheels spinning, but want to avoid creating tens or hundreds of keyframes by hand, you can use *expressions* instead. With expressions, you can create relationships between layer properties and use one property's keyframes to dynamically animate another layer. For example, if you set rotation keyframes for a layer and then apply the Drop Shadow effect, you can use an expression to link the Rotation property's values with the Drop Shadow effect's Direction values; that way, the drop shadow changes with the layer as it rotates.

Expressions are based on the JavaScript language, but you don't need to know JavaScript to use them. You can create expressions by using simple examples and modifying them to suit your needs, or by chaining objects and methods together.

You work with expressions in the Timeline panel or the Effect Controls panel. You can use the pick whip to create expressions, or you can enter and edit expressions manually in the expression field—a text field in the time graph under the property.

For more about expressions, see After Effects Help.

Duplicating an animation using the pick whip

Now you need to lighten the view through the window. To do this, you'll use the pick whip to duplicate the animation you just created. You can use the pick whip to create expressions that link the values of one property or effect to another.

1 Press the Home key, or move the current-time indicator to the beginning of the time ruler.

2 Select the Window Lit layer, and press T to reveal its Opacity property.

3 Alt-click (Windows) or Option-click (Mac OS) the Opacity stopwatch for the Window Lit layer to add an expression for the default Opacity value, 100%. The words *transform.opacity* appear in the time ruler for the Window Lit layer.

4 Click the pick whip icon (⊚) on the Window Lit Expression: Opacity line, and drag it to the Opacity property name in the Background Lit layer. When you release the mouse, the pick whip snaps, and the expression in the Window Lit layer time ruler now reads *"thisComp.layer("Background Lit").transform.opacity."* This means that the Opacity value for the Background Lit layer (0%) replaces the previous Opacity value (100%) for the Window Lit layer.

5 Drag the current-time indicator from 0:00 to 5:00. Notice that the Opacity values for the two layers match.

6 Go to the beginning of the time ruler, and then press the spacebar to preview the animation again. Notice that the sky outside the window lightens as the room inside the window does.

7 Press the spacebar to stop playback.

8 Hide the Window Lit and Background Lit layers' properties to keep the Timeline panel tidy for your next task.

9 Choose File > Save to save your project.

Animating movement in the scenery

The scenery outside the window is unrealistically static. For one thing, the sun should actually rise. In addition, shifting clouds and flying birds would bring this scene to life.

Animating the sun

To make the sun rise in the sky, you'll set keyframes for its Position, Scale, and Opacity properties.

1 In the Timeline panel, select the Sun layer, and expand its Transform properties.

2 Go to 4:07, and click the stopwatch icons (Ö) to set keyframes for the Position, Scale, and Opacity properties at their default values.

3 Go to 3:13.

4 Still working with the Sun layer, set its Scale to **33, 33%** and its Opacity to **10%**. After Effects adds a keyframe for each property.

5 Press the End key, or move the current-time indicator to the end of the composition.

6 For the Position property of the Sun layer, set the y value to **18**, and then set the Scale values to **150, 150%**. After Effects adds two keyframes.

You've just set keyframes that instruct the sun to move up and across the sky, and to become slightly larger and brighter as it rises.

7 Hide the Sun layer's properties.

Animating the birds

Next, you'll animate the motion of the birds flying by. To create the animation faster, you'll take advantage of the Auto-Keyframe option. When Auto-Keyframe is enabled, After Effects automatically creates a keyframe whenever you change a value.

1 Select the Birds layer in the Timeline panel, and press P to reveal its Position property.

2 From the Timeline panel menu, choose Enable Auto-Keyframe.

A red stopwatch icon appears at the top of the Timeline panel to remind you that Auto-Keyframe is selected.

3 Go to 4:20, and set the Position values for the Birds layer to **200, 49**. After Effects automatically adds a keyframe.

● **Note:** While the Auto-Keyframe option can make your life easier, it can also create more keyframes than you intended. Choose Enable Auto-Keyframe only when you need it for a specific task, and remember to disable it when you're done with that task!

4 Go to 4:25, and set the Position values of the Birds layer to **670, 49**. After Effects adds a keyframe.

5 Select the Birds layer, and press P to hide its Position property.

Animating the clouds

Next, you'll animate the clouds drifting across the sky.

1 Select the Clouds layer in the Timeline panel, and expand its Transform properties.

2 Go to 5:22, and click the stopwatch icon (🕙) for the Position property to set a Position keyframe at the current value (406.5, 58.5).

3 Still at 5:22, set the Opacity for the Clouds layer to **33%**.

After Effects automatically adds a keyframe, because Auto-Keyframe is still enabled.

4 Choose Enable Auto-Keyframe from the Timeline panel menu to deselect it.

5 Go to 5:02, and set the Clouds layer Opacity value to **0%**.

After Effects adds a keyframe, even though you disabled Auto-Keyframe.
After Effects adds a keyframe whenever you change the value for a property that already has a keyframe in the timeline.

6 Go to 9:07, and set the Clouds layer Opacity value to **50%**. After Effects adds a keyframe.

7 Press the End key, or move the current-time indicator to the last frame of the composition.

8 Set the Position of the Clouds layer to **456.5**, **48.5**. After Effects adds a keyframe.

Previewing the animation

Now, see how it all comes together.

1 Press the Home key, or go to 0:00.

2 Press F2 or click an empty area in the Timeline panel to deselect everything, and then press the spacebar to preview the animation.

The sun rises in the sky, the birds fly by (very quickly), and the clouds drift. So far, so good! However, there's a fundamental problem: These elements all overlap the window frame—the birds even appear to be flying inside the room. You'll solve this next.

3 Press the spacebar to stop playback.

4 Hide the properties for the Clouds layer, and then choose File > Save.

Adjusting the layers and creating a track matte

To solve the problem of the sun, birds, and clouds overlapping the window frame, you must first adjust the hierarchy of the layers within the composition. Then you'll use an alpha track matte to allow the outside scenery to show through the window, but not appear to be inside the room.

Precomposing layers

You'll start by precomposing the Sun, Birds, and Clouds layers into one composition.

1 Shift-click to select the Sun, Birds, and Clouds layers in the Timeline panel.

2 Choose Layer > Pre-compose.

3 In the Pre-compose dialog box, name the new composition **Window Contents**. Make sure the Move All Attributes Into The New Composition option is selected, and select Open New Composition. Then click OK.

A new Timeline panel named Window Contents appears. It contains the Sun, Birds, and Clouds layers you selected in step 1 above. The Window Contents composition also appears in the Composition window.

4 Click the sunrise Timeline panel to see the contents of the main composition. Notice that the Sun, Birds, and Clouds layers have been replaced by the Window Contents layer, which refers to the Window Contents composition.

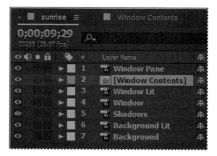

Creating the track matte

Now, you will create the track matte to hide the outside scenery behind all areas of the image except the windowpane. To do that, you'll duplicate the Window Lit layer and use its alpha channel.

About track mattes and traveling mattes

When you want one layer to show through a hole in another layer, set up a *track matte*. You'll need two layers—one to act as a matte, the other to fill the hole in the matte. You can animate either the track matte layer or the fill layer. When you animate the track matte layer, you create a *traveling matte*. If you want to animate the track matte and fill layers using identical settings, you can precompose them.

You define transparency in a track matte using values from either its alpha channel or the luminance of its pixels. Using luminance is handy when you want to create a track matte from a layer without an alpha channel, or a layer imported from a program that can't create an alpha channel. In both alpha-channel mattes and luminance mattes, pixels with higher values are more transparent. In most cases, you use a high-contrast matte so that areas are either completely transparent or completely opaque. Intermediate shades should appear only where you want partial or gradual transparency, such as along a soft edge.

After Effects preserves the order of a layer and its track matte after you duplicate or split the layer. Within the duplicated or split layers, the track matte layer remains on top of the fill layer. For example, if your project contains layers X and Y, where X is the track matte and Y the fill layer, duplicating or splitting both of these layers results in the layer order XYXY.

| A | B | C |

Anatomy of a traveling matte
A. *Track matte layer: a solid with a rectangular mask, set to Luma Matte. The mask is animated to travel across the screen.*
B. *Fill layer: a solid with a pattern effect.*
C. *Result: The pattern is seen in the track matte's shape and added to the image layer, which is below the track matte layer.*

1 In the sunrise Timeline panel, select the Window Lit layer.

2 Choose Edit > Duplicate.

3 Drag the duplicate layer, Window Lit 2, up in the layer stack so that it's above the Window Contents layer.

4 Click Toggle Switches/Modes at the bottom of the Timeline panel to display the TrkMat column, so you can apply the track matte.

5 Select the Window Contents layer, and choose Alpha Matte "Window Lit 2" from the TrkMat pop-up menu.

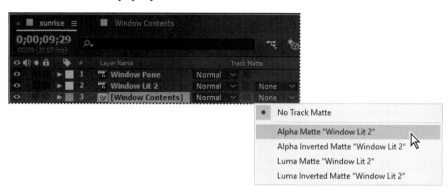

The alpha channel of the layer above (Window Lit 2) is used to set transparency for the Window Contents layer, so the scenery outside the window shows through the transparent areas of the windowpane.

6 Press the Home key or move the current-time indicator to the beginning of the time ruler, and then press the spacebar to preview the animation. Press the spacebar again when you're done.

7 Choose File > Save to save your project.

Adding motion blur

The birds will look more authentic if they include motion blur. You'll add the motion blur and then set the shutter angle and phase, which control the intensity of the blur.

1 Switch to the Window Contents Timeline panel.

2 Go to 4:22—the middle of the birds' animation. Then select the Birds layer, and choose Layer > Switches > Motion Blur to turn on motion blur for the layer.

3 Click the Enable Motion Blur button () at the top of the Timeline panel to display the motion blur for the Birds layer in the Composition panel.

4 Choose Composition > Composition Settings.

5 In the Composition Settings dialog box, click the Advanced tab, and reduce the Shutter Angle to **30** degrees.

The Shutter Angle setting imitates the effect of adjusting a shutter angle on a real camera, which controls how long the camera aperture is open, gathering light. Larger values create more motion blur.

6 Change the Shutter Phase to **0** degrees, and then click OK.

Animating the shadows

It's time to turn your attention to the shadows cast on the table by the clock and the vase. In a realistic time-lapse image, those shadows would shorten as the sun rises.

There are a few ways to create and animate shadows in After Effects. For example, you could use 3D layers and lights. In this project, however, you'll use the Corner Pin effect to distort the Shadows layer of the imported Photoshop image. Using the Corner Pin effect is like animating with the Photoshop Free Transform tool—the effect distorts an image by repositioning each of its four corners. You can use it to stretch, shrink, skew, or twist an image, or to simulate perspective or movement that pivots from the edge of a layer, such as a door opening.

1 Switch to the sunrise Timeline panel, and make sure you're at the beginning of the time ruler.

● **Note:** If you don't see the controls, choose View Options from the Composition panel menu. In the View Options dialog box, select the Handles and Effect Controls options, and then click OK.

2 Select the Shadows layer in the Timeline panel, and then choose Effect > Distort > Corner Pin. Small circles appear around the corner points of the Shadows layer in the Composition panel.

You'll start by setting the four corners of the Shadows layer to correspond to the four corners of the glass tabletop. Begin about midway into the animation, when the sun is high enough to start affecting the shadow.

▶ **Tip:** The lower right corner of the Shadows layer is offscreen. To adjust that corner, switch to the Hand tool (✋), and drag up in the Composition panel so that you can see some of the pasteboard below the image. Then switch back to the Selection tool (▶), and drag the lower right corner-pin handle to the approximate location of the lower right corner of the glass tabletop.

3 Go to 6:00, and then drag each of the four corner-pin handles to the respective corners of the glass tabletop. Notice that the x and y coordinates update in the Effect Controls panel.

If you have trouble getting the shadows to look right, you can manually enter the values shown in the figure that follows step 4.

4 Set a keyframe for each corner at 6:00 by clicking the stopwatch icon (🕑) for each position in the Effect Controls panel.

5 Press the End key, or move the current-time indicator to the last frame of the composition.

6 Using the Selection tool (▶), shorten the shadows: Drag the two lower corner-pins about 25% closer to the back edge of the tabletop. You may also need to move the two upper corners in slightly so that the bases of the shadows still align properly with the vase and the clock. Your corner-pin values should be similar to those in the figure below; you can enter the values directly if you prefer not to drag the corners. After Effects adds keyframes.

7 If necessary, select the Hand tool (✋), and drag the composition down to center it vertically in the Composition panel. Then switch back to the Selection tool, and deselect the layer.

8 Go to 0:00, and then press the spacebar to preview the entire animation, including the corner-pin effect. When you're done, press the spacebar again.

9 Choose File > Save to save your project.

Adding a lens flare effect

In photography, when bright light (such as sunlight) reflects off the lens of a camera, it causes a flare effect. Lens flares can be bright, colorful circles and halos, depending on the type of lens in the camera. After Effects offers a few lens flare effects. You'll add one now to enhance the realism of this time-lapse photography composition.

1 Go to 5:10, where the sun is shining brightly into the lens of the camera.

2 With no layers selected in the Timeline panel, choose Layer > New > Solid.

3 In the Solid Settings dialog box, name the layer **Lens Flare,** and click the Make Comp Size button. Then set the Color to black by clicking the swatch and setting all the RGB values to 0 in the Solid Color dialog box. Click OK to return to the Solid Settings dialog box.

4 Click OK to create the Lens Flare layer.

5 With the Lens Flare layer selected in the sunrise Timeline panel, choose Effect > Generate > Lens Flare from the After Effects menu bar.

The Composition panel and the Effect Controls panel display the visual and numeric default Lens Flare settings, respectively; you'll customize the effect for this composition.

6 Drag the Flare Center cross-hairs icon (⊕) in the Composition panel to the center of the sun. Since you cannot see the sun in the Composition panel, position the cross-hairs so that the x,y coordinates in the Effect Controls or Info panel are approximately 455, 135.

▶ **Tip:** You can also enter the Flare Center values directly in the Effect Controls panel.

7 In the Effect Controls panel, change the Lens Type to 35mm Prime, a more diffuse flare effect.

8 Make sure you're still at 5:10. In the Effect Controls panel, click the stopwatch icon (Ŏ) for the Flare Brightness property to set a keyframe at the default value of 100%.

9 Adjust the brightness of the lens flare to peak when the sun is highest:

 • Go to 3:27, and set the Flare Brightness value to **0%**.

 • Go to 6:27, and set the Flare Brightness value to **0%** as well.

 • Go to 6:00, and set the Flare Brightness to **100%**.

10 With the Lens Flare layer selected in the Timeline panel, choose Layer > Blending Mode > Screen to change the blending mode.

▶ **Tip:** You can also choose Screen from the Mode pop-up menu in the Timeline panel.

11 Press the Home key or move the current-time indicator to the beginning of the time ruler, and then press the spacebar to preview the Lens Flare effect. When you're done, press the spacebar again.

12 Choose File > Save to save your project.

Adding a video animation

● **Note:** You'll learn more about 3D layers in Lessons 11, "Using 3D Features," and 12, "Working with the 3D Camera Tracker."

The animation now looks very much like a time-lapse photo—except the clock isn't working yet! The hands of the clock should be spinning quickly to show the progress of time. To show this, you will add an animation that was created specifically for this scene. The animation was created in After Effects as a set of 3D layers that are lit, textured, and masked to blend into the scene.

1. Bring the Project panel forward. Close the sunrise Layers folder, and then double-click an empty area in the panel to open the Import File dialog box.

2. In the Lessons/Lesson06/ Assets folder, select the clock.mov file, and click Import or Open.

The QuickTime movie clock.mov now appears at the top of the Project panel.

3. Click in the sunrise Timeline panel to make it active, and then go to the beginning of the time ruler. Drag the clock.mov footage item from the Project panel to the top of the layer stack in the Timeline panel.

4. Preview the animation by pressing the spacebar. Press the spacebar again to stop playback when you're done.

5. Choose File > Save to save the project.

Rendering the animation

To prepare for the next task—retiming the composition—you need to render the sunrise composition and export it as a movie.

1 Select the sunrise composition in the Project panel, and then choose Composition > Add To Render Queue.

The Render Queue panel opens. Depending on the size of your screen, you may need to maximize the panel to see all the settings.

2 (Optional) Double-click the Render Queue panel tab to make the panel larger.

3 Accept the default Render Settings in the Render Queue panel. Then click the blue, italicized words *Not Yet Specified* next to the Output To pop-up menu.

4 Navigate to the Lessons/Lesson06/Assets folder, and name the file **Lesson06_retime.avi** (Windows) or **Lesson06_retime.mov** (Mac OS). Then click Save.

5 Expand the Output Module group, and then choose Import from the Post-Render Action menu. After Effects will import the movie file after it's rendered.

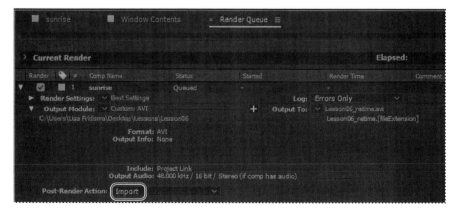

6 Hide the Output Module section.

7 Click the Render button in the Render Queue panel.

After Effects displays a progress bar as it renders and exports the composition, and plays an audio alert when it is finished. It also imports the resulting movie file into the project.

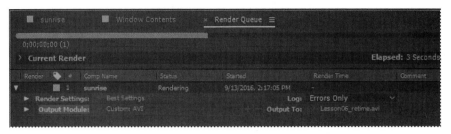

8 When After Effects has finished rendering and exporting the composition, double-click the Render Queue panel tab if you maximized the panel earlier. Then click the x in the Render Queue tab to close the Render Queue panel.

Retiming the composition

▶ **Tip:** You can get even finer control with the Timewarp effect, which you'll use in Lesson 13, "Advanced Editing Techniques."

So far, you have created a straightforward time-lapse simulation. That's fine, but After Effects offers more ways to play with time using the time-remapping feature. Time remapping lets you dynamically speed up, slow down, stop, or reverse footage. You can also use it to do things like create a freeze-frame result. The Graph Editor and the Layer panel are a big help when remapping time, as you'll see in the following exercise, when you retime the project so that the time-lapse speed changes over the course of the movie.

For this exercise, you'll use the movie that you just imported as the basis of a new composition, which will be easier to remap than the original.

1 Drag the Lesson06_retime movie onto the Create A New Composition button (🖵) at the bottom of the Project panel.

After Effects creates a new composition named Lesson06_retime, and displays it in the Timeline and Composition panels. Now you can remap all of the elements of the project at once.

2 With the Lesson06_retime layer selected in the Timeline panel, choose Layer > Time > Enable Time Remapping.

After Effects adds two keyframes, at the first and last frames of the layer, visible in the time ruler. A Time Remap property also appears under the layer name in the Timeline panel; this property lets you control which frame is displayed at a given point in time.

3 Double-click the Lesson06_retime layer name in the Timeline panel to open it in the Layer panel.

The Layer panel provides a visual reference of the frames you change when you remap time. It displays two time rulers: The time ruler at the bottom of the panel displays the current time. The Source Time ruler, just above the time ruler, has a remap-time marker that indicates which frame is playing at the current time.

4 Drag the current-time indicator across the time ruler in the Timeline panel, and notice that the source-time and current-time markers in the two Layer panel rulers are synchronized. That will change as you remap time.

5 Go to 4:00, and change the Time Remap value to **2:00**.

This remaps time so that frame 2:00 plays at 4:00. In other words, the composition now plays back at half-speed for the first four seconds of the composition.

6 Press the spacebar to preview the animation. The composition now runs at half-speed until 4:00, and at a faster speed thereafter. Press the spacebar again when you have finished previewing the animation.

Viewing time remapping in the Graph Editor

Using the Graph Editor, you can view and manipulate all aspects of effects and animations, including effect property values, keyframes, and interpolation. The Graph Editor displays changes in effects and animations as a two-dimensional graph, with playback time represented horizontally (from left to right). In layer bar mode, in contrast, the time ruler represents only the horizontal time element, without a graphical display of changing values.

1 Make sure the Time Remap property is selected for the Lesson06_retime layer in the Timeline panel.

2 Click the Graph Editor button (⬚) to display the Graph Editor.

The Graph Editor displays a time-remap graph that shows a white line connecting the keyframes at 0:00, 4:00, and 10:00. The angle of the line is shallow up to 4:00, and then becomes steeper. The steeper the line, the faster the playback time.

Using the Graph Editor to remap time

When remapping time, you can use the values in the time-remap graph to determine and control which frame of the movie plays at which point in time. Each Time Remap keyframe has a time value associated with it that corresponds to a specific frame in the layer; this value is represented vertically on the time-remap graph. When you enable time remapping for a layer, After Effects adds a Time Remap keyframe at the start and end points of the layer. These initial Time Remap keyframes have vertical time values equal to their horizontal position.

By setting additional Time Remap keyframes, you can create complex motion effects. Every time you add a Time Remap keyframe, you create another point at which you can change the playback speed or direction. As you move the keyframe up or down in the time-remap graph, you adjust which frame of the video is set to play at the current time.

You'll have some fun with the timing of this project.

1 In the time-remap graph, drag the middle keyframe vertically from 2 up to 10 seconds.

2 Drag the last keyframe down to 0 seconds.

3 Go to 0:00, and then press the spacebar to preview the results. Watch the time ruler and Source Time ruler in the Layer panel to see which frames are playing at any given point in time.

▶ **Tip:** Watch the Info panel as you drag to see more information as you adjust the keyframe.

The animation progresses rapidly over the first four seconds of the composition, and then plays in reverse for the rest of the composition.

4 Press the spacebar to stop the preview.

Having fun yet? Keep going.

5 Ctrl-click (Windows) or Command-click (Mac OS) the last keyframe to delete it. The composition is still in fast-forward mode for the first 4 seconds, but now it holds on a single frame (the last frame) for the rest of the composition.

6 Press the Home key or move the current-time indicator to the beginning of the time ruler, and then press the spacebar to preview the animation. Press the spacebar again when you're done.

● **Note:** Pressing Ctrl or Command temporarily activates the Add Vertex tool.

7 Ctrl-click (Windows) or Command-click (Mac OS) the dotted line at 6:00 to add a keyframe at 6:00 with the same value as the keyframe at 4:00.

8 Ctrl-click (Windows) or Command-click (Mac OS) at 10:00 to add another keyframe, and then drag it down to 0 seconds.

The animation progresses rapidly, holds for two seconds on the last frame, and then runs in reverse.

9 Go to the beginning of the composition, and then press the spacebar to preview the change. Press the spacebar again when you're done.

Adding an Easy Ease Out

You'll soften the shift in time that occurs at 6 seconds with an Easy Ease Out.

1 Click to select the keyframe at 6:00, and then click the Easy Ease Out button (⤴)at the bottom of the Graph Editor. This slows the shift into reverse—the footage runs slowly in reverse at first, and then gradually speeds up.

▶ **Tip:** You can refine the amount of ease on this transition further by dragging the Bezier handle that appears out of the right side of the keyframe at 6:00. If you drag it to the right, the transition is softer; if you drag it down or to the left, the transition is more pronounced.

2 Choose File > Save to save your work so far.

Scaling the animation in time

Finally, use the Graph Editor to scale the entire animation in time.

1 Click the Time Remap property name in the Timeline panel to select all of the Time Remap keyframes.

2 Make sure the Show Transform Box button (⊞) at the bottom of the Graph Editor is selected; a free-transform selection box should be visible around all of the keyframes.

Tip: If you press
Ctrl (Windows) or
Command (Mac OS)
while you drag, the
entire free-transform
box scales around the
center point, which you
can also drag to offset. If
you press Alt (Windows)
or Option (Mac OS)
and drag one corner
of the free-transform
box, the animation is
skewed in that corner as
you drag. You can also
drag one of the right
transform handles to the
left to scale the entire
animation so that it
happens more quickly.

3 Drag one of the upper transform handles from 10 seconds to 5 seconds.

The entire graph shifts, reducing the top keyframe values and slowing playback.

4 Press the Home key or move the current-time indicator to the beginning of the
time ruler, and then press the spacebar to preview the change. Press the spacebar
again when you're done.

5 Choose File > Save.

Congratulations. You've completed a complex animation, including shifts in time.
You can render and export the time-remap project if you'd like. Follow the instruc-
tions in "Rendering the animation" in this lesson, or see Lesson 14, "Rendering and
Outputting," for detailed instructions on rendering and exporting a composition.

Review questions

1 Why would you import a layered Photoshop file as a composition?

2 What is the pick whip, and how do you use it?

3 What is a track matte, and how do you use it?

4 How do you remap time in After Effects?

Review answers

1 When you import a layered Photoshop file into After Effects as a composition, After Effects preserves the layer order, transparency data, and layer styles from the source Photoshop document. It also preserves other features, such as adjustment layers and type.

2 The pick whip creates expressions that link the values of one property or effect to another layer. The pick whip is also a way to create parenting relationships. To use the pick whip, simply drag the pick whip icon from one property to another.

3 When you want one layer to show through a hole in another layer, you can use a track matte. To create a track matte, you need two layers: one to act as a matte, and another to fill the hole in the matte. You can animate either the track matte layer or the fill layer. When you animate the track matte layer, you create a traveling matte.

4 There are several ways to remap time in After Effects. Time remapping lets you dynamically speed up, slow down, stop, or reverse footage. When remapping time, you can use the values in the time-remap graph in the Graph Editor to determine and control which frame of the movie plays at which point in time. When you enable time remapping for a layer, After Effects adds a Time Remap keyframe at the start and end points of the layer. By setting additional Time Remap keyframes, you can create complex motion effects. Every time you add a Time Remap keyframe, you create another point at which you can change the playback speed or direction.

7 WORKING WITH MASKS

Lesson overview

In this lesson, you'll learn how to do the following:

- Create a mask using the Pen tool.

- Change a mask's mode.

- Edit a mask shape by controlling vertices and direction handles.

- Feather a mask edge.

- Replace the contents of a mask shape.

- Adjust the position of a layer in 3D space to blend it with the rest of a shot.

- Create a reflection effect.

- Modify a mask using the Mask Feather tool.

- Create a vignette.

This lesson will take approximately an hour to complete. Download the project files for this lesson, following the instructions in the Getting Started section under "Accessing the lesson files and Web Edition," if you haven't already done so. As you work on this lesson, you'll preserve the start files. If you need to restore the start files, download them from your Account page.

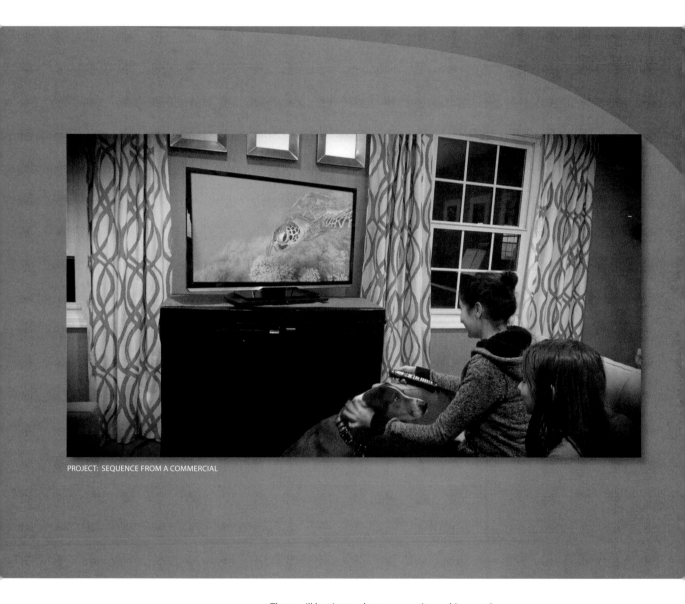

PROJECT: SEQUENCE FROM A COMMERCIAL

There will be times when you won't need (or want) everything in a shot to be included in the final composite. Use masks to control what appears.

About masks

A mask in Adobe After Effects is a path, or outline, that is used to modify layer effects and properties. The most common use of masks is to modify a layer's alpha channel. A mask consists of segments and vertices: *Segments* are the lines or curves that connect vertices. *Vertices* define where each segment of a path starts and ends.

A mask can be either an open or a closed path. An open path has a beginning point that is not the same as its end point; for example, a straight line is an open path. A closed path is continuous and has no beginning or end, such as a circle. Closed-path masks can create transparent areas for a layer. Open paths cannot create transparent areas for a layer, but are useful as parameters for an effect. For example, you can use an effect to generate a running light around a mask.

A mask belongs to a specific layer. Each layer can contain multiple masks.

You can draw masks in common geometric shapes—including polygons, ellipses, and stars—with the shape tools, or you can use the Pen tool to draw an arbitrary path.

Getting started

In this lesson, you will create a mask for the screen of a television and replace the screen's original content with a movie. Then you'll adjust the positioning of the new footage so that it fits the perspective of the shot. Finally, you'll polish the scene by adding a reflection, creating a vignette effect, and adjusting the color.

Begin by previewing the movie and setting up the project.

1 Make sure the following files are in the Lessons/Lesson07 folder on your hard disk, or download them from your Account page at www.peachpit.com now:

 • In the Assets folder: Turtle.mov, Watching_TV.mov

 • In the Sample_Movies folder: Lesson07.avi, Lesson07.mov

2 Open and play the Lesson07.avi sample movie in Windows Media Player or the Lesson07.mov sample movie in QuickTime Player to see what you will create in this lesson. When you are done, close Windows Media Player or QuickTime Player. You may delete the sample movies from your hard disk if you have limited storage space.

When you begin the lesson, restore the default application settings for After Effects. See "Restoring default preferences" on page 2.

3 Start After Effects, and then immediately hold down Ctrl+Alt+Shift (Windows) or Command+Option+Shift (Mac OS) to restore default preferences settings. When prompted, click OK to delete your preferences. Close the Start window.

After Effects opens to display a new, untitled project.

4 Choose File > Save As > Save As, and navigate to the Lessons/Lesson07/ Finished_Project folder.

5 Name the project **Lesson07_Finished.aep**, and then click Save.

Creating the composition

You'll import two footage items for this exercise. Then, you'll create the composition based on the aspect ratio and duration of one of the footage items.

1 Double-click an empty area of the Project panel to open the Import File dialog box.

2 Navigate to the Lessons/Lesson07/Assets folder, Shift-click to select the Turtle.mov and Watching_TV.mov files, and then click Import or Open.

3 Select the Watching_TV.mov footage item in the Project panel, and drag it onto the Create A New Composition button (🖼) at the bottom of the panel.

After Effects creates a composition named Watching_TV, and opens it in the Composition and Timeline panels.

4 Choose File > Save to save your work so far.

Creating a mask with the Pen tool

The TV screen is currently blank. To fill it with the video of a sea turtle, you need to mask the screen.

1 Press the Home key, or move the current-time indicator to the beginning of the time ruler.

2 Zoom in to the Composition panel until the TV screen nearly fills the view. You may need to use the Hand tool (✋) to reposition the view in the panel.

3 Make sure the Watching_TV.mov layer is selected in the Timeline panel, and then select the Pen tool (✒) in the Tools panel.

> **Tip:** You can also create a mask using the mocha shape plug-in, which comes with After Effects, and then import it into After Effects. To learn more about using the plug-in, see After Effects Help.

The Pen tool creates straight lines or curved segments. The TV appears to be rectangular, so you'll try using straight lines first.

4 Click the upper left corner of the TV screen to place the first vertex.

5 Click the upper right corner of the TV screen to place the second vertex. After Effects connects the two points with a segment.

6 Click to place a third vertex in the lower right corner of the TV screen, and then click to place a fourth vertex in the lower left corner of the screen.

7 Move the Pen tool over the first vertex (in the upper left corner). When a circle appears next to the pointer (as in the middle image below), click to close the mask path.

Editing a mask

The mask looks pretty good, but instead of masking the information *inside* the monitor, the mask has removed everything *outside* the monitor. You need to invert the mask. You'll also use Bezier curves to create a more accurate mask.

Inverting the mask

For this project, you need everything inside the mask to be transparent and everything outside the mask to be opaque. You'll invert the mask now.

▶ **Tip:** Pressing the M key twice in quick succession displays all mask properties for the selected layer.

1 Select the Watching_TV.mov layer in the Timeline panel, and press the M key to see the Mask Path property for the mask.

There are two ways to invert this mask: by choosing Subtract from the Mask Mode pop-up menu, or by selecting the Inverted option.

2 Select the Inverted option for Mask 1.

The mask inverts.

3 Press F2, or click an empty area of the Timeline panel, to deselect the Watching_TV.mov layer.

About mask modes

Blending modes for masks (mask modes) control how masks within a layer interact with one another. By default, all masks are set to Add, which combines the transparency values of any masks that overlap on the same layer. You can apply one mode to each mask, but you cannot change a mask's mode over time.

The first mask you create interacts with the layer's alpha channel. If that channel doesn't define the entire image as opaque, then the mask interacts with the layer frame. Each additional mask that you create interacts with masks located above it in the Timeline panel. The results of mask modes vary depending on the modes set for the masks higher up in the Timeline panel. You can use mask modes only between masks in the same layer. Using mask modes, you can create complex mask shapes with multiple transparent areas. For example, you can set a mask mode that combines masks and sets the opaque area to the regions where the masks intersect.

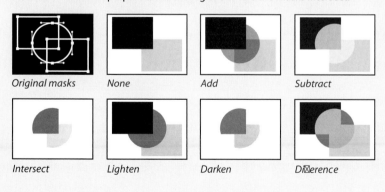

| Original masks | None | Add | Subtract |
| Intersect | Lighten | Darken | Difference |

If you look closely at the TV, you will probably see portions of the screen still appearing around the edges of the mask.

These errors will certainly call attention to changes being made to the layer, and they need to be fixed. To fix them, you'll change the straight lines to subtle curves.

Creating curved masks

Curved or freeform masks use Bezier curves to define the shape of the mask. Bezier curves give you the greatest control over the shape of the mask. With them, you can create straight lines with sharp angles, perfectly smooth curves, or a combination of the two.

1 In the Timeline panel, select Mask 1, the mask for the Watching_TV.mov layer. Selecting Mask 1 makes the mask active and also selects all the vertices.

2 In the Tools panel, select the Convert Vertex tool (∧), which is hidden behind the Pen tool.

3 In the Composition panel, click any of the vertices. The Convert Vertex tool changes the corner vertices to smooth points.

4 Switch to the Selection tool (▶), click anywhere in the Composition panel to deselect the mask, and then click the first vertex that you created.

Two direction handles extend off the smooth point. The angle and length of these handles control the shape of the mask.

5 Drag the right handle of the first vertex around the screen. Notice how this changes the shape of the mask. Notice also that the closer you drag the handle to another vertex, the less the shape of the path is influenced by the direction handle of the first vertex, and the more it is influenced by the direction handle of the second vertex.

Click the vertex. Drag the handle.

6 Once you are comfortable moving the handles, position the handle of the upper left vertex as in the preceding figure. As you have seen, you can create very fluid shapes.

Breaking direction handles

By default, the direction handles of any smooth point are connected to one another. As you drag one handle, the opposite handle moves as well. However, you can break this connection to get greater control over the shape of the mask, and you can create sharp points or long, smooth curves.

1 Select the Convert Vertex tool (⌐) in the Tools panel.

2 Drag the right direction handle of the upper left vertex. The left direction handle remains stationary.

3 Adjust the right direction handle until the top segment of the mask shape more closely follows the curve of the TV in that corner. It doesn't have to be perfect.

4 Drag the left direction handle of the same vertex until the left segment of the shape more closely follows the curve of the TV in that corner.

▶ **Tip:** If you make a mistake, press Ctrl+Z (Windows) or Command+Z (Mac OS) to undo your last action. You can also change the zoom level and use the Hand tool to reposition the image in the Composition panel as you work.

Drag the right direction handle of the upper left vertex, and then the left direction handle, to follow the curve of the TV screen.

Tip: Again, you may need to adjust your view in the Composition panel as you work. You can drag the image with the Hand tool. To temporarily switch to the Hand tool, press and hold the spacebar.

5 For each of the remaining corner points, click with the Convert Vertex tool, and then repeat steps 2–4 until the mask's shape more closely matches the curvature of the TV. If you need to shift a corner point, use the Selection tool.

6 When you're done, deselect the Watching_TV.mov layer in the Timeline panel to check the edge of your mask. You should not see any of the TV screen.

7 Choose File > Save to save your work.

Creating a Bezier mask

You used the Convert Vertex tool to change a corner vertex to a smooth point with Bezier handles, but you could have created a Bezier mask in the first place. To do so, click in the Composition panel with the Pen tool where you want to place the first vertex. Then click where you want to place the next vertex, and drag in the direction you want to create a curve. When you are satisfied with the curve, release the mouse button. Continue to add points until you've created the shape you want. Close the mask by either clicking on the first vertex or double-clicking the last vertex. Then switch to the Selection tool to refine the mask.

Feathering the edges of a mask

The mask looks good, but you need to soften the edges a bit.

1 Choose Composition > Composition Settings.

2 Click the Background Color box, and choose white for the background color (R=**255**, G=**255**, B=**255**). Then click OK to close the Color Picker, and OK again to close the Composition Settings dialog box.

The white background allows you to see that the edge of the TV screen looks a little too sharp and unrealistic. To address this, you'll feather, or soften, the edges.

3 Select the Watching_TV.mov layer in the Timeline panel, and press the F key to display the Mask Feather property for the mask.

4 Increase the Mask Feather amount to **1.5**, **1.5** pixels.

5 Hide the properties for the Watching_TV.mov layer, and then choose File > Save to save your work.

Replacing the content of the mask

You are now ready to replace the background with the video of a sea turtle and blend it with the overall shot.

1 In the Project panel, select the Turtle.mov file, and drag it to the Timeline panel, placing it below the Watching_TV.mov layer.

2 Choose Fit Up To 100% from the Magnification Ratio pop-up menu at the bottom of the Composition panel so that you can see the whole composition.

3　Select the Selection tool (▶), and then drag the Turtle.mov layer in the Composition panel until the anchor point is centered in the TV screen.

Zooming and panning by touch

If you're using a touch-enabled device, such as a Microsoft Surface, Wacom Cintiqu Touch, or multi-touch trackpad, you can use your fingers to zoom and pan. Touch gestures let you zoom and pan in the Composition, Layer, Footage, and Timeline panels.

To zoom: Pinch two fingers closer together to zoom in, or move them further apart to zoom out.

To pan: Move two fingers in unison to pan up, down, left, or right in the panel's current view.

Repositioning and resizing the clip

The sea turtle clip is too big for the TV screen, so you'll resize it as a 3D layer, which will give you more control over its shape and size.

1　With the Turtle.mov layer selected in the Timeline panel, click the 3D switch (⬡) for the layer.

2　Press the P key to show the Position property for the Turtle.mov layer.

The Position property for a 3D layer has three values: From left to right, they represent the x, y, and z axes of the image. The z axis controls the depth of the layer. You can see these axes represented in the Composition panel.

Note: You'll learn more about 3D layers in Lessons 11, "Using 3D Features," and 12, "Working with the 3D Camera Tracker."

3 Make sure the Selection tool is selected, and then position the pointer in the Composition panel over the red arrow so that a small *x* appears. The red arrow controls the x (horizontal) axis of the layer.

4 Drag left or right as necessary to center the clip horizontally in the monitor screen.

5 Position the pointer in the Composition panel over the green arrow so that a small *y* appears. Then drag up or down as necessary to position the clip vertically in the monitor screen.

6 Position the pointer in the Composition panel over the blue cube where the red and green arrows meet so that a small *z* appears. Then drag down and to the right to increase the depth of field, so that the Turtle.mov layer appears smaller.

7 Continue to drag the x, y, and z axes until the entire clip fits into the TV screen, as shown in the following image. Our final x, y, and z values are approximately **390, 146, 825**.

Tip: You can also enter the Position values directly in the Timeline panel instead of dragging in the Composition panel.

Rotating the clip

The video clip fits better, but you need to rotate it slightly to improve the perspective.

1 Select the Turtle.mov layer in the Timeline panel, and press the R key to reveal its Rotation properties.

Again, since this is a 3D layer, you can control rotation on the x, y, and z axes.

2 Change the X Rotation value to **1** degree and the Y Rotation value to **−40** degrees. This swivels the layer to match the perspective of the TV screen.

3 Change the Z Rotation value to **1** degree to align the layer with the TV screen.

Your composition should now resemble the preceding image.

4 Hide the properties for the Turtle.mov layer, and then choose File > Save to save your work.

Adding a reflection

The masked image looks convincing, but you can make it look even more realistic by adding a reflection to the TV screen.

1 Click an empty area in the Timeline panel to deselect all layers, and then choose Layer > New > Solid.

2 In the Solid Settings dialog box, name the layer **Reflection**, click the Make Comp Size button, change the Color to white, and then click OK.

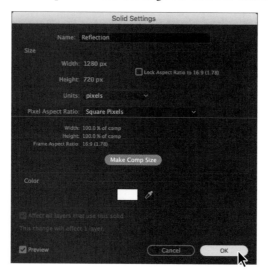

Instead of trying to exactly re-create the shape of the Watching_TV.mov layer's mask, it is easier to copy it to the Reflection layer.

3 Select the Watching_TV.mov layer in the Timeline panel, and press the M key to display the Mask Path property for the mask.

4 Select Mask 1, and then choose Edit > Copy or press Ctrl+C (Windows) or Command+C (Mac OS).

5 Select the Reflection layer in the Timeline panel, and then choose Edit > Paste or press Ctrl+V (Windows) or Command+V (Mac OS).

 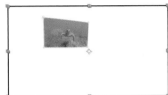

This time, you want to keep the area inside the mask opaque and make the area outside the mask transparent.

6 Select the Watching_TV.mov layer, and then press U to hide the mask properties.

7 Select the Reflection layer in the Timeline panel, and press the F key to reveal the Mask 1 Mask Feather property for the layer.

8 Change the Mask Feather value to **0** (zero).

9 Deselect the Inverted option. The Reflection layer now obscures the Turtle.mov layer.

10 Zoom in to see the screen, and then select the Mask Feather tool (✔), hidden beneath the Convert Vertex tool (⅄) in the Tools panel.

When you feather a mask, the width of the feather is the same all the way around the mask. The Mask Feather Tool lets you vary the feathering width at points you define on the closed mask.

11 Click the Reflection layer in the Timeline panel to select it. Then click the lower left vertex to create a feather point.

12 Click the feather point again, and without releasing the mouse button, drag that feather point inward so that only the center of the screen is reflected, and so that the feather point is positioned as shown in the image below.

Currently the feather extends evenly across the mask. You'll add more feather points for greater flexibility.

13 Click in the center of the top of the mask to create another feather point. Then drag the feather point down slightly, into the mask.

14 Right-click or Control-click the feather point you just created, and choose Edit Radius. Change the Feather Radius to **0**, and click OK.

This is a good start, but the sides slope in too sharply. You'll add more feather points to change the angle.

15 Add another feather point by clicking the left edge of the matte, about one-third of the way from the top.

16 Add a similar feather point on the right side.

The shape of the reflection is good, but it's obscuring the image. You'll change the opacity to reduce its effect.

17 Select the Reflection layer in the Timeline panel, and then press the T key to reveal the Opacity property. Change its value to **10%**.

18 Press T to hide the Opacity property, and then press F2 or click an empty area in the Timeline panel to deselect all layers.

Applying a blending mode

To create unique interactions between layers, you may want to experiment with blending modes. Blending modes control how each layer blends with, or reacts to, layers beneath it. Blending modes for layers in After Effects are identical to blending modes in Adobe Photoshop.

1 From the Timeline panel menu, choose Columns > Modes to display the Mode pop-up menu.

2 Choose Add from the Reflection layer's Mode pop-up menu.

This creates a hard glare on the TV screen image and boosts the colors underneath.

3 Choose File > Save to save your work.

Creating a vignette

A popular effect in motion graphic design is to apply a vignette to the composition. This is often done to simulate light variations of a glass lens. It creates an interesting look that focuses the attention on the subject and sets the shot apart.

1 Zoom out to see the whole image.

2 Choose Layer > New > Solid.

3 In the Solid Settings dialog box, name this layer **Vignette**, click the Make Comp Size button, change the Color to black (R=**0**, G=**0**, B=**0**), and then click OK.

In addition to the Pen tool, After Effects provides tools that let you easily create square and elliptical masks.

4 In the Tools panel, select the Ellipse tool (⬤), hidden behind the Rectangle tool (⬛).

5 In the Composition panel, position the cross-hairs pointer in the upper left corner of the image. Drag to the opposite corner to create an elliptical shape that fills the image. Adjust the shape and position using the Selection tool, if necessary.

6 Expand the Mask 1 property in the Vignette layer to display all of the mask properties for the layer.

7 Choose Subtract from the Mask 1 Mode pop-up menu.

8 Increase the Mask Feather amount to **200, 200** pixels.

Your composition should now resemble the following figure.

Even with this large feather amount, the vignette is a bit intense and constricting. You can give the composition more breathing room by adjusting the Mask Expansion property. The Mask Expansion property represents, in pixels, how far from the original mask edge you are expanding or contracting the adjusted edge.

9 Increase Mask Expansion to **90** pixels.

10 Hide the properties for the Vignette layer, and then choose File > Save.

Adjusting the timing

The sea turtle video shouldn't appear until the girl turns on the TV. You'll adjust the Turtle.mov layer's start point and animate the mask accordingly.

1 Go to 2:00, and then drag the Turtle.mov layer so that it begins at 2:00.

2 Select the Watching_TV.mov layer, and press MM to see the mask properties.

3 Click the stopwatch icon next to Mask Expansion to create a keyframe at 2:00.

4 Go to 1:23, and change the Mask Expansion value to **−150** pixels to reveal the blank TV screen.

5 Go to the beginning of the time ruler, and click the Add Or Remove Keyframe At Current Time icon to add a keyframe for the mask expansion property.

6 Hide the properties for all layers, and press the spacebar to preview your movie.

Tips for creating masks

If you have worked with Adobe Illustrator or Photoshop, or similar applications, you're probably familiar with masks and Bezier curves. If not, here are a few additional tips to help you create them effectively:

- Use as few vertices as possible.

- You can close a mask by clicking the starting vertex. To open a closed mask, click a mask segment, choose Layer > Mask And Shape Path, and deselect Closed.

- To add points to an open path, press Ctrl (Windows) or Command (Mac OS), and click the last point on the path with the Pen tool. When the point is selected, you can continue adding points.

Trimming the work area

▶ **Tip:** Alternatively, you can change the duration of the movie to 11:17. To do so, choose Composition > Composition Settings, and then type **11.17** in the Duration box.

The Turtle clip is shorter than the Watching_TV clip. Currently, the girls are watching a blank screen at the end of the movie. You'll move the work area end point to the end of the Turtle.mov layer so only that portion of the movie will render.

1 Go to 11:17, the last frame of the Turtle.mov layer.

2 Press N to move the work area end point to the current time.

3 Choose File > Save to save your work.

In this lesson, you have worked with the mask tools to hide, reveal, and adjust portions of a composition to create a stylized inset shot. Next to keyframes, masks are probably the most-used feature of After Effects.

Review questions

1 What is a mask?

2 Name two ways to adjust the shape of a mask.

3 What is a direction handle used for?

4 What is the difference between an open mask and a closed mask?

5 How is the Mask Feather tool useful?

Review answers

1 A mask in After Effects is a path, or outline, that is used to modify layer effects and properties. The most common use of masks is to modify a layer's alpha channel. A mask consists of segments and vertices.

2 You can adjust the shape of a mask by dragging individual vertices or by dragging a segment.

3 A direction handle is used to control the shape and angle of a Bezier curve.

4 An open mask can be used to control effects or the placement of text; it does not define a region of transparency. A closed mask defines a region that will affect the alpha channel of a layer.

5 The Mask Feather tool lets you vary the width of feathering at different points on a mask. With the Mask Feather tool, click to add a Feather point, and then drag it.

8 DISTORTING OBJECTS WITH THE PUPPET TOOLS

Lesson overview

In this lesson, you'll learn how to do the following:

- Place Deform pins using the Puppet Pin tool.

- Define areas of overlap using the Puppet Overlap tool.

- Stiffen parts of an image using the Puppet Starch tool.

- Animate the position of Deform pins.

- Record animation using the Puppet Sketch tool.

- Animate facial expressions with Character Animator.

 This lesson will take approximately an hour to complete. Download the project files for this lesson, following the instructions in the Getting Started section under "Accessing the lesson files and Web Edition," if you haven't already done so. As you work on this lesson, you'll preserve the start files. If you need to restore the start files, download them from your Account page.

PROJECT: ANIMATED ILLUSTRATION

Pull, squash, stretch, and otherwise deform objects on the screen using the Puppet tools. Whether you're creating realistic animations, fantastic scenarios, or modern art, the Puppet tools will expand your creative freedom.

Getting started

Using the Puppet tools in After Effects, you can add natural motion to raster images and vector graphics. Three tools create pins to define the point of deformation, areas of overlap, and areas that should remain more rigid. An additional tool, the Puppet Sketch tool, lets you record animation in real time. In this lesson, you'll use the Puppet tools to animate a character slipping on a banana peel.

Start by previewing the final movie and then setting up the project.

1 Make sure the following files are in the Lessons/Lesson08 folder on your hard disk, or download them from your Account page at www.peachpit.com now:

 • In the Assets folder: backdrop.psd, banana.psd, man.psd

 • In the Sample_Movies folder: Lesson08.avi, Lesson08.mov

2 Open and play the Lesson08.avi sample movie in Windows Media Player or the Lesson08.mov sample movie in QuickTime Player to see what you will create in this lesson. When you are done, close Windows Media Player or QuickTime Player. You may delete the sample movies from your hard disk if you have limited storage space.

When you begin this lesson, restore the default application settings for After Effects. See "Restoring default preferences" on page 2.

3 Start After Effects, and then immediately hold down Ctrl+Alt+Shift (Windows) or Command+Option+Shift (Mac OS). When prompted, click OK to delete your preferences. Close the Start window.

After Effects opens to display a blank, untitled project.

4 Choose File > Save As > Save As.

5 In the Save As dialog box, navigate to the Lessons/Lesson08/ Finished_Project folder.

6 Name the project **Lesson08_Finished.aep**, and then click Save.

Importing footage

You'll import three Adobe Photoshop files, which you'll use to create the scene.

1 Choose File > Import > File.

2 Navigate to the Lessons/Lesson08/
 Assets folder. Shift-click to select
 the backdrop.psd, banana.psd,
 and man.psd files, and then click
 Import or Open. The footage items
 appear in the Project panel.

Creating the composition

As with any project, you need to create a new composition.

1 Choose Composition > New Composition.

2 Name the composition **Walking Man**.

3 Choose NTSC DV from the Preset pop-up menu. The preset automatically
 sets the width, height, pixel aspect ratio, and frame rate for the composition.

4 In the Duration field, type **500** to specify 5 seconds, and then click OK.

After Effects opens the new composition in the Timeline and Composition panels.

Adding the background

It's easier to animate a character in context, so first you'll add the background to the composition.

1 Press the Home key, or move the current-time indicator to the beginning of the composition.

2 Drag the backdrop.psd file to the Timeline panel.

3 Click the Lock icon (🔒) for the layer to prevent accidental changes to it.

Scaling an object

Next, you'll add the banana peel. At its default size, it's large enough to do real damage to anyone who slips on it. You'll scale it to a more proportional size for the scene.

1 Drag the banana.psd file from the Project panel to the top layer in the Timeline panel.

2 Select the banana.psd layer in the Timeline panel, and press S to display its Scale property.

3 Change the Scale value to **15%**.

4 Press P to display the layer's Position property.

5 Change the Position to **160, 420**. The banana peel moves to the left side of the composition.

6 Hide the properties for the banana.psd layer.

Adding the character

The last element in the scene is the character himself. You'll add him to the composition and then scale and position him appropriately.

1 Drag the man.psd file from the Project panel to the top of the layer stack in the Timeline panel.

2 Select the man.psd layer, and press S to display its Scale property.

3 Change the Scale value to **15%**.

4 Press P to display the Position property, and change the Position to **575, 300**.

● **Note:** In the original drawing, the character had already slipped on the banana peel and was falling. To make it easier to animate, the character has been modified to be more upright. Sometimes you can make your work easier by making some adjustments before animation.

5 Press P again to hide the Position property for the layer.

6 Choose File > Save to save your work so far.

About the Puppet tools

The Puppet tools turn raster and vector images into virtual marionettes. When you move the string of a marionette, the body part attached to that string moves; pull the string attached to the hand, and the hand goes up. The Puppet tools use pins to indicate where strings would be attached.

The Puppet effect deforms parts of an image based on the positions of pins that you place and animate. These pins determine which parts of the image should move, which parts should remain rigid, and which parts should be in front when areas overlap.

There are three kinds of pins, each placed by a different tool:

- The Puppet Pin tool (✦) places and moves Deform pins, which deform a layer.
- The Puppet Overlap tool (✦) places Overlap pins, which indicate the parts of an image that should be in the front when areas overlap.
- The Puppet Starch tool (✦) places Starch pins, which stiffen parts of the image so that they are distorted less.

● **Note:** The mesh is calculated at the frame where the Deform pins are applied. If you add more pins anywhere in the timeline, they are placed based on the original position of the mesh.

As soon as you place a pin, the area within an outline is automatically divided into a mesh of triangles. Each part of the mesh is associated with the pixels of the image, so as the mesh moves, so do the pixels. When you animate a Deform pin, the mesh deforms more in the area closest to the pin, while keeping the overall shape as rigid as possible. For example, if you animate a pin in a character's hand, the hand and arm will be deformed, but most of the character will remain in place.

Adding Deform pins

Deform pins are the main component of the Puppet effect. Where you place these pins and how you position them determine how the objects move on the screen. You'll place Deform pins and display the mesh that After Effects creates to determine the area of influence for each pin.

When you select the Puppet Pin tool, the Tools panel displays the Puppet tool options. Each pin has its own properties in the Timeline panel, and After Effects automatically creates an initial keyframe for each pin.

1 Select the Puppet Pin tool () in the Tools panel.

2 In the Composition panel, place a Deform pin in the character's right arm, near the wrist. You may find it helpful to zoom in to see the character more clearly.

● **Note:** Be careful! The character's right arm is on the left side of the image, and vice versa. Pin the character according to *his* left and right, not yours!

A yellow dot representing the Deform pin appears in the Composition panel. If at this point you were to use the Selection tool (▶) to move the Deform pin, the entire character would move with it. You need more pins to keep the other parts of the mesh in place.

3 Using the Puppet Pin tool, place another Deform pin in the left arm near the wrist.

Now you can move the right hand with the Selection tool. The more pins you place, the smaller the area of influence for each pin, and the less each area will stretch. If you experimented, undo any stretching by pressing Ctrl+Z (Windows) or Command+Z (Mac OS).

4 Place additional Deform pins in the man's right and left legs (near the ankles), torso (near the bottom of the tie), and forehead.

5 In the Timeline panel, expand the Mesh 1 > Deform properties. Each Deform pin is listed. To keep track of each pin, you'll rename them.

6 Select Puppet Pin 1, press Enter or Return, and rename the pin **Right Arm**. Press Enter or Return again to accept the new name.

7 Rename the remaining pins (Puppet Pin 2 through Puppet Pin 6) **Left Arm**, **Right Leg**, **Left Leg**, **Torso**, and **Head**, respectively.

8 Select Show in the options section of the Tools panel to display the distortion mesh.

Tip: You can extend the mesh beyond the outline of the layer in order to ensure a stroke is included in the deformation. To expand the mesh, increase the Expansion property in the options section of the Tools panel.

9 Change the Triangles value in the options section of the Tools panel to **300**.

The Triangles setting determines how many triangles are included in the mesh. Increasing the number of triangles results in a smoother animation, but also increases rendering time.

Defining areas of overlap

Note: You must select the Show option separately for each Puppet tool. You can also place pins without viewing the mesh.

Normal human movement requires the arms to swing, so as the character walks across the screen, portions of his right arm and leg will be behind other areas of his body. You'll use the Puppet Overlap tool to define the areas that should appear in front when areas overlap.

1 Zoom in, and use the Hand tool (✋) to position the man in the Composition window so that you can see his torso and legs clearly.

2 Select the Puppet Overlap tool (🖈), which is hidden behind the Puppet Pin tool in the Tools panel.

3 Select Show in the options area of the Tools panel to view the distortion mesh.

Tip: If the mesh doesn't appear when you select Show, click outside the path shape in the Composition panel.

4 In the options area of the Tools panel, change In Front to **100%**.

The In Front value determines the apparent proximity to the viewer; setting the value to 100% prevents those parts of the body that are overlapped from showing through.

5 Click intersections in the mesh to place Overlap pins on the right side of the character's torso and left leg, which are the areas that should remain in the front. As you add a pin, you may want to adjust its Extent value in the options area of the Tools panel. The Extent value determines how far the overlap influence extends for the pin; the affected area appears lighter in the Composition panel. Use this image as a guide.

Stiffening an area

The character's arms and legs should move as he walks, but his torso should stay fairly firm. You'll use the Puppet Starch tool to add Starch pins where you want the character to be stiffer.

1 Select the Puppet Starch tool (⋯), which is hidden behind the Puppet Overlap tool in the Tools panel.

2 Select Show in the options area of the Tools panel to display the distortion mesh.

3 Place Starch pins on intersections to stiffen the lower half of the torso, as in the image at right.

4 Hide the properties for the man.psd layer in the Timeline panel.

5 Choose File > Save to save your work so far.

● **Note:** The Amount value determines how rigid the area will be. Typically, a low value is fine; higher values make the area more rigid. You can also use negative numbers to reduce the rigidity of another pin.

Animating pin positions

The Deform, Overlap, and Starch pins are in place. Now you can change the Deform pin positions to animate the character. The Overlap pins keep the front areas in the front, and the Starch pins keep specific areas (in this case, the torso) from moving too much.

Creating a walking cycle

Initially, the character should be walking across the screen. To create a realistic walking cycle, keep in mind that as humans walk, wave patterns develop in the motion path. You'll create a wave pattern in the pin positions. However, the values will vary slightly to add a bit of randomness, and to keep the character from looking too much like a robot.

1 Select the man.psd layer in the Timeline panel, and then press U to display all the keyframes for the layer.

2 Press Home, or move the current-time indicator to the beginning of the timeline.

Squash and stretch

As the character moves, his body squashes and stretches. Squash and stretch is a traditional animation technique that adds realism and weight to objects. It's an exaggeration of the effect that occurs in real life when a moving object comes into contact with a stationary object, such as the ground. When squashing and stretching are applied correctly, the volume of the character doesn't change.

The easiest way to understand the principle of squash and stretch is to view an animation of a bouncing ball. As the ball lands, it partially flattens, or squashes. As it bounces up, it stretches.

To see squash and stretch in action, open the Squash_and_stretch.aep project file in the Lesson08/End_Project_Files folder.

3 In the Timeline panel, change the position of the Deform pins as follows:

- Head: **845, 295**
- Torso: **821.5, 1210**
- Left Leg: **1000.5, 1734**
- Right Leg: **580.5, 1734**
- Left Arm: **1384.5, 1214.7**
- Right Arm: **478.5, 1108**

Note: After Effects automatically creates keyframes when you place Deform pins, so you don't need to click the stopwatch for each pin before setting its initial position.

Note: All the values listed here depend on where the deform pins were placed. You may need to adjust the values for keyframes to compensate for changes in the deform pin positions.

4 To complete the walking cycle, move the pins to the positions at the times indicated in the chart below. Where the chart says "Add keyframe," click the Add Or Remove Keyframe At Current Time button (♦) in the Timeline panel to create a keyframe at the pin's current position.

Note: To add a keyframe, click the diamond (between two arrows) on the left side of the Timeline panel.

TIME	HEAD	TORSO	LEFT LEG	RIGHT LEG	LEFT ARM	RIGHT ARM
0:07	593, 214	570.5, 1095	604, 1614.5			
0:15	314, 295	312.5, 1210	118.5, 1748.3	Add keyframe (♦)	886.5, 1208	−325.5, 1214.7
0:18	−6, 217	37.5, 1098.3		352.5, 1618.6		
1:00	−286, 295	−253.5, 1210	Add keyframe (♦)	−561.5, 1734	−121.5, 1234.7	Add keyframe (♦)
1:07	−614, 218.3	−530, 1094	−70.3, 1628.8			
1:15	−883, 300.7	−803.5, 1213.3	−1003.5, 1728.7	Add keyframe (♦)	Add keyframe (♦)	−1309.5, 1101.3
1:23	−1153, 212.7	−1055.5, 1099.7	−789.3, 1609.4			
2:00	−1412, 319.3	−1283.5, 1213	−1003.4, 1728.7	−1545.5, 1740.7	−1147.5, 1241.3	Add keyframe (♦)
2:08	−1622, 246	−1505.5, 1099.7	−996, 1617	−1926.5, 1677.1		

▶ **Tip:** The Timeline panel measures time in seconds and frames, depending on the frames-per-second (fps) rate. So 1:15 equals 1 second and 15 frames. At 29.97 fps, 1:15 is frame 45.

Animating a slip

The character steps on a banana peel, loses his balance, and falls. The falling movements occur more quickly than the walking cycle. To surprise the viewer, you'll animate the character to fall off the screen.

1 Choose File > Save to save the work you've just done.

2 Move the current-time indicator to 2:11, and then change the position of the Left Leg pin to **–2281**, **1495.3**.

3 At 2:15, move the Deform pins to the following positions:

- Head: **–1298**, **532.7**
- Torso: **–1667.5**, **1246.3**
- Left Leg: **–2398.8**, **1282.7**
- Right Leg: **–2277.5**, **874**
- Left Arm: **–1219.5**, **1768**
- Right Arm: **–1753.5**, **454.7**

4 At 2:20, make the character fall off the screen by moving the Deform pins to the following positions:

- Head: **–1094**, **2452.7**
- Torso: **–1643.5**, **3219.7**
- Left Leg: **–2329.5**, **2682**
- Right Leg: **–2169.5**, **2234**
- Left Arm: **–1189.5**, **3088**
- Right Arm: **–1597.5**, **2654.7**

5 Hide the properties for the man.psd layer, and save your work so far.

Moving an object

Of course, when the man slips on the banana peel, the banana peel moves, too. It should slide out from beneath the man's feet and fly off the screen. You didn't add any pins to the banana, and you don't need them. Instead, you'll move the entire layer, using its Position and Rotation properties.

1 Move the current-time indicator to 2:00.

2 Select the banana.psd layer in the Timeline panel, and press P to display its Position property.

3 Press Shift+R to also display the layer's Rotation property.

▶ **Tip:** To view multiple layer properties at the same time, press the Shift key while you press the keyboard shortcut for the additional layer property.

4 Click the stopwatch icons (⏱) next to Position and Rotation to create initial keyframes for each property.

5 Move to 2:06, and change the Position to **80**, **246** and the Rotation to **19** degrees.

6 Move to 2:15, and change the Position to **−59**, **361**, so that the banana peel moves completely off the screen.

7 At 2:15, change the Rotation to **42** degrees, so that the peel continues to rotate slightly as it moves off the screen.

8 Choose Fit Up To 100% in the Magnification pop-up menu at the bottom of the Composition panel so you can see the entire composition. Then press the spacebar to preview your animation. If necessary, adjust the Position property for the Deform pins in the Timeline panel. Then choose File > Save.

▶ **Tip:** To make the animation appear more natural, you can use roving keyframes. Roving keyframes aren't linked to a specific time; they change according to the keyframes near them. To make a keyframe a roving keyframe, right-click or Control-click it, and choose Rove Across Time.

Recording animation

Changing the Position property for each pin at each keyframe worked, but you probably found the process to be slow and tedious. If you were creating a much longer animation, you'd quickly tire of entering precise numbers for each keyframe. Instead of manually animating keyframes, you can use the Puppet Sketch tool to drag the objects into position in real time. After Effects starts recording the motion as soon as you begin dragging a pin, and it stops recording when you release the mouse button. The composition moves forward through time as you move the pin. When you stop recording, the current-time indicator returns to the point at which you began recording, so that you can record the path for another pin during the same time period.

Experiment with this method of animation as you re-create the slipping motion using the Puppet Sketch tool.

Tip: By default, the motion is played back at the speed at which it was recorded. To change the ratio of recording speed to playback speed, click Record Options in the Tools panel, and change the Speed value before recording.

1　Choose File > Save As > Save As, and name the project **Motionsketch.aep**. Save it in the Lesson08/Finished_Project folder.

2　Move the current-time indicator to 2:08.

3　In the Timeline panel, select the man.psd layer and press U to display all the keyframes for the layer..

4　Delete all keyframes after 2:08.

The walking cycle remains, but you've removed the keyframes that animate the character slipping and falling.

5　Select the Puppet Pin tool (✱) in the Tools panel.

6　In the Timeline panel, select Puppet to see the pins in the Composition panel.

7　Press F2 to deselect all layers, and then select a pin in the Composition panel, and press Ctrl (Windows) or Command (Mac OS) to activate the Puppet Sketch tool (a clock icon appears next to the pointer).

8　Continue to hold down Ctrl or Command as you drag the pin into a new position. Release the mouse button when you've finished. The current-time indicator returns to 2:08.

9　Press Ctrl or Command, and drag another pin into position. Use the outline of the character to guide you.

10　Continue using the Puppet Sketch tool to move all the pins through the animation until you're satisfied with the movement.

11　Preview the final animation.

Now you've used all the Puppet tools to create a realistic, engaging animation. Remember that you can use the Puppet tools to deform and manipulate many kinds of objects, not just drawn art. And watch out for banana peels!

Act it out with Adobe Character Animator

If you identify strongly with your characters, you might want to use Adobe Character Animator instead of creating cumbersome keyframes. It's especially useful if you're creating a long scene or you need to match the character's mouth to speech. It's also a lot of fun.

Character Animator is included in an Adobe Creative Cloud membership. With it, you can import a character you've created in Photoshop or Illustrator, and then act out the facial gestures and head movements the character should make in front of your webcam; your character mirrors your gestures on the screen. If you speak, the character's mouth moves to match your words.

You can move other body parts, such as legs and arms, using keyboard shortcuts or your mouse or tablet. And you can set up dangling behavior so that, for example, if a rabbit's head moves to the left, its ears dangle with it.

How much control you have over your character depends on how you set up the layers in the character file in Photoshop or Illustrator. You can keep it pretty simple, or you can create detailed layers to control individual components separately. Character Animator includes a template to help you map your own character to layer names that the application will recognize, such as Head, Left Arm, and so on. It also includes some entertaining interactive tutorials to help you get started.

(continued on next page)

Act it out with Adobe Character Animator *(continued)*

Tips for a smooth animation experience:

- Create different layers for different moving parts. For example, draw the mouth on one layer, the right eye on another, the left leg on its own layer, and so forth.

- Name layers so that Character Animator will recognize them. It looks for certain words, such as "pupil," to map the character to the image in the camera. You can name the layers in Photoshop or Illustrator, or you can tag them in Character Animator.

- Especially at first, consider using an existing character file as a template. It'll be easier to get the layer names right.

- Practice your facial and other gestures in Character Animator before recording. Once you've set your Rest Pose, try out different mouth shapes, eyebrow raises, head waggles, and other movements to see how subtle or exaggerated movements translate for your character.

- Speak into the microphone as you record. Many mouth shapes are triggered by audio cues, such as "uh-oh," and the character's mouth movements will be synced to your words automatically.

- Try animating objects that don't have faces and bodies. For example, you can use Character Animator to animate clouds floating, a flag waving, or flowers opening. Be creative and have fun!

Review questions

1 What's the difference between the Puppet Pin tool and the Puppet Overlap tool?

2 When would you use the Puppet Starch tool?

3 Describe two methods of animating pin positions.

Review answers

1 The Puppet Pin tool creates Deform pins, which define the position of a portion of the image as the image is deformed. The Puppet Overlap tool creates Overlap pins, which determine which areas of an object remain in front when two areas overlap.

2 Use the Puppet Starch tool to add Starch pins to an area that you want to remain more rigid while other areas of the object are distorted.

3 You can manually animate pin positions by changing the value of the Position property for each pin in the Timeline panel. To animate pin positions more quickly, use the Puppet Sketch tool: With the Puppet Pin tool selected, press Ctrl or Command, and drag a pin to record its movement.

9 USING THE ROTO BRUSH TOOL

Lesson overview

In this lesson, you'll learn how to do the following:

- Extract a foreground object from the background using the Roto Brush tool.

- Correct the segmentation boundary across a span of frames.

- Touch up a matte with the Refine Edge Tool.

- Freeze a matte across a clip.

- Animate properties for creative effects.

- Track a face in footage.

 This lesson will take approximately an hour to complete. Download the project files for this lesson, following the instructions in the Getting Started section under "Accessing the lesson files and Web Edition," if you haven't already done so. As you work on this lesson, you'll preserve the start files. If you need to restore the start files, download them from your Account page.

PROJECT: TV COMMERCIAL

With the Roto Brush tool, you can quickly separate a foreground object from a background across many frames. You can achieve professional results in a fraction of the time you'd spend performing the same task with traditional rotoscoping.

About rotoscoping

When you draw or paint on the frames of a movie, you're *rotoscoping*. For example, a common use of rotoscoping is to trace an object, using the path as a mask to separate it from the background so you can work with it separately. Traditionally in After Effects, you drew masks, animated the mask paths, and then used the masks to define a matte. (A *matte* is a mask used to hide part of an image so that another image can be superimposed.) While effective, this is a time-intensive, tedious process, especially if the object moves a great deal or the background is complex.

If a background or foreground object is a consistent, distinct color, you could use color keying to separate the object from the background. If the subject was shot against a green or blue background (green screen or blue screen), keying is usually much easier than rotoscoping.

The Roto Brush tool in After Effects is much faster than conventional rotoscoping, and for movies with complex backgrounds, it's much easier than keying. You use the Roto Brush tool to define the foreground and background elements. Then, After Effects creates a matte, and tracks the movement of the matte over time. The Roto Brush tool does much of the work for you, leaving only a little cleanup work to be done.

Getting started

In this lesson, you'll use the Roto Brush tool to isolate a young boy from a wet winter background so you can color-treat the background without affecting the boy. To finish up the project, you'll add an animated title.

First, you'll preview the final movie and set up your project.

1 Make sure the following files are in the Lessons/Lesson09 folder on your hard disk, or download them from your Account page at www.peachpit.com now:

 • In the Assets folder: boy.mov, Facetracking.mov

 • In the Sample_Movies folder: Lesson09.avi, Lesson09.mov

2 Open and play the Lesson09.avi sample movie in Windows Media Player or the Lesson09.mov sample movie in QuickTime Player to see what you will create in this lesson. When you are done, close Windows Media Player or QuickTime Player. You may delete the sample movies from your hard disk if you have limited storage space.

When you begin this lesson, restore the default application settings for After Effects. See "Restoring default preferences" on page 2.

3 Start After Effects, and then immediately hold down Ctrl+Alt+Shift (Windows) or Command+Option+Shift (Mac OS). When prompted, click OK to delete your preferences. Close the Start window.

After Effects opens to display an empty, untitled project.

4 Choose File > Save As > Save As.

5 In the Save As dialog box, navigate to the Lessons/Lesson09/ Finished_Project folder.

6 Name the project **Lesson09_Finished.aep**, and then click Save.

Creating the composition

You need to import one footage item for this lesson.

1 Choose File > Import > File.

2 Navigate to the Lessons/Lesson09/Assets folder, select the boy.mov file, and then click Import or Open.

3 Drag the boy.mov clip onto the Create A New Composition button (⊞) at the bottom of the Project panel.

After Effects creates a composition named boy, based on the settings in the boy.mov file. The composition is three seconds long, with a frame size of 1920 x 1080. The movie file was shot at a rate of 29.97 frames per second.

4 Choose File > Save to save the project so far.

Creating a segmentation boundary

You use the Roto Brush tool to specify which parts of the clip are in the foreground and which are in the background. You add strokes to distinguish the two, and then After Effects creates a segmentation boundary between the foreground and background.

Creating a base frame

To use the Roto Brush tool to isolate a foreground object, you start by adding strokes to a base frame to identify foreground and background areas. You can start on any frame in the clip, but in this exercise, you'll use the first frame as the base frame. Then you'll add the strokes that identify the boy as the foreground object.

1 Move the current-time indicator across the time ruler to preview the footage.

2 Press the Home key to move the current-time indicator to the beginning of the time ruler.

3 Select the Roto Brush tool (🖌) in the Tools panel.

You use the Roto Brush tool in the Layer panel, so you'll open it now.

4 Double-click the boy.mov layer in the Timeline panel to open the clip in the Layer panel.

5 Choose Fit from the Magnification Ratio pop-up menu at the bottom of the Layer panel if you don't see the entire image.

By default, the Roto Brush tool creates green foreground strokes. You'll start by adding strokes to the foreground—the boy. Generally, it's most efficient to start with broad strokes and then use smaller brushes to refine the border.

6 Choose Window > Brushes to open the Brushes panel. Set up a hard round 100-pixel brush. (You may need to resize the Brushes panel to see the options.)

When you're drawing strokes to define the foreground object, follow the skeletal structure of the subject. Unlike traditional rotoscoping, you don't need to define a precise boundary around the object. Start with broad strokes, and work down to small regions as After Effects determines where the boundary is supposed to be.

▶ Tip: You can quickly zoom in and out of the Layer panel using the scroll wheel on your mouse.

7 Draw a green stroke from the boy's head down toward the bottom of the clip.

A magenta outline identifies the boundaries After Effects created for the foreground object. After Effects recognized only about half of the boy, because you initially sampled only a small area of the subject. You'll help After Effects find the boundary by adding some more foreground strokes.

8 Still using a large brush, draw a green stroke from left to right across the boy's coat, including the black strip on the right.

▶ Tip: To increase or decrease the brush size quickly, press Ctrl (Windows) or Command (Mac OS) as you drag. Drag right to increase the brush size, or left to decrease it.

9 Use a smaller brush to add any neglected areas to the foreground.

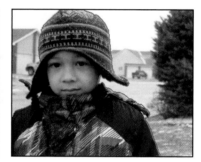

It can be tricky to get some areas without accidentally adding background as well. It's okay if you haven't captured every detail in the foreground. You'll use background strokes to remove any extraneous areas of the matte.

10 Press Alt (Windows) or Option (Mac OS) to switch to the red background stroke brush.

11 Add red strokes to background areas you want to exclude from the matte. Switch back and forth between the foreground and background brushes to fine-tune the matte. Don't forget to deselect the area under the boy's hat where the background shows through. In fact, one click may be all it takes to exclude that area from the matte.

Don't worry about being exact about your brush strokes. Just make sure the matte is within 1 to 2 pixels of the edge of the foreground object. You'll have an opportunity to refine the matte later. However, After Effects uses the information on the base frame to adjust the matte for the rest of the span, so you want the matte to be accurate.

12 Click the Toggle Alpha button (⬛) at the bottom of the Layer panel. The selected area is white against a black background, so you can see the matte clearly.

13 Click the Toggle Alpha Overlay button (⬛) at the bottom of the Layer panel. The foreground area appears in color, and the background has a red overlay.

14 Click the Toggle Alpha Boundary button (⬛) at the bottom of the Layer panel to see the outline around the boy again.

As you use the Roto Brush tool, the Alpha Boundary is the best way to see how accurate your boundary is, because you can see everything in the frame. However, the Alpha and Alpha Overlay options let you see your matte without the distraction of the background.

Refining the boundary across the initial span

You used the Roto Brush tool to create a base frame, which includes a segmentation boundary that divides the foreground from the background. After Effects applied the segmentation boundary across a span of frames. The Roto Brush span appears below the time ruler at the bottom of the Layer panel. As you move forward and backward through the footage, the segmentation boundary moves with the foreground object (in this case, the boy).

1 Extend the span range by dragging the end of the span to 1:00 in the Layer panel.

You'll step through the frames in the span and make adjustments to the segmentation boundary as necessary.

▶ **Tip:** To move forward one frame, press the 2 key on your keyboard; to move back one frame, press the 1 key.

2 Press the 2 key on your main keyboard (not the numeric keypad) to move forward one frame.

Working from the base frame, After Effects tracks the edge of the object and attempts to follow its movement. Depending on how complex your foreground and background elements are, the boundary may or may not conform exactly to the area you hoped it would. In this case, you may notice changes to the segmentation boundary along the boy's right sleeve (the left edge of the clip) as more of the coat is revealed in the frame. Likewise, the flaps of the cap and the edges of the hood need some adjustment, which means you need to refine the segmentation.

Note: As it propagates the segmentation boundary for a frame, After Effects caches that frame. Cached frames have a green bar in the time ruler. If you jump ahead to a frame further along the span, After Effects may take longer to calculate the boundary.

3 Using the Roto Brush tool, paint foreground and background strokes to refine the matte for this frame. If the matte is accurate, you don't need to paint any strokes.

If you make a stroke you don't like, you can always undo the stroke and try again. As you move through the span, each change you make affects the frames after it. The more you refine your selection, the better the overall results will be. You may find it useful to move forward a few frames to see how changes affect the boundary.

4 Press the 2 key again to move forward to the next frame.

5 Use the Roto Brush tool to add to the foreground or subtract from the background as necessary to refine the boundary.

6 Repeat steps 4 and 5 until you reach 1:00.

Adding new base frames

After Effects creates an initial Roto Brush span of 40 frames (20 in each direction). As you move through the frames, the span range may increase automatically, or you can drag to extend the span. However, the further you move from the base frame, the longer After Effects takes to propagate, or calculate, the segmentation for each frame, especially if the shot is complex. If the scene changes significantly, it may be better to create multiple base frames for your footage than to have one really long span. The scene in this project remains fairly consistent, so you could extend the span and make additional adjustments as needed. However, you'll create additional base frames to gain experience using the tools, learn to connect spans, and see how the segmentation shifts as you move further from a base frame.

You've reached 1:00 in the refining process. Now you'll add a new base frame to the project.

1 Go to 1:20 in the Layer panel. This frame isn't included in the initial span, so the segmentation boundary includes the entire frame.

2 Use the Roto Brush tool to add foreground and background strokes, defining the segmentation boundary.

A new base frame (represented by a blue rectangle) is added to the time ruler, and the Roto Brush span extends several frames behind and ahead of the new base frame. Depending on how far the initial span propagated, there may be a gap between the two spans. If so, you'll connect the two.

3 If necessary, drag the left edge of the new span to the edge of the previous span.

4 Press 1 to move backward one frame (from the new base frame), and then refine the segmentation boundary.

5 Continue to move backward through the span, refining the segmentation boundary until you reach the frame at 1:00.

6 Move back to the base frame at 1:20, and then press 2 to move forward, correcting the segmentation boundary for each frame if necessary.

7 When you reach the end of the span, drag the right edge to the end of the clip, and continue to refine each frame in the footage as needed. Pay special attention to the left earflap of the cap when it crosses in front of the tree. The dark areas overlap, making it more difficult to get a consistent edge. Remember that you are trying to get the segmentation boundary as close to the edge of the foreground object as possible.

8 When you have completed refining the segmentation boundary for the entire clip, choose File > Save to save your work so far.

Fine-tuning the matte

Roto Brush does a pretty good job, but there may be stray bits of background in the matte, or foreground areas that weren't included. You'll clean those up by refining the edge.

Adjusting the Roto Brush & Refine Edge effect

When you use the Roto Brush tool, After Effects applies the Roto Brush & Refine Edge effect to the layer. You can modify the effect using settings in the Effect Controls panel. You'll use those settings to further refine the edge of the matte.

1 Press the spacebar to play the clip in the Layer panel; press the spacebar again to end the preview when you've seen the whole clip.

As you preview the clip, you may notice that the segmentation boundary area jumps around quite a bit. You'll use the Reduce Chatter setting to make it smoother.

2 In the Effect Controls panel, increase the Feather amount to **10**, and increase Reduce Chatter to **20%**.

The Reduce Chatter value determines how much influence the current frame has when performing a weighted average across adjacent frames. Depending on how tight your matte was, you may need to increase Reduce Chatter to 50%.

3 Preview the clip again. Notice how much smoother the edge of the matte has become.

Refine Soft Matte and Refine Hard Matte effects

After Effects includes two related effects for refining mattes: Refine Soft Matte and Refine Hard Matte. The Refine Soft Matte effect does the same thing as Refine Edge Matte, except it applies the effect to the entire matte at a constant width. If you need to capture subtle variations across an entire matte, use this effect.

The Refine Hard Matte effect performs the same edge refinements as the Roto Brush when Fine-Tune Roto Brush Matte is turned on in the Roto Brush & Refine Edge effect in the Effect Controls panel.

Using the Refine Edge tool

The boy's coat and face have hard edges, but his cap is fuzzy, and the Roto Brush tool didn't pick up the nuanced edge. The Refine Edge tool lets you include fine details such as wisps of hair in designated areas of the segmentation boundary.

Though it might be tempting to use the Refine Edge tool immediately after creating the base frame, it's best to wait until you've refined the segmentation boundary across the entire clip. Because of the way After Effects propagates the segmentation boundary, using the Refine Edge tool too early results in a matte that is difficult to use.

1 Zoom in so that you can see the edges of the cap clearly. Enlarge the Layer panel if necessary, and use the Hand tool to move the layer so you can see the entire cap.

2 Select the Refine Edge tool (✍), hidden beneath the Roto Brush tool in the Tools panel, and then move to the beginning of the clip in the Layer panel.

The cap is relatively soft, so a small brush size will work well. For a fuzzier object, you might have better results with a much larger brush. The brush needs to overlap the stray edges that emerge from the object.

3 Change the brush size to **10** pixels.

When you use the Refine Edge tool, draw strokes across or along the edges of the matte.

4 In the Layer panel, move the Refine Edge tool over the edge of the cap, straddling the segmentation boundary and including the fuzzy variations. You can use multiple strokes to move the tool around the entire cap.

When you release the mouse, After Effects switches to the Refine Edge X-ray view so that you can see how the Refine Edge tool changes the matte, capturing the detail in the edges.

5 Move to the second base frame in the Layer panel (1:20), and then repeat steps 1–4 to complete the rotoscoping process.

6 Zoom out to see the entire scene, resize the Layer panel if you enlarged it, and then choose File > Save to save your work.

● **Note:** Use the Refine Edge tool only after you have cleaned up the matte across the entire clip.

Freezing your Roto Brush tool results

You've put a fair amount of time and effort into creating the segmentation boundary across the entire clip. After Effects has cached the segmentation boundary so it can recall it without having to make the calculations again. To keep that data easily accessible, you'll *freeze* it. This reduces the processing demands on your system so you can work faster in After Effects.

Once the segmentation is frozen, you cannot edit it unless you unfreeze it. Refreezing the segmentation is time-consuming, so it's best to refine the segmentation boundary as much as possible before freezing.

1 Click the Freeze button in the lower right area of the Layer panel.

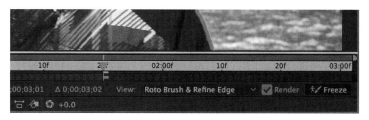

Depending on your system, this may take a while.

The Freezing Roto Brush dialog box displays a progress bar as it freezes the Roto Brush and Refine Edge tool data. Freezing may take a few minutes, depending on your system. As After Effects freezes the information for each frame, the cache line turns blue. When it has finished freezing, a blue warning bar appears above the time ruler in the Layer panel, reminding you that the segmentation is frozen.

2 Click the Toggle Alpha Boundary button (▣) in the Layer panel to see the matte. Then click the Toggle Transparency Grid button (▦). Move the time marker across the time ruler to see the subject without the distractions of the background.

3 Click the Toggle Alpha Boundary button again to see the boundary.

4 Choose File > Save.

After Effects saves the frozen segmentation information with the project.

Changing the background

There are many reasons to isolate a foreground image from a background. Often, you want to replace the background entirely, moving the subject to a different setting. But rotoscoping is also useful if you simply want to change the foreground or background without modifying the other. In this lesson, you'll make the background blue to enhance the theme of winter and help the subject stand out.

1 Close the Layer panel to return to the Composition panel, and then move the current-time indicator to the beginning of the timeline.

The Composition panel displays the composition, which includes only the boy.mov layer, consisting only of the foreground you isolated from the clip.

2 Hide the properties for the boy.mov layer, if they're visible.

3 Click the Project tab to display the Project panel. Then drag another copy of the boy.mov clip from the Project panel to the Timeline panel, and place it below the original boy.mov layer.

4 Click the new layer, press Enter or Return, and rename the layer **Background**.
 Then press Enter or Return again.

5 With the Background layer selected, choose Effect > Color Correction >
 Hue/Saturation in the After Effects menu bar.

6 In the Effect Controls panel, do the following:

 • Select Colorize.

 • Change Colorize Hue to **–122** degrees.

 • Change Colorize Saturation to **29**.

 • Change Colorize Lightness to **–13**.

7 Choose File > Increment And Save.

If you save incrementally, you can return to earlier versions of your project to make adjustments later. This can be very useful if you're experimenting or want to try alternative effects. The Increment And Save feature preserves the previously saved version of the project and creates a new project with the same name, with an increasing number added to the filename.

Adding animated text

You're nearly done. All you need to do is to add the animated title between the boy and the background.

1 Deselect all layers, and then move the current-time indicator to the beginning of the time ruler.

2 Choose Layer > New > Text.

A new text layer appears in the Timeline panel at the top of the layer stack, and a cursor appears in the Composition panel.

3 Type **WINTER BLUES** in the Composition panel.

4 Select all the text in the Composition panel, and then do the following in the Character panel:

- Choose Myriad Pro for the font.
- Choose Black or Semibold for the font style.
- Type **300** px for the font size.
- Choose Optical from the Kerning menu.
- Select white for the fill color.
- Select black for the stroke color.
- Make sure the stroke width is 1 px and Stroke Over Fill is selected.

5 Select the text layer in the Timeline panel to deselect the text. Then press
 T to reveal the layer's Opacity property. Change the Opacity to **40%**.

6 Click the Effects & Presets tab to open the panel, and then type **Glow** in the search
 box. Double-click the Glow preset under Stylize.

The text gains some texture. The default settings are fine.

7 Drag the WINTER BLUES layer in the Timeline panel down to position it
 between the boy.mov and Background layers. Then move the current-time
 indicator to the beginning of the time ruler, if it's not already there.

You'll animate the text so that it moves left behind the boy while he crosses to the right
of the frame.

8 With the WINTER BLUES
 layer selected, press P to reveal
 its Position property. Change
 the Position to **1925, 540**.
 Click the stopwatch icon (⏱)
 for the Position property to
 set a keyframe.

The text moves offscreen, so it's not visible when the movie begins.

9 Move the current-time
 indicator to 3:01 (the end
 of the clip), and change the
 Position to **−1990, 540**.

The text moves to the left. After Effects creates a keyframe.

10 Deselect all layers in the Timeline panel, and move the current-time indicator to the beginning of the time ruler. Press the spacebar to preview the clip.

11 Choose File > Save to save your work.

Outputting your project

Render your movie to complete the project.

1 Choose File > Export > Add To Render Queue.

2 In the Render Queue panel, click the blue words *Best Settings*.

3 In the Render Settings dialog box, choose Half from the Resolution pop-up menu, and make sure Use Comp's Frame Rate is selected in the Frame Rate area. Then click OK.

4 Click the blue text next to Output Module. Then, at the bottom of the Output Module Settings dialog box, choose Audio Output Off, and click OK.

5 Click the blue text next to Output To. In the Output Movie To dialog box, navigate to the Lesson09/Finished_Project folder, and click Save.

6 Click Render in the top right corner of the Render Queue panel.

7 Save and close the project.

Congratulations! You've separated a foreground object from the background, including tricky details, modified the background, and animated some text to complete the movie. You're ready to use the Roto Brush tool on your own projects.

Extra credit

Tracking faces

The face-tracking feature in After Effects makes it easier to track a face or specific facial features, such as lips or eyes. Previously, tracking a face required roto brushing or complex keying.

● **Note:** If you open the Lesson09_extra_credit.aep file, you may need to relink the Facetracking.mov asset.

1 Choose File > New > New Project. Double-click in the Project panel to open the Import File dialog box, and then navigate to the Lessons/Lesson09/Assets folder. Select the Facetracking.mov file, and click Import or Open.

2 Drag the Facetracking.mov clip onto the Create A New Composition button at the bottom of the Project panel.

3 Select the Facetracking.mov layer in the Timeline panel. Then, select the Ellipse tool, hidden by the Rectangle tool in the Tools panel.

4 Drag an elliptical mask roughly covering the face.

5 Right-click the Mask 1 layer, and choose Track Mask.

6 In the Tracker panel, choose Face Tracking (Outline Only) from the Method menu.

The Face Tracking (Outline Only) option tracks the entire face. The Face Tracking (Detailed Features) option tracks the outline plus the lips, eyes, and other distinctive facial features. You can export detailed facial data for use in Character Animator, or you can use it in After Effects to apply effects or to match it with another layer, such as an eye patch or a hat.

(continued on next page)

Extra credit (continued)

7 Click the Track Forward button in the Tracker panel.

The Tracker tracks the face, changing the mask's shape and position as the face moves.

8 Press the Home key to return to the beginning of the timeline, and then move the current-time indicator across the time ruler to see how the mask moves with the face.

9 In the Effects & Presets panel, search for **Bright**. Then drag the Brightness and Contrast effect onto the Facetracking.mov layer in the Timeline panel.

10 Expand Effects > Brightness & Contrast > Compositing Options in the Timeline panel.

11 Click the + icon next to Compositing Options. Choose Mask 1 from the Mask Reference 1 menu, and increase Brightness to **50**.

The masked area of the face brightens, but nothing else does. This setting is too bright, and the edge of the mask is too abrupt. You'll make it more subtle.

12 Reduce the Brightness to **20**.

13 Expand the Mask 1 properties. Change the Mask Feather property to **70**, **70** pixels.

14 Save the project to the Lesson09/Finished_Project folder. Then close the file.

You can use the face tracker to blur a face, brighten it, or add any other effect. You can also invert the mask to affect everything but the face.

Review questions

1 When should you use the Roto Brush tool?

2 What is the segmentation boundary?

3 When should you use the Refine Edge tool?

Review answers

1 Use the Roto Brush tool any time you would have used traditional rotoscoping. It's particularly useful for removing a foreground element from the background.

2 The segmentation boundary is the boundary between the foreground and background. The Roto Brush tool adjusts the segmentation boundary as you progress through the frames in the Roto Brush span.

3 Use the Refine Edge tool when you need to rotoscope objects with fuzzy or wispy edges. The Refine Edge tool creates partial transparency for areas of fine detail, such as hair. Use the Refine Edge tool only after you've adjusted the segmentation boundary across the entire clip.

10 PERFORMING COLOR CORRECTION

Lesson overview

In this lesson, you'll learn how to do the following:

- Use a transition to move from one clip to another.

- Use the Levels effect to correct the color in a shot.

- Use the mask tracker to track part of a scene.

- Remove an area using the Keylight (1.2) effect.

- Use the Auto Levels effect to remove a color cast.

- Key out an area using the Color Range effect.

- Correct colors using Synthetic Aperture Color Finesse 3.

- Use the CC Toner effect to create a mood.

- Copy an object in the scene with the Clone Stamp tool.

 This lesson will take approximately an hour to complete. Download the project files for this lesson, following the instructions in the Getting Started section under "Accessing the lesson files and Web Edition," if you haven't already done so. As you work on this lesson, you'll preserve the start files. If you need to restore the start files, download them from your Account page.

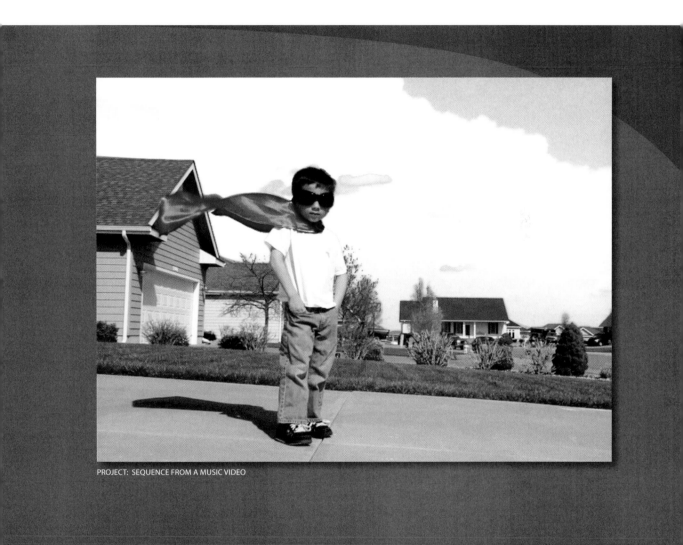

PROJECT: SEQUENCE FROM A MUSIC VIDEO

Most shots require some degree of color correction
and color grading. With Adobe After Effects, you
can easily remove color casts, brighten images, and
change the mood of a clip.

Getting started

As the term implies, color correction is a way of altering or adapting the color of a captured image. Strictly speaking, *color correction* is the act of adjusting the color in a shot to correct errors in white balance and exposure, and to ensure color consistency from one shot to another. However, you can use the same color-correction tools and techniques to perform *color grading*, which is the subjective manipulation of color to focus attention on a key element in a shot or create a color palette for a specific visual look.

In this lesson, you will correct the color of a video clip that was shot without the proper white-balance setting. First, you'll combine two clips from a longer video of a young superhero taking off and flying through the sky. Then, you'll apply a variety of color-correction effects to clean up and enhance the image. You'll also use mask tracking and motion tracking to replace the sky with more dramatic clouds.

First, you'll preview the final movie and set up your project.

1 Make sure the following files are in the Lessons/Lesson10 folder on your hard disk, or download them from your Account page at www.peachpit.com now:

 • In the Assets folder: storm_clouds.jpg, superkid_01.mov, superkid_02.mov

 • In the Sample_Movies folder: Lesson10.avi, Lesson10.mov

● **Note:** This lesson includes the SA Color Finesse 3 effect, which requires registration. If you open the Lesson10_end file, you may be prompted to register the effect.

2 Open and play the Lesson10.avi sample movie in Windows Media Player or the Lesson10.mov sample movie in QuickTime Player to see what you will create in this lesson. When you are done, close Windows Media Player or QuickTime Player. You may delete the sample movies from your hard disk if you have limited storage space.

When you begin this lesson, restore the default application settings for After Effects. See "Restoring default preferences" on page 2.

3 Start After Effects, and then immediately hold down Ctrl+Alt+Shift (Windows) or Command+Option+Shift (Mac OS). When prompted, click OK to delete your preferences. Close the Start window.

After Effects opens to display an empty, untitled project.

4 Choose File > Save As > Save As.

5 In the Save As dialog box, navigate to the Lessons/Lesson10/ Finished_Project folder.

6 Name the project **Lesson10_Finished.aep**, and then click Save.

Creating the composition

You'll create a new composition based on the two superkid movie files.

1 Choose File > Import > File.

2 Navigate to the Lessons/Lesson10/Assets folder, Shift-click to select the storm_ clouds.jpg, superkid_01.mov, and superkid_02.mov files, and then click Import or Open.

3 In the Project panel, deselect the assets you imported. Select the superkid_01. mov file and Shift-click the superkid_02.mov file, and drag the files onto the Create A New Composition button (▣) at the bottom of the Project panel.

4 In the New Composition From Selection dialog box, do the following:

- Make sure Single Composition is selected.

- In the Options area, choose superkid_01.mov from the Use Dimensions From menu.

- Select Sequence Layers.

- Select Overlap.

- For Duration, enter **0:18**.

- Choose Dissolve Front Layer from the Transition menu.

- Click OK.

● **Note:** You can add transitions after you've created a composition by selecting the layers, choosing Animation > Keyframe Assistant > Sequence Layers, and then selecting the options.

When Sequence Layers is selected, After Effects places the layers in sequence rather than placing them both to start at 0:00. You specified an overlap of 18 frames and a cross-dissolve transition so that the first clip dissolves into the second.

After Effects creates a new composition named for the superkid_01.mov file, and displays it in the Composition and Timeline panels.

5 Select the superkid_01 composition in the Project panel, press Enter or Return, and rename the composition **Taking Flight**. Press Enter or Return again to accept the change.

6 Press the spacebar to preview the clips, including the transition, and then press the spacebar again to stop the preview.

7 Choose File > Save to save your work so far.

Previewing your project on a video monitor

If possible, perform color correction on a video monitor instead of a computer monitor. The gamma values between a computer monitor and a broadcast monitor vary greatly. What may look good on a computer screen may be too bright and washed out on a broadcast monitor. Always be sure your video or computer monitor is properly calibrated before performing color correction. For instructions on calibrating a computer monitor, see After Effects Help.

Mercury Transmit is a software interface that Adobe digital video applications use to send video frames to external video displays. Video device manufacturers AJA, Blackmagic Design, Bluefish444, and Matrox provide plug-ins that route the video frames from Mercury Transmit to their hardware. The same Mercury Transmit plug-ins work in Adobe Premiere Pro, Prelude, SpeedGrade, and After Effects. Mercury Transmit can also use monitors connected to your computer's video card and FireWire-connected DV devices without an additional plug-in.

1 With a video monitor connected to your computer system, start After Effects.

2 Choose Edit > Preferences > Video Preview (Windows) or After Effects CC > Preferences > Video Preview (Mac OS). Then select Enable Mercury Transmit.

3 Choose a device from the list. Devices with names such as AJA Kona 3G or Blackmagic Playback represent video devices connected to your computer. Adobe Monitor devices are the computer monitors connected to your video card. Adobe DV requires a DV device connected to a FireWire port on your computer.

4 To change the options for your video device, click Setup next to its name. More options may be available in the device's control panel or management application.

5 Click OK to close the Preferences dialog box.

Adjusting color balance with levels

After Effects provides several tools for color correction. Some may do the job with a single click, but understanding how to adjust colors manually gives you the greatest freedom to achieve the look you want. You'll use the Levels effect to adjust the shadows, remove the blue cast, and make the image pop a little more. You'll work on the clips individually, starting with the second clip.

Note: An additional color-correction tool, called Adobe SpeedGrade, is available with Adobe Creative Cloud membership. To learn about SpeedGrade, see adobe.com/products/speedgrade.

1 Go to 4:00 in the time ruler.

2 Select the superkid_02.mov layer in the Timeline panel.

3 Press Enter or Return, rename the layer **Wide Shot**, and then press Enter or Return to accept the new name.

4 With the Wide Shot layer selected, choose Effect > Color Correction > Levels (Individual Controls).

The Levels (Individual Controls) effect may be a little intimidating at first, but it can give you great control over your shot. It remaps the range of input color or alpha channel levels onto a new range of output levels, functioning much the same as the Levels adjustment in Adobe Photoshop.

The Channel menu specifies the channel to be modified, and the histogram shows the number of pixels with each luminance value in the image. When the selected channel is RGB, you can adjust the overall brightness and contrast of the image.

To remove a color cast, you must first know which areas of the image are supposed to be gray (or white or black). In this shot, the driveway is gray, the shirt is white, and the shoes and goggles are black.

Note: You may need to resize the Info panel to see the values.

5 Open the Info panel. Then, move the cursor over the white frame of the garage. As you move the cursor, the RGB values change in the Info panel.

Tip: For an even more accurate number, sample multiple areas of the image that are gray or white, average those values, and then use those numbers to determine the adjustments.

In one area of the garage, the RGB values are R=186, G=218, B=239. To determine what the values should be, divide 255 (the highest possible RGB value) by the highest value in the sample. That gives you 255 divided by 239 (the blue value), or 1.08. To equalize the colors so that blue is no longer prominent, multiply 1.08 by the original red and green values (186 and 218, respectively). The new values (rounded) are 200 for red and 233 for green.

6 In the Effect Controls panel, expand the Red and Green properties.

7 For the Red Input White value, enter **200**; for the Green Input White value, enter **233**.

The blue cast is gone, and the image appears warmer.

For each channel, the Input settings increase the value, while the Output settings decrease the value. For example, lowering the Red Input White value adds red to the highlights in the shot, and increasing the Red Output White value adds red to the shadows or dark areas in the shot.

Performing the math lets you zero in on the appropriate settings quickly. If you prefer, you could experiment with the settings to find the best values for the footage you're using.

8 Hide the Levels (Individual Controls) properties in the Effect Controls panel.

Adjusting color balance with Color Finesse 3

You used the Levels effect to adjust the color balance in the second clip. Now you'll use Synthetic Aperture Color Finesse 3 to do the same for the first clip. Synthetic Aperture Color Finesse 3 is a third-party plug-in that installs with After Effects. It offers a number of ways to correct and enhance an image, along with a variety of tools to measure the results. The clip is in pretty good shape, but some fine-tuning will result in a better project.

Note: Synthetic Aperture Color Finesse 3 is a powerful color-correction plug-in. Once you're familiar with it, you can use it to perform a wide variety of color corrections.

1 Press the Home key, or move the current-time indicator to the beginning of the time ruler.

2 Select the superkid_01.mov layer in the Timeline panel, press Enter or Return, rename the layer **Close Shot**, and press Enter or Return to accept the new name.

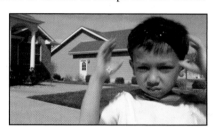

3 With the Close Shot layer selected, choose Effect > Synthetic Aperture > SA Color Finesse 3. Register if prompted to do so.

Experienced users may find the simplified interface controls the most efficient way to adjust the color of an image, but the full interface is helpful to truly master the effect. You'll use the full interface.

4 In the SA Color Finesse 3 area of the Effect Controls panel, click Full Interface.

SA Color Finesse 3 opens in its own window. The upper left area of the window provides different scopes that measure the results in different ways. You make adjustments using controls in the bottom area of the window.

Tip: In other applications, the RGB Waveform scope may be called the RGB Parade scope.

5 In the upper left area of the window, click RGB WFM to select the RGB Waveform scope.

The RGB Waveform scope displays the luminance range in each of the RGB channels, measured from 0 to 100%. Generally, luminance shouldn't exceed 100%, but in this clip, the luminance of the blue channel does, which means some areas of detail are clipped. Leveling the luminance values will improve the overall image.

Tip: When you change a value on a tab, a check mark appears next to the tab to indicate you've adjusted the controls.

6 On the far left side of the lower area of the window, click the RGB tab to activate the controls. (Click the tab itself; if you just check the box, the controls aren't displayed.)

7 Click Master to activate the color controls for the entire image.

In this shot, the green channel appears to have the most even luminance, so you'll use it as a baseline to adjust the other two channels.

8 Move the Master Gamma slider to **1.08**—the same value you used to adjust the color balance in the second clip using the Levels effect.

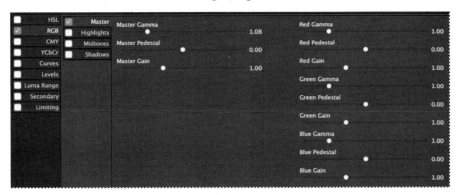

● **Note:** We're providing the values to use for this clip, but you can also experiment with the sliders to balance the colors. As you become more familiar with the controls, you'll know intuitively which changes to make.

The Master Gamma slider adjusts the midtone values in the overall image without affecting the black and white values. Increasing the value to 1.08 brightens the image slightly.

9 Click the Highlights tab to activate it.

Sliders on the Highlights tab adjust the bright portions of the image.

On all the tabs, Gamma sliders affect the midtones for a channel. Pedestal correction adds a fixed offset to the channel's pixel values; you can use it to boost an image's overall brightness, but doing so will also make the blacks brighter. Gain adjusts an image's "brightness" by multiplication so that lighter pixels are affected more than darker pixels, effectively raising the white point.

10 Increase the Red Pedestal to **.04**. Then lower the Blue Gamma value to **.84**, and decrease the Blue Pedestal value to **−.08**.

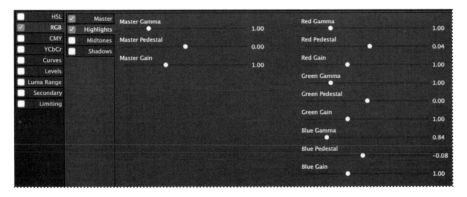

Increasing the Red Pedestal value bumped up the peak luminance values for the red channel, and decreasing the Blue Pedestal value lowered the peak luminance value for the blue channel. The luminance peaks for each channel are now close to 100.

11 Click the Midtones tab to activate it. Then increase the Red Gamma to **1.23** and the Blue Gamma to **1.12**.

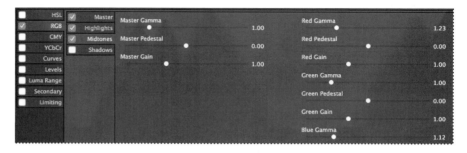

Sliders on the Midtones tab affect only the midtones of the image. The large gray range of colors in each channel are now more similar.

12 Click the Shadows tab to activate it. Then increase the Red Pedestal value to **.02** and the Red Gain to **1.07**. Lower the Blue Gamma value to **.91**.

Sliders on the Shadows tab affect the darker areas of the image, which appear at the bottom of the RGB waveform.

13 Click OK in the lower right corner to accept the changes and close the SA Color Finesse 3 window.

● **Note:** To learn more about SA Color Finesse 3, within the plug-in's interface, choose Help > View Color Finesse User's Guide or Help > View Color Finesse Online Knowledge Base.

Before

After

14 Choose File > Save to save your work.

Replacing the background

These shots were taken on a clear day with few clouds. To add a little drama, you'll key out the sky and replace it with storm clouds. You'll start by using the rigid mask tracker to mask the sky, and then key out the sky color. Then you'll replace it with another image.

Using the mask tracker

The mask tracker transforms a mask so that it follows the motion of an object or objects in a movie. It's similar to the face tracker you used in the Extra Credit project in Lesson 9. You can use it to mask a moving object so that you can apply a special effect to it, for example. In this case, you'll use it to track the sky as it shifts in a handheld camera. There is a great deal of blue in this clip in shadows, the cape, and other areas, so it would be difficult to key out the sky without first isolating it.

1 Go to 2:22—the last frame in the first clip before the transition begins.

2 Select the Close Shot layer in the Timeline panel. Then select the Pen tool (✐) from the Tools panel.

3 In the Composition panel, draw a mask that follows the roofline of the buildings. Complete the mask above the image in the Composition panel, as shown below. It's okay if the mask cuts off the boy's head, because his head doesn't contain blue and won't be keyed out.

4 With the Close Shot layer selected in the Timeline panel, press the M key to display the Mask properties.

5 Choose None from the Mask Mode menu.

Mask modes (blending modes for masks) control how masks within a layer interact with one another. By default, all masks are set to Add, which combines the transparency values of any masks that overlap on the same layer. While Add is chosen, areas outside the mask disappear. Choosing None from the Mask Mode menu reveals the entire clip in the Composition panel, not just the masked area, so it's easier to edit.

● **Note:** You'll learn more about tracking objects in Lesson 13, "Advanced Editing Techniques." For help working with track points, see "Moving and resizing the track points" on page 330.

6 Right-click or Control-click Mask 1, and choose Track Mask.

After Effects opens the Tracker panel. The mask tracker does not alter the shape of the mask to follow a shape; the mask remains the same shape but the tracker can change its position, rotation, or scale based on the motion in the clip. You'll use it to track the edges of the buildings without having to manually adjust and track the mask. Because the scene was shot without a tripod, you'll track the position, scale, and rotation of the mask.

7 In the Tracker panel, choose Position, Scale & Rotation from the Method menu. Click the Track Selected Masks Backward button (◄) to begin tracking backward from 2:22.

● **Note:** If the mask requires adjustment on more than a few frames, delete it and draw the mask again.

8 When the tracking is complete, manually preview the clip to see the mask. If it slips out of place, adjust the mask on individual frames. You can shift the entire mask or reposition individual points, but don't delete any points, as that will change the mask for all the frames that follow.

Keying out the sky with Keylight (1.2)

Now that you've masked the sky, you'll key out the blue in the area that you masked. First, you'll duplicate the layer, and then apply mask modes to isolate the mask.

1 Go to 2:02. Then, select the Close Shot layer, and choose Edit > Duplicate.

After Effects adds an identical layer, named Close Shot 2, above the Close Shot layer.

2 Select the Close Shot layer, and choose Subtract from its Mask Mode menu.

3 Select the Close Shot 2 layer, press M to display its Mask properties, and choose Add from its Mask Mode menu.

When you apply the Subtract mask mode, the influence of the mask is subtracted from the masks above it in the stacking order. The Add mask mode adds the mask to the masks above it. In this case, you're ensuring that only the sky will be selected in the Close Shot 2 layer. If you zoom in to the Composition window while no layers are selected, you can see a faint line where the two layers intersect.

4 Select the Close Shot layer, and press the M key twice quickly to show all of the mask properties for the layer. Reduce the Mask Expansion value to **–1.0**.

The Mask Expansion setting determines how far, in pixels, from the mask path the influence of the mask on the alpha channel extends. You've shrunk the mask on the Close Shot layer so that the two masks don't overlap.

5 Hide the properties for the Close Shot layer.

6 Select the Close Shot 2 layer, and choose Effect > Keying > Keylight (1.2).

The Keylight 1.2 effect options appear in the Effect Controls panel.

7 Select the eyedropper next to Screen Colour, and then sample an area of the sky near the boy's head.

Most of the sky is keyed out, but if your mask overlapped any of the shadowy areas of the buildings, they're probably affected too. You'll use Screen Balance to fix that.

8 Change the Screen Balance to **0**.

The buildings lighten up.

Screen Balance determines how saturation is measured: With a balance of 1, saturation is measured against the smaller of the other two components in the color; with a balance of 0, it's measured against the larger of the two; with a balance of 0.5, it's measured from the average of the two. Generally speaking, blue screens work best with a balance around .95 and green screens with a balance around 0.5, but it varies depending on the colors in the image. For many clips, try setting the balance closer to 0, and then closer to 1, to see what works best.

9 Click the Toggle Transparency Grid button (▒) in the Composition panel to see the keyed-out area clearly.

10 Expand the Screen Matte category in the Effect Controls panel, and then change the Clip White value to **67**.

The screen matte is the matte that remains when you've keyed out other parts of the image. Sometimes parts of the matte are accidentally keyed out. The Clip White value turns the gray (transparent) pixels to white (opaque).

This process is very similar to adjusting Levels for a layer. Anything above the Clip White value is considered pure white. Likewise, the Clip Black value makes anything below the value completely black.

11 Make sure Final Result is chosen in the View menu at the top of the Keylight (1.2) area in the Effect Controls panel.

12 Hide the properties for the Close Shot 2 layer.

Adding a new background

With the original sky keyed out, you're ready to add the clouds to the scene.

1 Click the Project tab to display the Project panel, and then drag the storm_clouds.jpg file to the Timeline panel, placing it below the Close Shot layer.

2 Drag the end of the storm_clouds layer to align with the end of the Close Shot layer.

Now the clouds are there, but they're not very dramatic. You'll make them larger and adjust their position.

3 Press the S key to display the Scale property for the layer, and change the amount to **222%**.

4 Press Shift+P to display the Position property for the layer, and change the value to **580.5**, **255.7**.

Color-correcting using Auto Levels

Although the storm clouds are dramatic, the contrast of the image and the color cast don't really match the foreground elements. You'll use the Auto Levels effect to correct that.

The Auto Levels effect automatically sets highlights and shadows by defining the lightest and darkest pixels in each color channel as white and black, and then redistributing intermediate pixel values proportionately. Because Auto Levels adjusts each color channel individually, it may remove or introduce a color cast. In this case, with the default settings applied, Auto Levels removes the orange cast and balances the shot.

1 With the storm_clouds layer selected in the Timeline panel, choose Effect > Color Correction > Auto Levels.

2 To brighten the clouds just a bit, change the White Clip value to **1.00%**.

The Black Clip and White Clip values determine how much of the shadows and highlights (respectively) are clipped to the new extreme shadow and highlight colors in the image. Setting the clipping values too high reduces detail in the shadows or highlights; 1% is as high as is typically recommended.

3 Choose File > Save to save your work.

Motion tracking the clouds

The clouds are in place, and they're looking good. But if you scrub through the clip, you'll notice that the clouds are static while the foreground moves due to camera motion. The clouds should travel with the foreground. You'll use motion tracking to solve this problem.

After Effects tracks motion by matching pixels from a selected area in a frame to pixels in each succeeding frame. Tracking points designate the areas to track.

1 Press the Home key, or move the current-time indicator to the beginning of the time ruler.

2 Select the Close Shot layer in the Timeline panel, right-click or Control-click the layer, and choose Track Motion.

After Effects displays the Close Shot layer in the Layer panel and makes the Tracker panel active.

3 In the Tracker panel, select the Position, Rotation, and Scale options.

After Effects displays two track points in the Layer panel. The outer box in each track point represents the search region (the area After Effects scans); the inner box is the feature region (what After Effects is searching for); the center "x" is the attach point.

4 Click an empty area in the inner box (the feature region) of the first track point, and drag the entire track point to the corner of the house on the left. You want to track an area with strong contrast.

5 Click an empty area in the feature region of the second track point, and drag the entire track point to the peak of the roof across from the first track point.

6 In the Tracker panel, click Edit Target. Then, in the Motion Target dialog box, choose 3. storm_clouds.jpg from the Layer menu. Click OK.

After Effects applies the tracking data to the target layer. In this case, it will track the motion of the Close Shot layer, and apply that tracking data to the storm_clouds.jpg layer so that they move in sync.

7 Click the Analyze Forward button (▶) in the Tracker panel.

After Effects analyzes the positions of the tracking regions frame by frame to track the camera movement in the clip.

8 When the analysis is complete, click Apply in the Tracker panel. Click OK to apply the data for both the x and y dimensions.

9 Switch back to the Composition panel, and scrub backward through the timeline. The clouds move with the foreground elements. Hide the Close Shot layer properties to keep the Timeline panel tidy.

Because you selected Scale in the Tracker panel, After Effects resized the layer as necessary to sync it with the Close Shot layer. The clouds are no longer in the same position. You'll adjust the anchor point for the layer.

10 Select the storm_clouds.jpg layer in the Timeline panel, and press the A key to display its Anchor Point property. Change the Anchor Point position to **313**, **601**.

11 Press A to hide the Anchor Point property, and choose File > Save to save your work so far.

Replacing the sky in the second clip

You'll use a similar process to replace the sky in the second clip, with a few differences. You'll use the Color Range effect to key out the sky instead of the Keylight (1.2) effect.

Creating the masks

As you did with the first clip, you'll start by drawing a mask to isolate the sky so you won't key out all the blue in the image. You'll use the mask tracker to ensure the mask stays in the right position throughout the clip.

1 Go to 2:23 in the time ruler—the first frame in the second clip.

2 Click the Video switch (the eye icon) in the Timeline panel for the Close Shot, Close Shot 2, and storm_clouds.jpg layers to hide them so that you can see the full Wide Shot clip clearly.

3 Select the Wide Shot layer in the Timeline panel.

4 Select the Pen tool (✐) in the Tools panel, and then follow the edges of the buildings to draw a mask around the bottom of the image, omitting the sky. Make sure the boy's blue pants are entirely within the shape you draw, so they won't be keyed out with the sky.

5 Select the Wide Shot layer again, and then press Ctrl+D (Windows) or Command+D (Mac OS) to duplicate the layer.

A new Wide Shot 2 layer appears above the original Wide Shot layer in the Timeline panel.

6 Select the original Wide Shot layer, and press the M key twice to reveal the mask properties for the layer. Change the Mask Expansion value to **1** pixel.

The influence of the mask expands by 1 pixel beyond its outline.

7 Select the Wide Shot 2 layer, press the M key twice to reveal the mask properties for the layer, and then select Inverted.

The area that is masked in the Wide Shot 2 layer is inverted: What is masked in the Wide Shot layer is not in the Wide Shot 2 layer, and vice versa. To see this clearly, temporarily hide the Wide Shot layer and then show it again.

8 Select Mask 1 in the Wide Shot 2 layer, right-click or Control-click Mask 1, and then choose Track Mask.

9 In the Tracker panel, choose Position from the Method menu, and then click the Track Selected Masks Forward button (▶).

The mask tracker tracks the mask as the camera moves.

10 When the analysis is complete, go to 2:23 in the time ruler again. Under the Wide Shot layer, right-click or Control-click Mask 1, and choose Track Mask.

11 In the Tracker panel, choose Position from the Method menu, and then click the Track Selected Masks Forward button (▶).

12 Hide the properties for all layers.

Keying out an area with the Color Range effect

The Color Range effect keys out a specified range of colors. This key effect is especially useful where the color to be keyed is unevenly lit. The sky in the Wide Shot clip ranges in color from a deep blue to a lighter shade near the horizon—a perfect candidate for the Color Range effect.

1 Go to 2:23 in the time ruler.

2 Select the Wide Shot 2 layer in the Timeline panel, and choose Effect > Keying > Color Range.

3 Select the Key Color eyedropper, next to the Preview window in the Effect Controls panel. Then, in the Composition panel, click a midtone blue color in the sky to sample it.

The keyed-out area appears black in the Preview window in the Effect Controls panel.

4 Select the Add To Key Color eyedropper in the Effect Controls panel, and then click another area of the sky in the Composition panel.

5 Repeat step 4 until the entire sky has been keyed out.

> **Tip:** Select the blue areas of the sky, but not the clouds. You don't want to key out parts of the boy's shirt.

Adding a new background

With the original sky keyed out, you're ready to add the clouds to the scene.

1 Click the Project tab to display the Project panel. Then drag the storm_clouds.jpg item from the Project panel to the Timeline panel, placing it below the Wide Shot layer.

2 With the storm_clouds layer selected in the Timeline panel, press the S key to display its Scale property, and then increase the Scale values to **150, 150%**.

▶ **Tip:** If you're typing the values, press Tab to jump between the fields.

3 With the storm_clouds layer still selected in the Timeline panel, press P to display its Position property. Then change the position values to **356, 205** or the position you prefer.

4 With the storm_clouds layer selected, choose Effect > Color Correction > Auto Levels. Change the White Clip value to **1.00%**.

Motion tracking the shot

Again, because the clip was shot without a tripod, the camera shifts. The clouds should shift with it. You'll track the motion to sync the clouds with the foreground elements, just as you did for the other clip.

1 Make sure the current-time indicator is at 2:23. Then select the Wide Shot layer, right-click or Control-click it, and choose Track Motion.

2 In the Tracker panel, select the Position, Rotation, and Scale options.

3 Click in the feature region (the inner box) of the first track point, and drag it to the right peak of the roof of the house in the center shot. Then, drag the feature region of the second track point to the peak of the house straight across from it, as in the illustration.

4 In the Tracker panel, click Edit Target. In the Motion Target dialog box, choose 6. storm_clouds.jpg from the Layer menu, and click OK. Make sure you select the second storm_clouds.jpg file, and not the first one (layer 3); you want the one that is associated with the Wide Shot layer.

5 Click the Analyze Forward button in the Tracker panel.

6 When the analysis is complete, click Apply in the Tracker panel. Click OK to apply the data to both the x and y dimensions.

7 Click the Composition: Taking Flight tab in the Composition panel to make it active. Then scrub through the clip to watch the clouds in sync with the other elements.

The clouds follow the movement of the camera, but because the layer was scaled, they may not be in the right position.

8 Hide the properties for all layers.

9 Make sure no layers are selected. Then, select the storm_clouds.jpg layer at the bottom of the layer stack, and press the A key to reveal the Anchor Point property. Adjust it so that it looks right. We used **941, 662**.

10 Make the Close Shot, Close Shot 2, and first storm_clouds.jpg layers visible again.

11 Choose File > Save to save your work so far.

Color grading

So far, the color changes you've made have been to correct inaccurate white balances or to match color between clips. You can also change color and tone to create a mood or otherwise enhance a movie. You'll make some final adjustments to give the entire movie a steely blue color, make the image soft and dreamy, and add a vignette.

Using CC Toner to map colors

CC Toner is a color-mapping effect based on the luminance of the source layer. You can map two (duotone), three (tritone), or five (pentone) colors. You'll use it to map a cold blue color to bright areas of the clip, a steely blue to the midtones, and a darker blue to darker areas of the clip.

1 Choose Layer > New > Adjustment Layer.

You can use an adjustment layer to apply an effect to all the layers beneath it at once. Because it's on a separate layer, you can also hide or edit the layer and automatically affect its influence on all the other layers.

2 Move the Adjustment Layer 1 layer to the top of the Timeline panel, if it's not already there.

3 Select the Adjustment Layer 1 layer, press Enter or Return, rename the layer **Steel Blue**, and press Enter or Return again.

4 Select the Steel Blue layer, and choose Effect > Color Correction > CC Toner.

5 In the Effect Controls panel, choose Pentone from the Tones menu. Then do the following:

- Click the Brights color swatch, and choose a cold blue color (we used R=**120**, G=**160**, B=**190**).

- Click the Midtones color swatch, and choose a darker, steely blue (we used R=**70**, G=**90**, B=**120**).

- Click the Darktones color swatch, and choose a much darker blue (we used R=**10**, G=**30**, B=**60**).

- Change the Blend With Original value to **75%**.

Adding a blur

You'll add a blur to the entire project. First you'll precompose the layers, and then you'll create a partially visible blurred layer.

1 Select all of the layers in the Timeline panel, and choose Layer > Pre-Compose.

Precomposing layers moves them to a new composition, making it easier to affect all the layers in a composition at once.

2 In the Pre-Compose dialog box, name the composition **Final Effect**, and select Move All Attributes Into The New Composition. Then click OK.

After Effects replaces all the layers in the Taking Flight composition with a single layer named Final Effect.

3 Select the Final Effect layer, and choose Edit > Duplicate to make a copy of it.

4 With the top layer selected, choose Effect > Blur & Sharpen > Gaussian Blur.

5 In the Effect Controls panel, change the Blurriness to **40**.

The effect is too strong. You'll reduce the opacity of the layer that contains the effect.

6 With the top layer selected, press the T key to reveal the Opacity property for the layer. Change its value to **30%**.

Adding a vignette

You'll use a new solid layer to create a vignette for the movie.

1 Choose Layer > New > Solid.

2 In the Solid Settings dialog box, do the following:

- Name the layer **Vignette**.

- Click the Make Comp Size button.

- Change the color to black (R=**0**, G=**0**, B=**0**).

- Click OK.

3 Select the Ellipse tool (●), hidden beneath the Rectangle tool (■) in the Tools panel, and then double-click the Ellipse tool to add an elliptical mask that is automatically sized to fit the layer.

4 In the Timeline panel, select the Vignette layer, and press the M key twice to reveal the mask properties. Change the Mask Mode to Subtract, and change the Mask Feather value to **300** pixels.

5 Press the T key to reveal the Opacity property, and change its value to **50%**.

6 Hide the properties for all layers.

7 Preview your movie!

8 Save the file.

Extra Credit

Cloning an object in a scene

You can copy an object, and then use motion tracking to ensure it remains in sync with the rest of the scene. You'll use the Clone tool to place a second light on the other side of the door in the background of the Close Shot clip. Cloning in After Effects is similar to cloning in Photoshop, but in After Effects, you can clone across the entire timeline, rather than in a single image.

1 Press the Home key, or move the current-time indicator to the beginning of the time ruler.

2 Double-click the lower Final Effect layer in the Timeline panel to open the Final Effect composition. You want to make the change to the copy of the composition that is not blurred.

3 Double-click the Close Shot layer in the Timeline panel to open it in the Layer panel. You can paint only on individual layers—not on the composition as a whole.

4 Select the Clone Stamp tool in the Tools panel. The Clone Stamp tool samples the pixels on a source layer and applies the sampled pixels to a target layer; the target layer can be the same layer or a different layer in the same composition. When you select the Clone Stamp tool, After Effects adds the Brushes and Paint panels to the stack.

5 Enlarge the Brushes panel if necessary, and then change the Diameter to **10** pixels and the Hardness value to **60%**.

6 Enlarge the Paint panel. Make sure the Mode is set to Normal and the Duration to Constant. The source should be set to Current Layer. Select Aligned and Lock Source Time, and make sure the Source Time is set to 0 frames.

The Constant setting applies the Clone Stamp effect from the current time forward. Because you're starting at the beginning of the timeline, the changes you make will affect every frame in the layer.

(continued on next page)

Extra credit *(continued)*

When Aligned is selected in the Paint panel, the position of the sample point—the clone position—changes for subsequent strokes to match the movement of the Clone Stamp tool in the target Layer panel so you can use multiple strokes to paint the entire cloned object. The Lock Source Time option lets you clone a single source frame.

7 In the Layer panel, position the cursor at the top of the lamp. Alt-click (Windows) or Option-click (Mac OS) to designate a source point for cloning.

8 Click next to the left side of the door, and then click and drag to clone the light. Be careful not to clone part of the door in the process. If you make a mistake, undo and start over with a new source point.

> **Tip:** If you make a mistake, just press Ctrl+Z (Windows) or Command+Z (Mac OS) to undo the stroke, and then try again.

9 When the second light is in place, scrub through the clip.

The cloned light remains stationary while the rest of the scene moves; it isn't in sync with the side of the building. You'll use tracking data to fix the problem.

10 In the Timeline panel, expand the properties for the Close Shot layer, and then expand the Motion Trackers, Tracker 1, and Track Point 1 properties. Then, still in the Close Shot layer, expand the Effects, Paint, Clone 1, and Transform Clone 1 properties.

11 Alt-click or Option-click the stopwatch for the Transform Clone 1 Position property to turn on the expression for the property. Drag its pick whip to the Track Point 1: Attach Point property, and release it. (You may need to enlarge the Timeline panel to see both properties at once.)

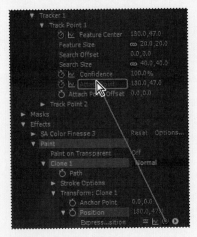

The expression you created ties the position of the cloned light to the tracking data you created for the clip earlier in the lesson. The light will travel with the image. But it may be in the wrong place. You can correct its relationship to the door by adjusting its anchor point.

12 Adjust the Transform: Clone 1: Anchor Point property until the light is positioned next to the door. Your values will probably be different from ours.

13 Scrub through the clip to verify that the light is positioned properly. When you're satisfied that it is, close the Close Shot tab in the Layer panel and the Final Effect composition tab in the Timeline panel. Preview the entire composition to see your work.

14 Choose File > Save to save your work.

Review questions

1 What's the difference between color correction and color grading?

2 What does the SA Color Finesse 3 effect do?

3 When would you use the mask tracker?

Review answers

1 Color correction is performed to correct errors in white balance and exposure or to ensure color consistency from one shot to another. Color grading is more subjective; its goals are to optimize the source material, to focus attention on a key element in the shot, or to create a color palette to match the visual look the director prefers.

2 SA Color Finesse 3 is a third-party plug-in installed with After Effects CC. It performs a wide variety of color-editing effects, such as isolating a color range for enhancement. SA Color Finesse 3 affects the original layer, ignoring any effects that have already been applied to the layer.

3 Use the mask tracker when you need to track a mask that does not change shape, but that does change position, scale, or rotation through a clip. For example, you can use it to track a person in an action shot, a wheel, or an area of the sky.

11 USING 3D FEATURES

Lesson overview

In this lesson, you'll learn how to do the following:

- Create a 3D environment in After Effects.

- Look at a 3D scene from multiple views.

- Create 3D text.

- Rotate and position layers along x, y, and z axes.

- Animate a camera layer.

- Add lights to create shadows and depth.

- Extrude 3D text in After Effects.

- Create a Cinema 4D layer to use in After Effects.

This lesson will take approximately an hour to complete. Download the project files for this lesson, following the instructions in the Getting Started section under "Accessing the lesson files and Web Edition," if you haven't already done so. As you work on this lesson, you'll preserve the start files. If you need to restore the start files, download them from your Account page.

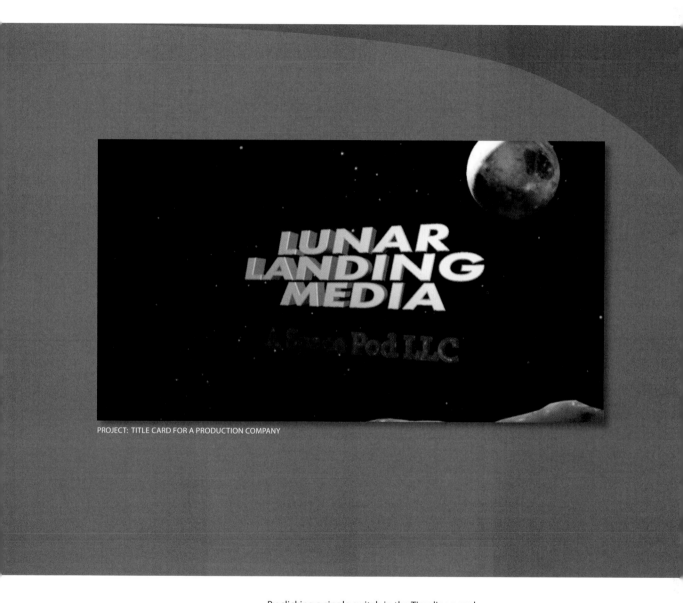

PROJECT: TITLE CARD FOR A PRODUCTION COMPANY

By clicking a single switch in the Timeline panel in After Effects, you can turn a 2D layer into a 3D layer, opening up a whole new world of creative possibilities. Maxon Cinema 4D Lite, included with After Effects, gives you even greater flexibility.

Getting started

Adobe After Effects can work with layers in two dimensions (x, y) or in three dimensions (x, y, z). So far in this book, you've worked primarily in two dimensions. When you specify a layer as three-dimensional (3D), After Effects adds the z axis, which lets you move the object forward and backward in space. By combining this depth with a variety of lights and camera angles, you can create animated 3D projects that take advantage of the full range of natural motion, lighting and shadows, perspective, and focusing effects. In this lesson, you'll explore how to create and animate 3D layers. Then you'll use Maxon Cinema 4D Lite (installed with After Effects) to add texture to 3D text for a title card for a fictional production company.

First, you'll preview the final movie and then set up the project.

1 Make sure the following files are in the Lessons/Lesson11 folder on your hard disk, or download them from your Account page at www.peachpit.com now:

 • In the Assets folder: Lunar.mp3, Space_Landscape.jpg

 • In the Sample_Movies folder: Lesson_11.avi, Lesson11.mov

2 Open and play the Lesson11.avi sample movie in Windows Media Player or the Lesson11.mov sample movie in QuickTime Player to see what you will create in this lesson. When you are done, close Windows Media Player or QuickTime Player. You may delete the sample movies from your hard disk if you have limited storage space.

When you begin this lesson, restore the default application settings for After Effects. See "Restoring default preferences" on page 2.

3 Start After Effects, and then immediately hold down Ctrl+Alt+Shift (Windows) or Command+Option+Shift (Mac OS). When prompted, click OK to delete your preferences. Close the Start window.

After Effects opens to display an empty, untitled project.

4 Choose File > Save As > Save As.

5 In the Save Project As dialog box, navigate to the Lessons/Lesson11/Finished_ Project folder. Name the project **Lesson11_Finished.aep**, and click Save.

6 Click the Create A New Composition button (⬛) at the bottom of the Project panel.

7 In the Composition Settings dialog box, do the following, and then click OK:

- Name the composition **Lunar Landing Media**.
- Choose HDTV 1080 24 from the Preset menu.
- Enter **3:00** for the Duration.
- Make sure the Background Color is black.

8 Choose File > Save.

Creating 3D text

In order to move something in 3D space, you need to make it a 3D object. Initially, any layer has only x (width) and y (height) dimensions, and can be moved only along those axes. But all you have to do to move a layer in three dimensions in After Effects is to turn on its 3D layer switch, which lets you manipulate the object along its z axis (depth). You'll create text, and then make it 3D.

1 Click in the Timeline panel to make it active.

2 Select the Horizontal Type tool (T) in the Tools panel.

After Effects adds the Character and Paragraph panels to the stack and opens the Character panel.

Note: If Futura PT is not available, install it using Typekit. Choose File > Add Fonts From Typekit, search for Futura PT, and sync it using Creative Cloud. Once you've synced the font, it will be available in all applications on your system.

3 Make the Character panel wider, if necessary, and then select the following settings:

- Font: Futura PT

- Font Style: Heavy Oblique

- Fill Color: White

- Stroke: None

- Font Size: **140** px

- Leading: **70** px

- Tracking: **20**%

- Vertical Scale: **65**%

4 Select All Caps. (You may need to drag the bottom of the Character panel to extend it in order to see all settings.)

5 Open the Paragraph panel, and select the Center Text alignment option.

6 Click anywhere in the Composition panel and type **Lunar Landing Media**, with each word on its own line, as in the image on the next page.

7 Select the Selection tool (▶).

8 In the Timeline panel, expand the Transform properties for the Lunar Landing Media layer, and change the Position property to **960, 470**.

The text is roughly centered in the composition.

9 In the Timeline panel, select the 3D Layer switch (⊕) for the Lunar Landing Media layer to give it three dimensions.

Three 3D Rotation properties appear in the Transform group for the layer, and properties that previously supported only two dimensions now display a third value for the z axis. In addition, a new property group named Material Options appears.

When the layer is selected, a color-coded 3D axis appears over the layer's anchor point in the Composition panel. The red arrow controls the x axis, the green arrow controls the y axis, and the blue arrow controls the z axis. At the moment, the z axis appears at the intersection of the x and y axes; it may be difficult to see against the black background. The letter x, y, or z appears when you position the Selection tool over the corresponding axis. When you move or rotate the layer while the pointer is over a particular axis, the layer's movement is restricted to that axis.

10 Hide the properties for the Lunar Landing Media layer.

Using 3D views

Sometimes the appearance of 3D layers can be deceptive. For example, a layer might appear to be scaling smaller along its x and y axes when it's actually moving along the z axis. You can't always tell from the default view in the Composition panel. The Select View Layout pop-up menu at the bottom of the Composition panel lets you divide the panel into different views of a single frame, so you can see your work from multiple angles. You specify different views using the 3D View pop-up menu.

1 At the bottom of the Composition panel, click the Select View Layout pop-up menu, and choose 4 Views, if your screen is large enough to display them. Otherwise, choose 2 Views - Horizontal.

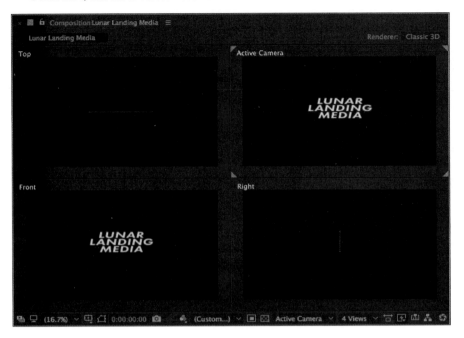

With 4 Views selected, the upper left quadrant displays the scene from the top (along the y axis). There, you can see the z axis, and it's clear that the text layer has no depth. The lower left quadrant shows the view from the front. The upper right quadrant displays what the camera sees, but because there is no camera in the scene, it's the same as the front view. The lower right quadrant shows the view from the right, as if you were observing it along the x axis.

With 2 Views - Horizontal selected, the left view shows the scene from the top, and the right shows the camera's view (currently the front view).

2 Click the Front view to make it active. (Blue corner tabs appear around the active view.) Then, from the 3D View pop-up menu, choose Custom View 1 to see the scene from a different perspective. (If your Composition window displays only two views, click the Top view, and choose Custom View 1 from the 3D View pop-up menu.)

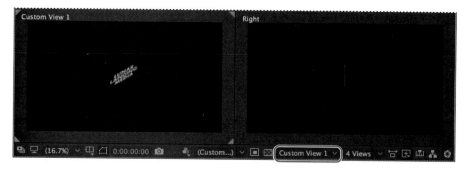

Viewing your 3D scene from different perspectives can help you align elements more accurately, view how layers are interacting with each other, and understand how objects, lights, and cameras are positioned in 3D space.

Importing a background

The text in your title card should appear to be moving in outer space. You'll import an image to use as a background.

1 Double-click an empty area of the Project panel to open the Import File dialog box.

2 Navigate to the Lesson11/Assets folder, and double-click the Space_Landscape.jpg file.

3 Drag the Space_Landscape.jpg item into the Timeline panel, placing it at the bottom of the layer stack.

4 Rename the Space_Landscape.jpg layer **Background**.

5 In the Timeline panel, select the Background layer, and then click the 3D Layer switch (⊕) to convert it to a 3D layer.

● **Note:** If you're displaying only two views, select the Active Camera view, and choose Right from the 3D View pop-up menu. Then complete step 6.

6 Make sure the Background layer is selected. Then, in the Right view in the Composition panel, drag the z-axis arrow (the blue arrow) to the right to move the Background layer further behind the text. Watch the other layers as you drag to see how the layer interacts with 3D space.

7 In the Timeline panel, press the P key to display the Position property for the Background layer. Change the Position to **960, 300, 150**.

8 Press P to hide the Position property, and then choose File > Save to save your work so far.

Adding 3D lights

You've created a 3D scene, but it doesn't yet look three-dimensional from the front. Adding light to a composition creates shadows that give depth to the scene. You'll create two new lights for your composition.

Creating a light layer

In After Effects, a *light* is a type of layer that shines light on other layers. You can choose from among four different types of lights—Parallel, Spot, Point, and Ambient—and modify them with various settings. Lights, by default, are directed toward a point of interest, which is the focus area of the scene.

1 Deselect all layers so that the new layer you create will appear at the top of the layer stack.

2 Press the Home key, or move the current-time indicator to the beginning of the time ruler.

3 Choose Layer > New > Light.

4 In the Light Settings dialog box, do the following:

 • Name the layer **Key Light**.

 • Choose Spot from the Light Type menu.

 • Set Color to a light orange (R=**255**, G=**235**, B=**195**).

 • Make sure Intensity is set to **100%** and Cone Angle to **90** degrees.

 • Make sure Cone Feather is set to **50%**.

 • Select the Casts Shadows option.

 • Set Shadow Darkness to **50%** and Shadow Diffusion to **150** pixels.

 • Click OK to create the light layer.

In the Timeline panel, the light layer is represented by a light bulb icon (💡). In the Composition panel, a wireframe illustrates the light's position, with a cross-hairs icon (⊕) representing the point of interest.

Positioning the spotlight

The point of interest for this light is currently pointed at the center of the scene. Because that's where the text layer is located, you don't need to adjust it. However, you'll change the light position so the scene looks less bleak.

1 Select the Key Light layer in the Timeline panel, and press the P key to reveal the Position property for the light layer.

2 In the Timeline panel, type **955, –102, –2000** in the Position property. The light is now in front of and above the object, aiming down.

Creating and positioning the fill light

The key light gives the scene a moody look, but it's still very dark. You'll add a fill light to lighten the darker areas.

1 Choose Layer > New > Light.

2 In the Light Settings dialog box, do the following:

- Name the layer **Fill Light**.

- Choose Spot from the Light Type menu.

- Set the Color to a light blue (R=**205**, G=**238**, B=**251**).

- Set Intensity to **50%** and Cone Angle to **90** degrees.

- Make sure Cone Feather is set to **50%**.

- Deselect Casts Shadows.

- Click OK to create the light layer.

3 In the Timeline panel, select the Fill Light layer, and press the P key to reveal its Position property.

4 Change the position to **2624**, **370**, **–1125**.

The text stroke, stars, and moon highlight are all much brighter now.

5 Hide the open properties for all layers, and choose File > Save.

Casting shadows and setting material properties

The scene is looking better, with a mix of warm and cool colors. However, it still doesn't look three-dimensional. You'll change the Material Options properties to determine how the 3D layers interact with the lights and shadows.

1 Select the Lunar Landing Media layer in the Timeline panel, and press the A key twice (AA) to reveal the Material Options properties for the layer.

The Material Options property group defines the surface properties of the 3D layer. You can also set shadow and light transmission values.

2 For Casts Shadows, click the word *Off* to toggle the setting on. (Make sure it says *On*, not *Only*.)

The text layer now casts shadows based on the lights in the scene.

3 Change the Diffuse value to **60%** and the Specular Intensity to **60%** so that the text layer reflects more of the light in the scene.

4 Increase the Specular Shininess to **15%** to give the surface a more metallic shine.

5 Hide the properties for the Lunar Landing Media layer.

Adding a camera

You've already seen that you can view a 3D scene from different perspectives. You can also view 3D layers from various angles and distances using layers called *cameras*. When you set a camera view for your composition, you look at the layers as though you were looking through that camera. You can view a composition through the active camera or through a named, custom camera. If you have not created a custom camera, then the active camera is the same as the default composition view.

So far, you have been viewing this composition primarily from the Top, Right, and Custom View 1 angles. Currently, the Active Camera view doesn't let you see your composition from any specific angle. To see everything you want to see, you'll create a custom camera.

1 Deselect all layers, and then choose Layer > New > Camera.

2 In the Camera Settings dialog box, choose 20mm from the Preset menu, and click OK.

The Camera 1 layer appears at the top of the layer stack in the Timeline panel (with a camera icon next to the layer name), and the Composition panel updates to reflect the new camera layer's perspective. The view should change slightly, because the 20mm preset shows a wider field of view than the default. If you didn't notice the scene change, toggle the visibility of the Camera 1 layer to see it, and then make sure it's visible.

3 Choose 2 Views - Horizontal from the Select View Layout pop-up menu at the bottom of the Composition panel. Change the view on the left to Right, and make sure the view on the right is set to Active Camera.

Like light layers, camera layers have a *point of interest* that can be used to determine what the camera looks at. By default, the camera's point of interest is the center of the composition. That's where your text currently is, so that point of interest works well.

4 Make sure the current-time indicator is at the beginning of the time ruler. Select the Camera 1 layer, and press the P key to reveal the Position property for the layer. Create an initial keyframe by clicking the stopwatch icon (Ò) next to the Position property.

5 Set the z-axis value to −**1000**.

The camera moves slightly closer to the text.

6 Go to 1:00.

7 Change the z-axis value to **−590.**

The camera moves much closer to the text.

8 Right-click (Windows) or Control-click (Mac OS) the second Position keyframe, and choose Keyframe Assistant > Easy Ease In.

9 Move the current-time indicator through the timeline to 1:00. As the camera moves through the scene, notice how the light reflects off the text layer and how the overall image is influenced by the wider camera lens.

10 Hide the Position property for the Camera 1 layer, and choose File > Save.

Extruding text in After Effects

Using the Cinema 4D renderer, you can extrude text and shapes within After Effects. You'll use the Geometry Options properties to make the text a little more interesting.

1 Expand the Lunar Landing Media layer in the Timeline panel.

2 Next to Geometry Options (currently dimmed), click Change Renderer.

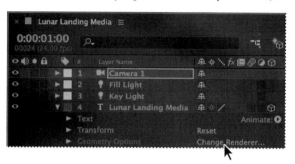

The Composition Settings dialog box opens, with the 3D Renderer tab active.

3 Choose Cinema 4D from the Renderer pop-up menu, and click Options.

4 Move the Quality slider to 32.

▶ **Tip:** To quickly open the options dialog box, click the wrench icon next to the renderer name at the top of the Composition panel.

5 Click OK to close the Cinema 4D Renderer Options dialog box, and then click OK again to close the Composition Settings dialog box.

The Cinema 4D renderer options include a single Quality value, which determines how the CINEMA 4D renderer draws 3D layers. A lower value results in faster rendering but lower rendering quality. Choose a Quality setting that balances rendering speed with the 3D rendering quality your project requires.

6 Expand Geometry Options for the Lunar Landing Media layer.

7 Choose Concave from the Bevel Style menu.

8 Change the Extrusion Depth to **50**.

9 Select the Lunar Landing Media layer, and press R to reveal the Rotation properties.

It's not obvious that you've extruded the text. You'll adjust the text's angle to show off the effect and to provide additional interest to the scene.

10 Change the Y Rotation to **17**.

11 Hide all properties for the layer.

Working with Cinema 4D Lite

After Effects installs a version of Maxon Cinema 4D that lets motion graphic artists and animators insert 3D objects directly into an After Effects scene without pre-rendering passes and potentially complicated file exchanges. You can continue to edit 3D objects in Cinema 4D Lite after you've added them to your After Effects composition.

● **Note:** After Effects uses a different coordinate numbering convention than other 3D applications. In After Effects, the upper left corner of the composition is considered 0, 0. In many 3D applications, including Maxon Cinema 4D, the center of the world (often the screen) is the origin, or 0, 0, 0 point. Additionally, the Y distance increases as the cursor moves down the screen in After Effects.

You'll use Cinema 4D Lite to create a textured subtitle, which you'll add to the After Effects scene below the main text.

Creating a new Cinema 4D layer

You can add a Cinema 4D layer to a composition in After Effects. When you add the layer, After Effects opens Cinema 4D Lite so you can create your 3D scene in a new C4D file. When you finish your work in Cinema 4D, save the file, and it will update automatically in After Effects. You can return to Cinema 4D to make additional changes to the layer.

1 Deselect all layers in the Timeline panel, and then choose Layer > New > Maxon Cinema 4D File. After Effects displays a Save As dialog box.

2 Name the file **subtitle.c4d**, and save it in the Lesson11/ Finished_Project folder.

3 Click Save.

Saving the file adds a C4D file to the Timeline panel, and After Effects opens the Cineware effect in the Effect Controls panel. Cineware creates and manages the link between After Effects and Cinema 4D.

Cinema 4D opens with an empty scene, displaying only the 3D grid.

● **Note:** You may be prompted to update Cinema 4D, or to register in order to access additional features. You can complete the exercise without doing either, but if you plan to use Cinema4D on your own projects, consider registering and updating the application.

A. Modes icon palette **B.** Viewport **C.** Tools icon palette **D.** Object Manager **E.** Material Manager
F. Timeline **G.** Coordinates Manager **H.** Attribute Manager

Creating 3D text in Cinema 4D

You'll start by creating the text.

1 In the Tools icon palette (below the menu bar), click and hold the triangle in the lower right corner of the Freehand icon to display its menu, and then select the Text tool.

A basic text spline appears in the middle of the scene.

2 In the text box in the Attribute Manager, type **A Space Pod LLC**.

3 In the Attribute Manager, change the text settings as follows:

- Font: Chapparal Pro
- Align: Middle
- Height: **40** cm

 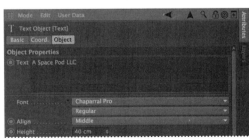

The view is currently from an angle. You want to see how the text looks from the front, so you'll change the camera view.

4 Choose Front from the Cameras menu above the Viewport.

5 In the Tools icon palette, click and hold the triangle in the lower right corner of the Subdivision Surface icon to view its menu, and then select Extrude.

6 In the Object Manager, select the Text object, and then drag it to the middle column to the right of Extrude to parent it. You'll know you've positioned it correctly when the cursor becomes a box with an arrow pointing down.

In the Object Manager, the Text object appears nested below the Extrude object, indicating the parent relationship. The text is now extruded, though you can't tell because you're viewing it from the front.

7 In the Object Manager, click the Extrude object to make it active (it turns bright orange).

8 In the Attribute Manager, select the Object tab, and then change the z-axis Movement value to **10** cm to reduce the extrusion depth.

Now, you'll enhance the text further by beveling the edges and making some adjustments.

9 In the Attribute Manager, select the Caps tab, and do the following:

- Choose Fillet Cap from the Start menu.
- Increase the Steps value to **2**.
- Decrease the Radius value to **3** cm.
- Choose Concave from the Fillet Type menu.

The changes you made give the text an interesting edge.

Adding texture to an object

Cinema 4D Lite comes with a number of preset surfaces you can apply to 3D objects. You'll add a subtle water texture to the text.

1 In the Materials Manager, click Create, and then choose Load Material Preset > Lite > Materials > Liquids >Water Turbulent.

2 In the Materials Manager, click the surface you just added, and drag it onto the text in the Viewport.

3 Choose File > Save.

Positioning the 3D object

Because you'll use the Cinema 4D camera in After Effects, you can position the text in Cinema 4D using the full range of 3D tools. You'll adjust the text in Cinema 4D so that it appears below the title text in After Effects and so that it tilts at the same angle as the other text.

1 Select the Move tool in the Tools icon palette.

2 Drag the green arrow (the y axis) down until the Y value for Position in the Coordinates Manager is about -165 cm.

3 Select the Scale tool in the Tools icon palette.

4 Drag the blue triangle to the upper right until the tool tip displays approximately 163%. (The XYZ values in the Size column in the Coordinates Manager should be approximately 449 cm, 70 cm, and 21 cm.)

5 Choose File > Save to save the file so far.

6 Return to After Effects to see how the text is currently positioned in the scene.

The text looks pretty good, but its angle isn't right. You'll fix that next.

7 Return to Cinema 4D Lite.

8 Select the Rotate tool in the Tools icon palette.

● **Note:** Cinema 4D
Lite displays values
for the H (heading), P
(pitch), and B (bank)
axes for rotation.

9 Drag the green horizontal bar to the left so that the H rotation value is about -22.

10 Adjust the inner blue circle to tilt the right edge of the text down just a bit, so that the B rotation value is about 2.6°.

Integrating the C4D layer in After Effects

Now, you'll return to After Effects to work with the 3D text in your project. You've already positioned the layer in Cinema 4D. In After Effects, you'll animate its opacity.

1 Save your file in Cinema 4D Lite, and return to After Effects.

2 Select the subtitle.c4d layer in the Timeline panel to display the Cineware effect in the Effect Controls panel.

While you're working with a Cinema 4D file in After Effects, you should usually choose Software or Standard (Draft) from the Renderer menu in the Cineware effect. However, when you prepare to render your final project, choose Standard (Final) from the Renderer menu.

The Software option uses a faster renderer that doesn't include all the features of the file. The Standard (Final) option renders more slowly, but it gives you a better view of what the Cinema 4D file looks like. You'll choose the Standard (Draft) option so that the grid doesn't show.

3　In the Effect Controls panel, choose Standard (Draft) from the Renderer menu.

4　Make sure the current-time indicator is at 1:00 in the timeline so you can see the final camera view.

5　(Optional) If you'd like to adjust the text position, return to Cinema 4D to tweak it, save the file, and return to After Effects again.

6　Press T to reveal the layer's Opacity property, and then click the stopwatch icon (⏱) to set a keyframe at 1:00.

7　Return to the beginning of the timeline, and change the Opacity to **20%**.

Finishing the project

As a final touch, you'll add an audio file for the title card. You're ready to import the audio file and prepare the file for rendering.

1 Select the Project tab, double-click an empty area of the Project panel, and then navigate to the Lesson11/Assets folder. Double-click the Lunar.mp3 file to import it.

2 Drag the Lunar.mp3 file from the Project panel to the bottom of the layer stack in the Timeline panel.

3 Select the subtitle.c4d layer in the Timeline panel.

4 Click the Effect Controls tab, and then, in the Effect Controls panel, choose Standard (Final) from the Renderer menu.

5 Choose File > Save, and then preview your movie.

You've created a simple 3D scene using After Effects and Cinema 4D Lite, but you've only just scratched the surface of what is possible. Experiment with your own projects to explore your options.

Review questions

1 What happens to a layer when you select its 3D Layer switch?

2 Why is it important to look at multiple views of a composition that contains 3D layers?

3 What is a camera layer?

4 What is a 3D light in After Effects?

Review answers

1 When you select a layer's 3D Layer switch in the Timeline panel, After Effects adds a third axis, the z axis, to the layer. You can then move and rotate the layer in three dimensions. In addition, the layer takes on new properties that are unique to 3D layers, such as the Materials Options property group.

2 The appearance of 3D layers can be deceptive, depending on the view in the Composition panel. By enabling 3D views, you can see the true position of a layer relative to other layers in the composition.

3 You can view After Effects 3D layers from any number of angles and distances using layers called *cameras*. When you set a camera view for your composition, you look at the layers as though you were looking through that camera. You can choose between viewing a composition through the active camera or through a named, custom camera. If you have not created a custom camera, then the active camera is the same as the default composition view.

4 In After Effects, a light is a type of layer that shines light on other layers. You can choose from among four different types of lights—Parallel, Spot, Point, and Ambient—and modify them with various settings.

12 WORKING WITH THE 3D CAMERA TRACKER

Lesson overview

In this lesson, you'll learn how to do the following:

- Track footage using the 3D Camera Tracker.

- Add camera and text elements to a tracked scene.

- Set a ground plane and origin.

- Create realistic shadows for new 3D elements.

- Lock elements to planes using null objects.

- Adjust camera settings to match real-world footage.

- Remove rolling shutter distortions from DSLR footage.

This lesson will take approximately one and a half hours to complete. Download the project files for this lesson, following the instructions in the Getting Started section under "Accessing the lesson files and Web Edition," if you haven't already done so. As you work on this lesson, you'll preserve the start files. If you need to restore the start files, download them from your Account page.

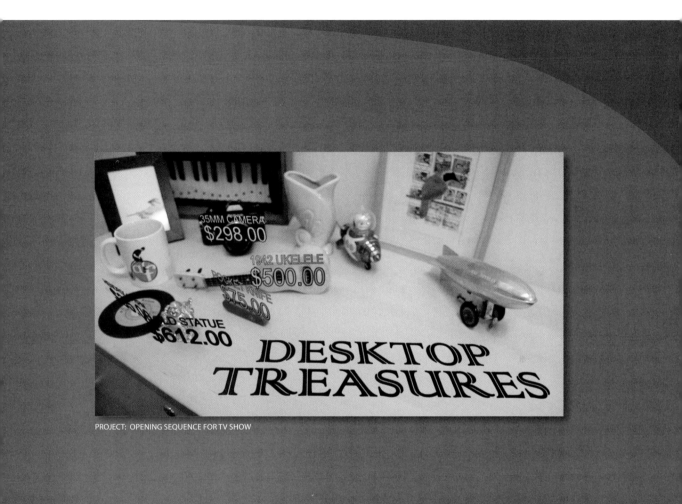

PROJECT: OPENING SEQUENCE FOR TV SHOW

The 3D Camera Tracker effect analyzes two-dimensional footage to create a virtual 3D camera that matches the original. You can use this data to add 3D objects that merge realistically with your scene.

About the 3D Camera Tracker effect

The 3D Camera Tracker effect automatically analyzes the motion present in existing 2D footage, extracts the position and lens type of the real camera that shot the scene, and creates a new 3D camera in After Effects to match it. The effect also overlays 3D track points onto the 2D footage, so you can easily attach new 3D layers onto the original footage.

These new 3D layers have the same movement and perspective changes as the original footage. The 3D Camera Tracker effect even helps create "shadow catchers," so your new 3D layers can appear to cast realistic shadows and reflections onto the existing footage.

The 3D Camera Tracker performs its analysis in the background. Therefore, you can work on other compositions while the footage is being analyzed.

Getting started

In this lesson, you'll create the opening scene for a fictional reality show that estimates the value of everyday objects found on office desks. You'll begin by importing the footage and tracking it with the 3D Camera Tracker effect. Then you'll add 3D text elements that track precisely with the scene. Finally, you'll animate the text, add audio, and enhance the footage to complete the show's introduction.

First, you'll preview the final movie and set up your project.

1 Make sure the following files are in the Lessons/Lesson12 folder on your hard disk, or download them from your Account page at www.peachpit.com now:

 • In the Assets folder: Desktop.mov, Treasures_Music.aif, Treasures_Title.psd

 • In the Sample_Movies folder: Lesson12.avi, Lesson12.mov

2 Open and play the Lesson12.avi sample movie in Windows Media Player or the Lesson12.mov sample movie in QuickTime Player to see what you will create in this lesson. When you are done, close Windows Media Player or QuickTime Player. You may delete the sample movies from your hard disk if you have limited storage space.

When you begin this lesson, restore the default application settings for After Effects. See "Restoring default preferences" on page 2.

3 Start After Effects, and then immediately hold down Ctrl+Alt+Shift (Windows) or Command+Option+Shift (Mac OS). When prompted, click OK to delete your preferences. Close the Start window.

After Effects opens to display an empty, untitled project.

4 Choose File > Save As > Save As.

5 In the Save As dialog box, navigate to the Lessons/Lesson12/Finished_Project folder.

6 Name the project **Lesson12_Finished.aep**, and then click Save.

Importing the footage

You need to import three footage items for this lesson.

1 Choose File > Import > File.

2 Navigate to the Lessons/Lesson12/Assets folder, Shift-click to select the Desktop.mov, Treasures_Music.aif, and Treasures_Title.psd files, and then click Import or Open.

3 Choose File > New > New Folder to create a new folder in the Project panel, or click the Create A New Folder button (▬) at the bottom of the panel.

4 Type **Footage** to name the folder, press Enter or Return to accept the name, and then drag the Desktop.mov and Treasures_Title.psd items into the Footage folder.

5 Make sure nothing is selected. Then create another folder, name it **Audio**, and drag the Treasures_Music.aif item into it.

6 Expand the folders so that you can see their contents.

Creating the composition

Now, you will create a new composition based on the aspect ratio and duration of the Desktop.mov file.

1 Drag the Desktop.mov item onto the Create A New Composition button (▣) at the bottom of the Project panel. After Effects creates a new composition named Desktop and displays it in the Composition and Timeline panels.

2 Drag the Desktop composition to an empty area of the Project panel to move it out of the Footage folder.

3 Drag the current-time indicator across the time ruler to preview the shot.

The camera moves around a desktop so that you can see the objects on it. You'll add labels and dollar amounts, animated in time with background music.

4 Choose File > Save to save the file.

Repairing rolling shutter distortions

Digital cameras with CMOS sensors—including video-capable DSLRs, popular for the creation of films, commercials, and television shows—typically have what is commonly known as a "rolling" shutter, which captures a frame of video one scan line at a time. Due to time lag between scan lines, not all parts of the image are recorded at exactly the same time, causing motion to ripple down the frame. If the camera or the subject is moving, the rolling shutter can cause distortions, such as leaning buildings and other skewed images.

The Rolling Shutter Repair effect attempts to correct this problem automatically. To use it, select the problem layer in the Timeline panel, and choose Effect > Distort > Rolling Shutter Repair.

Due to a rolling shutter distortion, the pillars of the building appear to be leaning.

After applying the effect, the building looks much more stable.

The default settings usually do the trick, but you may need to change the Scan Direction or the Method being used to analyze the footage.

If you plan to use the 3D Camera Tracker effect with footage on which you've used the Rolling Shutter Repair effect, precompose the footage first.

Tracking the footage

The 2D footage is in place. Now you'll have After Effects track it and interpolate where a 3D camera should be placed.

1 In the Timeline panel, click the Audio icon for the Desktop.mov layer to mute the audio.

You'll add a soundtrack later, and you don't want any ambient noise from this clip.

2 Right-click (Windows) or Control-click (Mac OS) the Desktop.mov layer in the Timeline panel, and choose Track Camera.

After Effects opens the Effect Controls panel and displays its progress as it analyzes the footage in the background. When the analysis is complete, many tracking points appear in the Composition panel. The size of a tracked point indicates its proximity to the virtual camera: Larger points are closer, and smaller points are further away.

The default analysis of the footage often yields satisfactory results, but you can perform a more detailed analysis to better solve the camera position.

3 In the Effect Controls panel, expand the Advanced category, and then select Detailed Analysis.

Depending on your system, this may take a while.

After Effects analyzes the footage again. If you're working with a slower machine and you suspect you'll need a detailed analysis, you can save time by selecting Detailed Analysis while the 3D Camera Tracker is performing its initial analysis. The detailed analysis may take a few minutes, depending on your system. Because the analysis is performed in the background, you could work on other aspects of your project while it progresses.

4 When the analysis is complete, choose File > Save to save your work so far.

Creating a ground plane, a camera, and the initial text

Note: You can also add a camera by clicking the Create Camera button in the Effect Controls panel.

You have a 3D scene, but it needs a 3D camera. You'll add a camera when you create the first text element, and then you'll add a second text element related to the first.

1 Press the Home key, or move the current-time indicator to the beginning of the time ruler.

2 In the Composition panel, hover the cursor over the hole in the record on the desk until the displayed target is in line with the plane and the perspective matches. (If you don't see the track points and target, click the 3D Camera Tracker effect in the Effect Controls panel to make it active.)

Note: If the size of the target makes it difficult to see the plane, resize the target by pressing Alt or Option as you drag from the center of the target.

When you hover the cursor between three or more neighboring track points that can define a plane, a semitransparent triangle appears between the points. Additionally, a red target shows the orientation of the plane in 3D space.

3 Right-click (Windows) or Control-click (Mac OS) the plane, and choose Set Ground Plane And Origin.

The ground plane and origin provide a reference point, setting a point where the coordinates are (0, 0, 0). Though nothing appears to change in the Composition panel using the Active Camera View, the ground plane and origin make it easier to change the camera's rotation and position.

4 Right-click (Windows) or Control-click (Mac OS) the same plane, and choose Create Text And Camera.

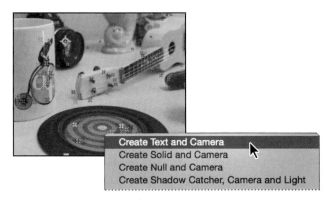

After Effects displays a large text item lying flat in the Composition panel. It also adds two layers to the Timeline panel: Text and 3D Tracker Camera. The 3D switch is enabled for the Text layer, but the Desktop.mov layer remains 2D. Because the text elements are the only ones that need to be positioned in 3D space, there is no reason to make the background footage layer a 3D layer.

5 Move the current-time indicator along the time ruler. The text remains in position, tracking with the camera. Return the current-time indicator to the beginning of the time ruler.

6 Double-click the Text layer in the Timeline panel to add the Character and Paragraph panels to the stacked panels on the right.

7 Open the Paragraph panel, and select Center Text for the alignment. The text is centered over the record.

8 Open the Character panel. Change the font to a sans serif font such as Arial Narrow or Helvetica Light. Then change the font size to **20** px, the stroke width to **1** px, and the stroke type to Fill Over Stroke. Make sure the fill color is white and the stroke color is black (the default colors).

The text looks great, but you want it to stand on end. You'll change its location in space, and then replace it with the price of the object.

● **Note:** Instead of entering values, you could use the Rotation tool to adjust the individual axes in the Composition panel.

9 Select the Text layer in the Timeline panel to exit text-editing mode. Then, press the R key to display the Rotation property of the layer, and change the Orientation values to **0, 350, 0** degrees.

Any new 3D layer you create uses the ground plane and origin to orient the layer in the scene. The Text layer was originally flat, with the Orientation of 270 degrees on the x axis. When you change that value to 0, the text becomes vertical.

10 Double-click the Text layer in the Timeline panel to make it active in the Composition panel.

When the text is editable, it appears to have a light red mask surrounding it.

11 With the text selected in the Composition panel, type **$35.00** to replace it.

So far, so good. Next, you want to label the item, and the label needs to stay with the price as the camera moves. You'll duplicate the layer, modify it, and then parent one layer to the other.

12 Select the $35.00 layer in the Timeline panel, and press Ctrl+D (Windows) or Command+D (Mac OS) to duplicate it.

13 Double-click the $35.2 layer, and type **HENDRIX 45 RPM** (in all capital letters) in the Composition panel.

The text is too large; it's the same size as the price text. You'll parent it to the $35.00 layer and then scale it.

14 Select the Hendrix 45 RPM layer in the Timeline panel, and press the P key to reveal the Position property for the layer. Drag the pick whip from the Hendrix layer to the $35.00 layer.

The Position value for the Hendrix layer changes to 0, 0, 0, because its position is related to the parent layer. However, you want the Hendrix layer to appear above the $35.00 layer, not in front of it.

15 Change the y-axis position value to **−18** to move the Hendrix label above the price text.

16 With the Hendrix layer selected, press the S key to reveal the Scale property, and change the Scale values to **37.4**, **37.4**, **37.4%**.

17 Close the open properties, and then choose File > Save to save your work so far.

Creating realistic shadows

You've set up your first text elements, but unlike true 3D objects, they aren't casting any shadows. You'll create a shadow catcher and a light to add depth to your video.

1 Press the Home key, or move the current-time indicator to the beginning of the time ruler.

2 Select the Desktop.mov layer in the Timeline panel, press the E key to display the 3D Camera Tracker effect, and then select the 3D Camera Tracker effect.

● **Note:** Be sure to select the 3D Camera Tracker effect in the DesktopC.mov layer, not the 3D Tracker Camera layer.

3 Select the Selection tool (▶) in the Tools panel. Then, in the Composition panel, hover until you find the same plane you used to create the text layer.

4 Right-click (Windows) or Control-click (Mac OS) the target, and choose Create Shadow Catcher And Light.

After Effects adds a light source to the scene. The default settings are applied, so a shadow appears in the Composition panel. However, you'll need to reposition the light to match the light in the source footage. The Shadow Catcher 1 layer that After Effects adds to the Timeline panel is a shape layer that has its material options set so that it accepts shadows only from the scene.

5 Select the Light 1 layer in the Timeline panel, and press the P key to reveal the Position property for the layer.

Tip: In a real-world project, it's ideal to work with the lighting plan that was used to shoot the original 2D scene. The goal is to have the new 3D lights match the original source lighting as closely as possible.

6 Enter the following values for the Position property to reposition the light: **1900, −2500, −375**.

7 Choose Layer > Light Settings.

You can change the intensity, color, and other attributes of the light in the Light Settings dialog box.

8 Name the light **Key Light**. Choose Point from the Light Type menu, and then select a slightly red color (we used R=232, G=214, B=213) to match the slight color cast in the room. Then change the Shadow Darkness to **15%** and the Shadow Diffusion to **100** px. Click OK.

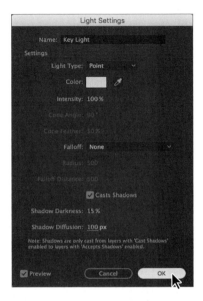

9 Select the Shadow Catcher 1 layer in the Timeline panel, and press the S key to reveal the Scale property.

10 Change the Scale value to **340%**.

Scaling the Shadow Catcher 1 layer changes the area in which shadows can appear for the light that was created with it.

Adding ambient light

The shadow looks better after the adjustments you made to the light, but it's now causing the text to appear black. You'll add ambient light to address this. Unlike a point light, ambient light creates a more diffuse light throughout the scene.

1 Deselect all layers, and then choose Layer > New > Light.

2 Name the light **Ambient Light**, choose Ambient from the Light Type menu, and change its Intensity value to **80%**. The light color should be the same as the color you selected for the point light.

3 Click OK to add the light to the scene.

4 Hide the properties for all layers in the Timeline panel, except for the Desktop.mov layer.

Creating additional text elements

▶ **Tip:** If a 3D object should be obscured by an object in the background, duplicate the background layer, move it to the top of the layer stack, and then use the Mask tool to create masks around portions of the foreground elements. You will need to animate these masks over time, but if you do it carefully, you can create a seamless composition.

You created the label for the Hendrix record. Now you need to perform the same tasks to create labels for the camera, gold statue, pocket knife, and ukulele. You'll use the same steps to create each label, but because the objects are in different places on the table, you'll need to use different orientation and scaling values, as listed in the following chart. You'll find it easiest to attach the label for each to the correct plane at different points in the time ruler.

OBJECT	POSITION IN TIME RULER (STEP 1)	ORIENTATION (STEP 5)	PRICE (STEP 6)	PRICE SCALE (STEP 7)	LABEL (STEP 9)
camera	3:00	0, 310, 0	$298.00	3000	35MM CAMERA
statue	5:00	0, 325, 0	$612.00	2000	GOLD STATUE
knife	7:00	0, 340, 0	$75.00	2500	POCKET KNIFE
ukulele	9:00	0, 310, 0	$500.00	3000	1942 UKULELE

1 Move the current-time indicator to get a better view of the object.

2 In the Timeline panel, select the 3D Camera Tracker (under the Desktop. mov layer) to make it active. (If you don't see the 3D Camera Tracker, press the E key to reveal it.)

● **Note:** Make sure you select the 3D Camera Tracker effect in the DesktopC.mov layer, not the 3D Tracker Camera layer.

3 Make sure the Selection tool (▶) is selected. Then, in the Composition panel, hover over an area so that the red target is parallel to the front of the object.

4 Right-click (Windows) or Control-click (Mac OS) the target, and choose Create Text.

5 Select the Text layer in the Timeline panel, and press the R key to reveal the Rotation values. Then change the Orientation values.

6 Double-click the Text layer to make it editable, and then type the price in the Composition panel.

7 Select the price layer in the Timeline panel, and press S to reveal the Scale property. Change the Scale value.

8 With the price layer selected, press Ctrl+D (Windows) or Command+D (Mac OS) to duplicate the layer.

9 Double-click the duplicate layer in the Timeline panel, and then type the label in the Composition panel.

10 Select the label layer in the Timeline panel, and press P to reveal its Position property. Then drag the pick whip from the label layer (e.g., 35MM CAMERA) to the price layer (e.g., $298.00).

● **Note:** If you turn on Caps Lock to type the label, be sure to turn it off again. Otherwise, you'll get unexpected results, and After Effects won't be able to update the layer name.

11 Change the y value of the Position property for the label layer to **−18** to move the label above the price.

12 Select the label layer again, and press S to reveal the Scale property. Change its Scale values to **50, 50, 50%**.

13 Hide the properties for the layers you just created.

14 Repeat steps 1–13 to label the additional objects, using the values in the chart on the previous page.

The labels all look good, but they may overlap in places that can make them hard to read. You can reposition them as necessary.

● **Note:** Your labels may look different from ours, depending on where you positioned each plane.

15 If you need to adjust a label, select the price layer for the object, and then use the Selection tool to adjust its position. Because you've parented the label layer to the price layer, adjusting the price moves both text layers.

16 Choose File > Save to save your work so far.

Locking a layer to a plane with a null object

The title card for the show should be flat on the table, using the same plane you used to attach text to the record. You'll use a null object to attach the title card to that plane. The title card is an Adobe Photoshop file.

1 Press the Home key, or move the current-time indicator to the beginning of the time ruler.

2 In the Timeline panel, select the 3D Camera Tracker (under the Desktop.mov layer) to make it active. (If you don't see the 3D Camera Tracker, press the E key to reveal it.)

3 Select the Selection tool (▶), and then move the cursor so that the target is lying flat over the record.

4 Right-click (Windows) or Control-click (Mac OS) the target, and choose Create Null.

After Effects adds a Track Null 1 layer to the top of the layer stack in the Timeline panel. Because you know that the record is on the same plane as the desktop, you can use this null object to position the title of the show in the open area of the desk, and still have it move correctly in relation to other elements and the camera in the scene.

5 Select the Track Null 1 layer in the Timeline panel, press Enter or Return, and change the name to **Desktop Null**. Press Enter or Return again to accept the name change.

6 From the Project panel, drag the Treasures_Title.psd asset to the Timeline panel, placing it directly above the Desktop Null layer.

7 Drag the pick whip from the Treasures_Title layer to the Desktop Null layer to parent the layer.

8 Click the 3D switch for the Treasures_Title layer to make it a 3D layer.

► **Tip:** Instead of dragging the pick whip, you could choose 2.Desktop Null from the Parent menu in the Treasures_Title layer.

Because you've parented the title layer to the null object, when it becomes a 3D layer it is automatically oriented to be flat on the desktop.

9 Move to the end of the time ruler so you can see how the title card is positioned.

You need to move the title to the empty area of the desktop, and then rotate it and resize it.

10 Select the Treasures_Title layer in the Timeline panel, and press R to reveal its Rotation property. Then change its Z Rotation value to **305** degrees.

11 Press the S key to reveal the Scale property, and change the Scale amount to **625%**.

12 With the Selection tool, move the title text into position, as in the image at the bottom of this page. If you need to resize the text, use the Selection tool to adjust the object's corner handles.

13 Click the Toggle Switches/Modes button at the bottom of the Timeline panel. Choose Luminosity from the Mode menu for the Treasures_Title layer.

14 Click the Toggle Switches/Modes button again to return to displaying switches.

15 Choose File > Save to save your work so far.

Animating the text

The 3D text elements, camera, and lighting are all complete, but you can make the introduction more interesting by animating the text to appear according to cues in the soundtrack. You'll add an audio track, and then animate the labels to appear when cash register sounds occur.

Animating the first text elements

You'll animate the record label and price to appear early in the intro, with the price cycling through characters until it arrives at the final text.

1 In the Project panel, drag the Treasures_Music.aif file from the Audio folder to the bottom of the layer stack in the Timeline panel.

2 Move the current-time indicator to the beginning of the timeline, and then press the spacebar to move the first few seconds of the composition into RAM. Press the spacebar to stop caching, go to the beginning of the time ruler, and press the spacebar again to preview what you cached.

Notice that the cash register sound occurs periodically. You'll animate the text to appear at those points.

3 Go to 1:00, and select the $35.00 layer. Press the S key to reveal the Scale property, and then change the Scale amount to **0%**. Click the stopwatch icon (⏱) to create an initial keyframe.

4 Go to 1:08, and change the Scale amount for the $35.00 layer to **3200%** so that the text is larger than its final size.

5 Go to 1:10, and change the Scale amount to **3000%**, the final value for the text.

6 Go to 1:00, and press S to hide the Scale property. Then click the arrow next to the $35.00 layer to reveal all its properties.

7 Next to the Text property, choose Character Offset from the Animate menu.

8 Expand Range Selector 1 in the Animator 1 properties. Then click the stopwatch next to Offset to create an initial keyframe, and make sure the value is **0%**.

9 Click the stopwatch to create an initial keyframe for Character Offset (under Character Range), and make sure its value is **0**.

10 Go to 1:12, and change the Range Selector 1 Offset value to **–100%**.

11 Click the word *Offset* to select both keyframes, right-click (Windows) or Control-click (Mac OS) one of the keyframes, and then choose Keyframe Assistant > Easy Ease.

12 Go to 1:17, and change the Character Offset value to **20**.

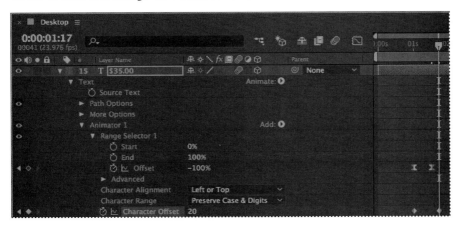

13 Preview the first two seconds of the composition.

The title of the record pops up as the text cycles through to the estimated price. The character offset values determine how the text cycles through characters to arrive at the final one.

Copying the animation to other text elements

Now that you've animated the text for the record, you can copy the animation for the other objects, placing the keyframes at the appropriate points in the time ruler.

1 Select the $35.00 layer, and press the U key to reveal only the properties that have keyframes.

2 In the time graph, drag a marquee around all the keyframes to select them.

3 Choose Edit > Copy to copy the keyframes and their values.

4 Go to 3:00, and select the $298.00 layer. Choose Edit > Paste to paste the keyframes and their values, beginning at the current time (3:00).

5 Go to 5:00, and select the $612.00 layer. Press Ctrl+V (Windows) or Command+V (Mac OS) to paste the keyframes and their values.

6 Go to 7:00, select the $75.00 layer, and press Ctrl+V (Windows) or Command+V (Mac OS).

7 Go to 9:00, select the $500.00 layer, and press Ctrl+V (Windows) or Command+V (Mac OS).

8 Hide the properties for all the layers, and then choose File > Save.

Adjusting the camera's depth of field

The intro is looking pretty good, but you can make the computer-generated elements more closely match the source footage if you adjust the depth of field for the 3D camera. You'll use the values that were used in the camera that shot the original footage, so the text that is further away from the camera appears to be more out of focus.

1 Select the 3D Tracker Camera layer in the Timeline panel.

2 Choose Layer > Camera Settings.

3 In the Camera Settings dialog box, do the following, and then click OK:

 • Select Enable Depth of Field.

 • Set the Focus Distance to **200** mm.

 • Change the F-Stop value to **5.6**.

 • Set the Focal Length to **27.2**.

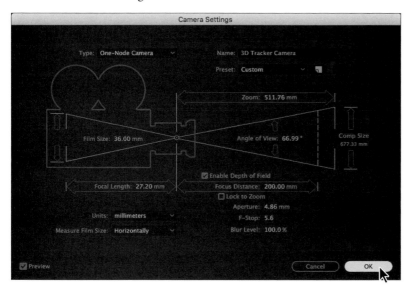

4 In the Timeline panel, select all of the layers except the audio layer. Then select the Motion Blur switch for one of the layers, applying it to all selected layers.

5 Click the Enable Motion Blur button (⬤) at the top of the Timeline panel to enable motion blur for all layers.

6 Choose File > Save to save your project.

Rendering the composition

You've done some complex work to create a scene that merges the added components with an existing tableau. To see the final results, you'll render the project. You'll learn more about rendering in Lesson 14, "Rendering and Outputting."

1 In the Project panel, select the Desktop composition.

2 Choose Composition > Add To Adobe Media Encoder Queue.

Adobe Media Encoder opens. Your composition is listed in the Queue panel with default output settings.

3 In the Queue panel, choose AVI (Windows) or QuickTime (Mac OS) in the Format column.

4 Choose NTSC DV Widescreen 24p in the Preset column.

5 Click the blue text in the Output File column, navigate to the Lesson12/ Finished_Project folder, and click Save.

6 Click the Start Queue button (▶) to begin rendering.

7 When Adobe Media Encoder has finished rendering the composition, play the movie to admire your work!

Review questions

1 What does the 3D Camera Tracker effect do?

2 How can you make an added 3D element look like it is the same size as elements that are farther from the camera?

3 What is the Rolling Shutter Repair effect?

Review answers

1 The 3D Camera Tracker effect automatically analyzes the motion present in existing 2D footage, extracts the position and lens type of the real camera that shot the scene, and creates a new 3D camera in After Effects to match it. The effect also overlays 3D track points onto the 2D footage, so you can easily attach new 3D layers onto the original footage.

2 To make an added 3D element appear to recede, so that it looks like it's farther from the camera, adjust its Scale property. Adjusting the Scale property keeps its perspective locked with the rest of the composition.

3 The Rolling Shutter Repair effect attempts to correct the "rolling" shutter problem that commonly occurs when you use digital cameras with CMOS sensors, which capture a frame of video one scan line at a time. Due to time lag between scan lines, not all parts of the image are recorded at exactly the same time, causing motion to ripple down the frame. If the camera or the subject is moving, the rolling shutter can cause distortions, such as leaning buildings and other skewed images. To use the effect, select the problem layer in the Timeline panel, and choose Effect > Distort > Rolling Shutter Repair.

13 ADVANCED EDITING TECHNIQUES

Lesson overview

In this lesson, you'll learn how to do the following:

- Stabilize a shaky camera shot.

- Use single-point motion tracking to track one object in a shot to another object in a shot.

- Perform multipoint tracking using perspective corner-pinning.

- Use Imagineer Systems mocha for After Effects to track motion.

- Create a particle system.

- Use the Timewarp effect to create slow-motion video.

 This lesson will take approximately two hours to complete. Download the project files for this lesson, following the instructions in the Getting Started section under "Accessing the lesson files and Web Edition," if you haven't already done so. As you work on this lesson, you'll preserve the start files. If you need to restore the start files, download them from your Account page.

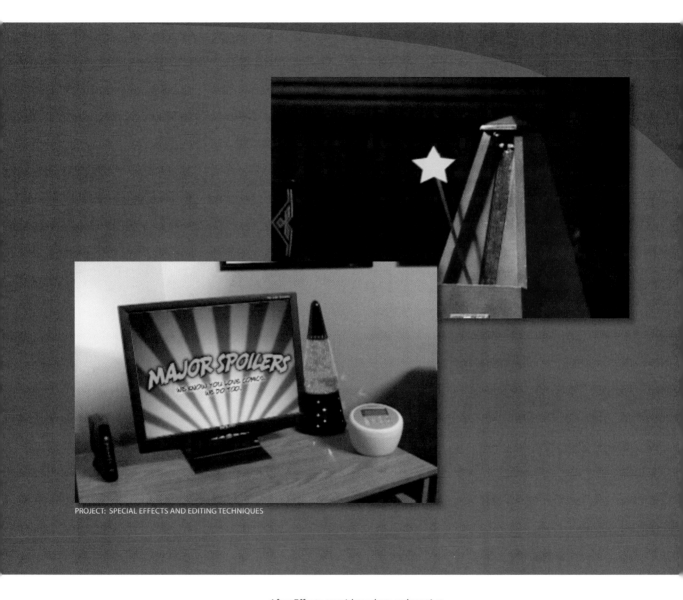

PROJECT: SPECIAL EFFECTS AND EDITING TECHNIQUES

After Effects provides advanced motion stabilization, motion tracking, high-end effects, and other features for the most demanding production environments.

Getting started

In previous lessons, you've used many of the essential 2D and 3D tools you need for motion graphics design. But Adobe After Effects also offers motion stabilization, motion tracking, advanced keying tools, distortion effects, the capability to retime footage using the Timewarp effect, support for high dynamic range (HDR) color images, network rendering, and much more. In this lesson, you will learn how to use Warp Stabilizer VFX to stabilize a handheld camera shot, how to track one object to another in an image so that their motion is synchronized, and how to use corner-pinning to track an object with perspective. Finally, you will explore two of the high-end digital effects available in After Effects: a particle system generator and the Timewarp effect.

This lesson includes multiple projects. Take a peek at all of them before beginning.

1 Make sure the following files are in the Lessons/Lesson13 folder on your hard disk, or download them from your Account page at www.peachpit.com now:

- In the Assets folder: flowers.mov, Group_Approach[DV].mov, majorspoilers. mov, metronome.mov, mocha_tracking.mov, multipoint_tracking.mov

- In the Sample_Movies folder, the AVI and MOV subfolders, each with the following files: Lesson13_Multipoint, Lesson13_Particles, Lesson13_Stabilize, and Lesson13_Timewarp

● **Note:** You can view these movies all at once or, if you don't plan to complete these exercises in one session, you can watch each sample movie just before you are ready to complete the associated exercise.

2 Open and play the sample movies in the Lesson13/Sample_Movies/AVI folder in Windows Media Player or play the Lesson13/Sample_Movies/MOV folder in QuickTime Player to see the projects you will create in this lesson.

3 When you're done, quit Windows Media Player or QuickTime Player. You may delete these sample movies from your hard disk if you have limited storage space.

Using Warp Stabilizer VFX

If you shoot footage using a handheld camera, you will probably end up with shaky shots. Unless this look is intentional, you'll want to stabilize your shots to eliminate unwanted motion.

Warp Stabilizer VFX in After Effects automatically removes extraneous jitters. When played back, the motion appears smooth, because the layer itself is scaled and moves incrementally to offset the unwanted movement.

Bicubic scaling

When you scale video footage or an image to a larger size, After Effects must sample data to add information where none existed before. You can choose which sampling method After Effects uses when scaling a layer. For details, see After Effects help.

Bilinear sampling is the method After Effects traditionally used. However, bicubic sampling uses a more complex algorithm that typically provides better results when color transitions are more gradual, as in nearly all real-world photographic images. Bilinear scaling may be a better option for sharp-edged graphics.

To choose a sampling method for a layer, select the layer, and choose Layer > Quality > Bicubic or Layer > Quality > Bilinear. Bicubic and bilinear sampling are available only for layers that are set to Best quality. (To change a layer's quality setting to Best, choose Layer > Quality > Best.) You can also use the Quality and Sampling layer switch to toggle between the Bilinear and Bicubic sampling methods.

If you need to scale an image by a large amount while preserving details, use the Detail-preserving Upscale effect instead. The effect preserves the sharpness of sharp lines and curves. For example, you can scale up from SD frame sizes to HD frame sizes, or from HD frame sizes to digital cinema frame sizes. This effect is very closely related to the Preserve Details resampling option in the Image Size dialog box in Photoshop. Note that using the Detail-preserving Upscale effect is slower than using either bilinear or bicubic scaling for the layer.

Setting up the project

As you start After Effects, restore the default application settings for After Effects. See "Restoring default preferences" on page 2.

1 Start After Effects, and then immediately hold down Ctrl+Alt+Shift (Windows) or Command+Option+Shift (Mac OS) to restore default preferences settings. When prompted, click OK to delete your preferences.

2 Close the Start window.

After Effects opens to display a new, untitled project.

3 Choose File > Save As > Save As.

4 In the Save As dialog box, navigate to the Lessons/Lesson13/Finished_ Projects folder.

5 Name the project **Lesson13_Stabilize.aep**, and then click Save.

Importing the footage

You need to import one footage item to start this project.

1 Double-click an empty area of the Project panel to open the Import File dialog box.

2 Navigate to the Lessons/Lesson13/ Assets folder. Select the flowers.mov file, and click Import or Open.

Creating the composition

You'll start by creating the composition.

1 Drag the flowers.mov clip in the Project panel onto the Create A New Composition button () at the bottom of the panel.

After Effects creates a new composition named flowers with the same pixel size, aspect ratio, frame rate, and duration of the source clip.

2 Click the Play button in the Preview panel to preview the footage. Press the spacebar to stop the preview when you've seen the whole clip.

This clip was shot with a handheld camera in the late afternoon. A slight breeze rustles the vegetation, and the camera moves unsteadily.

Applying Warp Stabilizer VFX

Warp Stabilizer VFX starts analyzing footage as soon as you apply it. Stabilization is a background process, so you can work on other compositions while it finishes. How long it takes depends on your system. After Effects displays a blue banner while it analyzes the footage and an orange banner while it applies stabilization.

1 Select the flowers.mov layer in the Timeline panel, and choose Animation > Warp Stabilizer VFX. The blue banner appears immediately.

2 When Warp Stabilizer VFX has finished stabilizing, and the orange banner has disappeared, press the spacebar to preview the changes.

3 Press the spacebar to stop the preview.

The clip is still shaky, but it's smoother than it was initially. Warp Stabilizer VFX moved and repositioned the footage. To see how it applied changes, view the effects in the Effect Controls panel. For example, the clip's borders were scaled up (to about 103%) to hide black gaps that occur when the image is repositioned in the stabilization process. You'll adjust the settings that Warp Stabilizer VFX uses.

Adjusting the Warp Stabilizer VFX settings

You'll change the settings in the Effect Controls panel to make the shot smoother.

1 In the Effect Controls panel, increase the Smoothness amount to **75%**.

Warp Stabilizer VFX immediately begins stabilizing again. It doesn't need to analyze the footage, because the initial analysis data is stored in memory.

Warp Stabilizer VFX settings

This is a summary of the Warp Stabilizer VFX settings to help you get started. To learn more about the settings, and to read more tips for using the effect successfully, see After Effects Help.

- **Result** controls the intended result. Smooth Motion makes camera movement smoother, but doesn't eliminate it; use the Smoothness setting to control how smooth the movement becomes. No Motion attempts to remove all of the camera motion.

- **Method** specifies the most complex operation the Warp Stabilizer VFX performs on the footage to stabilize it: Position, which is based on position data only; Position, Scale, Rotation, which uses these three types of data; Perspective, which effectively corner-pins the entire frame; or Subspace Warp (the default), which attempts to warp various parts of the frame differently to stabilize the entire frame.

- **Borders** settings adjust how borders (the moving edges) are treated for footage that is stabilized. Framing controls how the edges appear in a stabilizing result, and determines whether the effect crops, scales, or synthesizes edges using material from other frames.

- **Auto-scale** displays the current auto-scale amount, and allows you to set limits on the amount of auto-scaling.

- **Advanced** settings give you even greater control over the actions of the Warp Stabilizer VFX effect.

2 When Warp Stabilizer VFX has finished, preview the changes.

3 Press the spacebar to stop playback when you're done.

It's better, but still a little rough. The Auto-scale setting in the Effect Controls panel now displays 103.7%; the effect moved the frames more dramatically, requiring more scaling to eliminate black gaps around the edges.

Rather than change the amount Warp Stabilizer VFX smooths the footage, now you'll change its goal.

4 In the Effect Controls panel, choose No Motion from the Result menu.

With this setting, Warp Stabilizer VFX attempts to lock the camera in position. This requires even more scaling. When No Motion is selected, the Smoothness option is dimmed.

5 When the orange banner disappears, preview the changes again. Press the spacebar to stop the playback.

Now the camera stays in position, so that the movement you notice is the rustling of the flowers in the wind, not the shakiness of the camera. In order to achieve this effect, Warp Stabilizer VFX had to scale the clip to about 112% of its original size.

Fine-tuning the results

The default analysis works well most of the time, but sometimes you may need to massage the end results even further. In this project, the clip skews subtly in a few places, most noticeably at about the five-second mark. Casual viewers may not notice the problem, but a keen producer will. You'll change the method that Warp Stabilizer VFX uses to remove the skew.

1 In the Effect Controls panel, choose Position, Scale, Rotation from the Method menu.

2 Choose Stabilize Only from the Framing menu.

● **Note:** Scaling a video layer up degrades the image. A good rule of thumb is to increase the layer to no more than 115% the size of the original source.

3 Increase the Additional Scale to **114%**.

4 Preview the changes.

Now the shot looks rock-steady. The only movement is that caused by the wind rustling the flowers.

5 Press the spacebar to stop the playback when you're done.

6 Choose File > Save to save your work.

7 Choose File > Close Project.

As you have discovered, stabilizing a shot is not without its drawbacks. To compensate for the movement or rotation data applied to the layer, the frames must be scaled, which could ultimately degrade the footage. If you really need to use the shot in your production, this may be the best compromise.

▶ **Tip:** You can use Warp Stabilizer VFX advanced settings to achieve more complex effects, too. To learn more, see *Adobe After Effects CC Visual Effects and Compositing Studio Techniques*, available from Adobe Press.

Using single-point motion tracking

With the increase in the number of productions that incorporate digital elements into final shots, compositors need an easy way to synchronize computer-generated effects with film or video backgrounds. After Effects lets you do this with the capability to follow, or track, a defined area in the shot, and to apply that movement to other layers. These layers can contain text, effects, images, or other footage. The resulting visual effect precisely matches the original moving footage.

When you track motion in an After Effects composition that contains multiple layers, the default tracking type is Transform. This type of motion tracking tracks position and/or rotation to apply to another layer. When tracking position, this option creates one track point, and generates Position keyframes. When tracking rotation, this option creates two track points, and produces Rotation keyframes.

In this exercise, you will track a shape layer to the weighted arm of a metronome. This will be especially challenging, as the camera operator chose not to use a tripod.

Setting up the project

If you've just completed the first project, and After Effects is open, skip to step 3. Otherwise, restore the default application settings for After Effects. See "Restoring default preferences" on page 2.

1 Start After Effects, and then immediately hold down Ctrl+Alt+Shift (Windows) or Command+Option+Shift (Mac OS) to restore default preferences settings. When prompted, click OK to delete your preferences.

2 Close the Start window.

After Effects opens to display a new, untitled project.

3 Choose File > Save As > Save As.

4 In the Save As dialog box, navigate to the Lessons/Lesson13/Finished_ Projects folder.

5 Name the project **Lesson13_Tracking.aep**, and then click Save.

Creating the composition

You need to import one footage item to start this project. You'll use it to create the composition.

1 Double-click an empty area of the Project panel to open the Import File dialog box.

2 Navigate to the Lessons/Lesson13/Assets folder. Select the metronome.mov file, and then click Import or Open.

3 In the Project panel, drag the metronome.mov clip onto the Create A New Composition button at the bottom of the panel.

After Effects creates a new composition named metronome, with the same pixel size, aspect ratio, frame rate, and duration of the source clip.

4 Drag the current-time indicator across the time ruler to manually preview the footage.

Creating a shape layer

You're going to attach a star to the end of the metronome. First, you need to create the star. You'll use a shape layer.

1 Press the Home key, or move the current-time indicator to the beginning of the time ruler.

2 Click an empty area of the Timeline panel to deselect the layer.

3 Select the Star tool (⭐), hidden behind the Rectangle tool (▣) in the Tools panel.

● **Note:** If you don't see the Fill Color swatch, make sure you don't have a layer selected. When a layer is selected, shape tools draw masks.

4 Click the Fill Color swatch, and select a light yellow such as R=**220**, G=**250**, B=**90**. Click the word *Stroke*, select None in the Stroke Options dialog box, and click OK.

5 In the Composition panel, draw a small star.

6 Use the Selection tool (▶) to position the star over the weighted end of the pendulum arm.

7 Select Shape Layer 1 to see the layer's anchor point. Use the Pan Behind tool (✦) to move the anchor point to the center of the star shape, if it isn't already there.

Positioning the track point

After Effects tracks motion by matching pixels from a selected area in a frame to pixels in each succeeding frame. You create tracking points to specify the area to track. A track point contains a feature region, a search region, and an attach point. After Effects displays the track point in the Layer panel as it tracks.

You will track the metronome weight (the rhombus at the end of its arm) by placing tracking regions around the area that you'll track another layer to. With the star shape added to the Tracking composition, you are ready to position the track point.

1 Select the metronome.mov layer in the Timeline panel.

2 Choose Animation > Track Motion. The Tracker panel opens; increase its size if you can't see all the options.

After Effects opens the selected layer in the Layer panel. The Track Point 1 indicator is in the center of the image.

Notice the settings in the Tracker panel: Metronome.mov is selected in the Motion Source menu. The Current Track is Tracker 1, and the Motion Target is Shape Layer 1, because After Effects automatically sets the Motion Target to the layer immediately above the source layer.

Now, you'll position your track point.

3 Using the Selection tool (▶), move the Track Point 1 indicator (drag the empty portion of the inner box) in the Layer panel over the metronome weight.

4 Enlarge the search region (the outer box) to encompass the area around the pendulum. Then adjust the feature region (the inner box) within the weight.

● Note: In this exercise, you want the star to move atop the metronome weight. However, if you wanted an object to move in relationship to the tracked area but not on top of it, you could reposition the attach point accordingly.

Analyzing and applying tracking

Now that the search and feature regions are defined, you can apply the tracker.

● Note: The tracking analysis may take quite a while. The larger the search and feature regions, the longer After Effects takes to analyze tracking.

1 Click the Analyze Forward button (▶) in the Tracker panel. Watch the analysis to ensure the track point stays with the metronome weight. If it doesn't, press the spacebar to stop the analysis, and reposition the feature region. (See the sidebar "Checking for drift.")

2 When the analysis is complete, click the Apply button.

3 In the Motion Tracker Apply Options dialog box, click OK to apply the tracking to the x and y dimensions.

Checking for drift

As an image moves in a shot, the lighting, surrounding objects, and angle of the object can all change, making a once-distinct feature no longer identifiable at the subpixel level. It takes time to develop an eye for choosing a trackable feature. Even with careful planning and practice, you may often find that the feature region drifts away from the desired feature. Readjusting the feature and search regions, changing the tracking options, and trying again are all standard parts of digital tracking. When you notice drifting occurring, try the following:

1 Immediately stop the analysis by pressing the spacebar.

2 Move the current-time indicator back to the last good tracked point. You can see this in the Layer panel.

3 Reposition and/or resize the feature and search regions, being careful not to accidentally move the attach point. Moving the attach point will cause a noticeable jump in your tracked layer.

4 Click the Analyze Forward button to resume tracking.

The motion-tracking data is added to the Timeline panel, where you can see that the track data is in the metronome layer, but the results are applied to the Position property of the Shape Layer 1 layer.

4 Press the spacebar to preview the movie. The star not only follows the pendulum; it moves with the camera's movement.

5 When you're ready, press the spacebar to stop playback.

6 Hide the properties for both layers in the Timeline panel, choose File > Save, and then choose File > Close Project.

Motion tracking an element onto background footage can be fun. As long as you have a stable feature to track, single-point motion tracking can be quite easy.

Moving and resizing
the track points

In setting up motion tracking, it's often necessary to refine a track point by adjusting its feature region, search region, and attach point. You can resize or move these items independently or in groups by dragging with the Selection tool. The pointer icon changes to reflect one of many different activities.

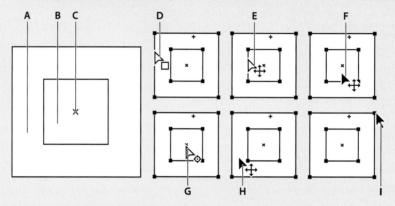

Track point components (left) and Selection tool pointer icons (right):
A. Search region B. Feature region C. Attach point D. Moves search region
E. Moves both regions F. Moves entire track point G. Moves attach point
H. Moves entire track point I. Resizes region

- To turn feature region magnification on or off, choose Magnify Feature When Dragging from the Tracker panel menu. A check mark appears next to the option when it's on.

- To move only the search region, using the Selection tool, drag the edge of the search region; the Move Search Region pointer (⬚) appears (D, above).

- To move just the feature and search regions together, Alt-drag (Windows) or Option-drag (Mac OS) with the Selection tool inside the feature or search region; the Move Both Regions pointer (✛) appears (E, above).

- To move only the attach point, using the Selection tool, drag the attach point; the Move Attach Point pointer (◇) appears (G, above).

- To resize the feature or search region, drag a corner handle (I, above).

- To move the feature region, search region, and attach point together, drag with the Selection tool inside the track point area (avoiding the region edges and the attach point); the Move Track Point pointer (✛) appears.

For more information about track points, see After Effects Help.

Using multipoint tracking

After Effects also offers two more advanced types of tracking that use multiple tracking points: parallel corner-pinning and perspective corner-pinning.

When you track using parallel corner-pinning, you simultaneously track three points in the source footage. After Effects calculates the position of a fourth point to keep the lines between the points parallel. When the movement of the points is applied to the target layer, the Corner Pin effect distorts the layer to simulate skew, scale, and rotation, but not perspective. Parallel lines remain parallel, and relative distances are preserved.

When you track using perspective corner-pinning, you simultaneously track four points in the source footage. When applied to the target footage, the Corner Pin effect uses the movement of the four points to distort the layer, simulating changes in perspective.

You'll attach an animation to a computer monitor using perspective corner-pinning. The effect is similar to the Lesson 7 project, but you'll use a different technique. If you haven't already watched the sample movie for this exercise, do so now.

Setting up the project

Start by launching After Effects and creating a new project.

1 If it's not already open, start After Effects, and then immediately hold down Ctrl+Alt+Shift (Windows) or Command+Option+Shift (Mac OS) to restore default preferences settings. When prompted, click OK to delete your preferences, and close the Start window.

After Effects opens to display an empty, untitled project.

2 Choose File > Save As > Save As.

3 In the Save As dialog box, navigate to the Lessons/Lesson13/ Finished_Projects folder.

4 Name the project **Lesson13_Multipoint.aep,** and then click Save.

5 Double-click an empty area of the Project panel to open the Import File dialog box, and then navigate to the Lessons/Lesson13/Assets folder.

6 Ctrl-click (Windows) or Command-click (Mac OS) both the majorspoilers.mov and multipoint_tracking.mov files, and then click Import or Open.

7 Press Ctrl+N (Windows) or Command+N (Mac OS) to create a new composition.

8 In the Composition Settings dialog box, do the following, and then click OK:

- Type **Multipoint_Tracking** in the Composition Name field.

- Choose NTSC DV from the Preset menu.

- Set the Duration to **7:05**—the length of the majorspoilers.mov file.

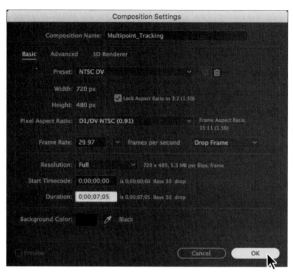

9 Drag the multipoint_tracking.mov item from the Project panel to the Timeline panel. Manually preview the footage, which is shaky because it was shot with a handheld camera.

Because you're positioning the majorspoilers.mov layer on the computer monitor, it will be fairly easy to place tracking markers on the flat plane. By default, the tracker tracks by luminance, so you will use the areas around the screen that have high contrast differences for tracking.

10 Press the Home key, or move the current-time indicator to the beginning of the time ruler.

11 Drag the majorspoilers.mov footage item from the Project panel to the Timeline panel, placing it at the top of the layer stack.

12 To make it easier to see the underlying movie as you place the tracking points, turn off the Video switch for the majorspoilers.mov layer in the Timeline panel.

Positioning the track points

You're ready to add the track points to the multipoint_tracking.mov layer.

1 Select the multipoint_tracking.mov layer in the Timeline panel.

2 Choose Window > Tracker to open the Tracker panel, if it isn't open.

3 In the Tracker panel, choose multipoint_tracking.mov from the Motion Source menu.

4 Select the multipoint_tracking.mov layer again, and then click Track Motion.

The desk scene opens in the Layer panel, with a track point indicator in the center of the image. However, you will be tracking four points in order to attach the animated movie to the computer screen.

5 Choose Perspective Corner Pin from the Track Type menu.

Three more track point indicators appear in the Layer panel.

Tip: Refer to the sidebar "Moving and resizing the track points" for help moving the track point regions.

6 Drag the track points to four different high-contrast areas of the image. The four corners of the computer screen provide excellent contrast. Use the image below as a guide. (Because the areas of high contrast are also where you want to attach the majorspoilers layer, you don't need to move the attach points.)

Applying the multipoint tracker

You're ready to analyze the data and apply the tracker.

1 Click the Analyze Forward button (►) in the Tracker panel. When the analysis is complete, click the Apply button to calculate the tracking.

Note: If the composition doesn't appear in the Composition panel, click in the Timeline window to move the current-time indicator and refresh the display.

2 Notice the results in the Timeline panel: You can see the Corner Pin and Position property keyframes for the majorspoilers layer and the track point data for the motion_tracking layer.

3 Make the majorspoilers layer visible again, move the current-time indicator to the beginning of the timeline, and preview the movie to see the results of the tracker.

4 When you're done watching the preview, press the spacebar to stop playback.

If you don't like the results, return to the Tracker panel, click the Reset button, and try again. With practice, you will become adept at identifying good feature regions.

5 Hide the layer properties to keep the Timeline panel neat, and choose File > Save to save your work.

6 Choose File > Close Project.

mocha for After Effects

In most cases, you'll get better and more accurate tracking results using mocha from Imagineer Systems to track points in video. A version of mocha is included with After Effects. To track using mocha, choose Animation > Track In Mocha AE.

One advantage of mocha for After Effects is that you don't have to accurately place tracking points to obtain a perfect track. Rather than using tracking points, mocha for After Effects uses a planar tracker, which attempts to track an object's translation, rotation, and scaling data based on the movement of a user-defined plane. Planes provide more detail to the computer than is possible with single-point and multi-point tracking tools.

When you work with mocha for After Effects, you need to identify planes in a clip that coincide with movement you want to track. Planes don't have to be tabletops or walls. For example, if someone is waving goodbye, you can use their upper and lower limbs as two planes. After you track the planes, you can export the tracking data for use in After Effects.

mocha for After Effects uses two different spline technologies for tracking: X splines and Bezier splines. X splines may work better for tracking, especially with perspective motion, but Bezier splines work well, too, and are the industry standard.

To learn more about mocha for After Effects, choose Help > Online Help or Help > Offline Help in mocha.

We've saved some tracking data for the computer monitor in mocha for After Effects, so that you can apply it in After Effects if you'd like. To apply the data, follow these steps:

1 Create a new project in After Effects, and import the majorspoilers.mov and mocha_tracking.mov files from the Lesson13/Assets folder. Create a new composition from the mocha_tracking.mov file, and then drag the majorspoilers. mov file to the top of the layer stack in the Timeline panel.

2 Open the mocha_data.txt file (in the Lesson13/Optional_Mocha_Tutorial folder) in a text editor such as WordPad or TextEdit. (Don't use Notepad on Windows. It doesn't retain the mocha formatting, so After Effects doesn't recognize its content on the clipboard.) Choose Edit > Select All, and then Edit > Copy to copy all the data.

3 In After Effects, select the majorspoilers.mov layer in the Timeline panel, and choose Edit > Paste. All the data is applied to the layer.

4 Preview the results.

Creating a particle simulation

After Effects includes several effects that do an excellent job of creating particle simulations. Two of them—CC Particle Systems II and CC Particle World—are based on the same engine. The major difference between the two is that Particle World enables you to move the particles in 3D space, rather than in a 2D layer.

In this exercise, you'll learn how to use the CC Particle Systems II effect to create a supernova that could be used as the opening of a science program or as a motion background. If you haven't already watched the sample movie for this exercise, do so now before continuing.

Setting up the project

Start by launching After Effects and creating a new composition.

1 If it's not already open, start After Effects, and then immediately hold down Ctrl+Alt+Shift (Windows) or Command+Option+Shift (Mac OS) to restore default preferences settings. When prompted, click OK to delete your preferences, and close the Start window.

After Effects opens to display an empty, untitled project.

2 Choose File > Save As > Save As.

3 In the Save As dialog box, navigate to the Lessons/Lesson13/ Finished_Projects folder.

4 Name the project **Lesson13_Particles.aep**, and then click Save.

You don't need to import any footage items for this exercise. However, you do need to create the composition.

5 In After Effects, press Ctrl+N (Windows) or Command+N (Mac OS).

6 In the Composition Settings dialog box, do the following, and then click OK:

 • Type **Supernova** in the Composition Name field.

 • Choose HDTV 1080 29.97 from the Preset pop-up menu.

 • Set the Duration to **10:00**.

Creating a particle system

You will build the particle system from a solid layer, so you'll create that next.

1 Choose Layer > New > Solid to create a new solid layer.

2 In the Solid Settings dialog box, type **Particles** in the Name box.

3 Click Make Comp Size to make the layer the same size as the composition. Then click OK.

Understanding Particle Systems II properties

Particle systems have a unique vocabulary. Some of the key settings are explained here for your reference. They're listed in the order in which they appear (top to bottom) in the Effect Controls panel.

Birth Rate Controls the number of particles generated per second. The value itself is arbitrary and does not equal the actual number of particles being generated. However, the higher the number, the more densely packed the particles become.

Longevity Determines how long the particles are visible.

Producer Position Controls the center point or origin of the particle system. The position is set based on the x, y coordinates. All particles emanate from this single point. You can control the size of the producer by making adjustments to the x and y radius settings. The higher these values, the larger the producer point will be. A high x value and a y value of zero (0) result in a line.

Velocity Controls the speed of particles. The higher the number, the faster the particles move.

Inherent Velocity % Determines how much of the velocity is passed along to the particles when the Producer Position is animated. A negative value causes the particles to move in the opposite direction.

Gravity Determines how fast particles fall. The higher the value, the faster the particles fall. A negative value causes particles to rise.

Resistance Simulates particles interacting with air or water, slowing over time.

Direction Determines which direction the particles flow. Use with the Direction Animation type.

Extra Introduces randomness into the movement of the particles.

Birth/Death Size Determines the size of the particles when they are created and when they expire.

Opacity Map Controls opacity changes for the particle over its lifetime.

Color Map Use with the Birth and Death colors to shade the particles over time.

4 With the Particles layer selected in the Timeline panel, choose Effect > Simulation > CC Particle Systems II.

5 Go to 4:00 to see the particle system.

A large stream of yellow particles appears in the Composition panel.

Customizing the particle effect

You will turn this stream of particles into a supernova by customizing the settings in the Effect Controls panel.

1 Expand the Physics property group in the Effect Controls panel. The Explosive Animation setting works fine for this project, but instead of the particles falling down, you want them to flow out in all directions, so change the Gravity value to **0.0**.

2 Hide the Physics property group, and expand the Particle property group. Then choose Faded Sphere from the Particle Type menu.

Now the particles look intergalactic. Don't stop there, though.

3 Change the Death Size to **1.50**, and increase the Size Variation to **100%**.

This allows the particles to change birth size randomly.

4 Reduce the Max Opacity to **55%** to make the particles semitransparent.

5 Click the Birth Color swatch, and change the color to R=**255**, G=**200**, B=**50** to give the particles a yellow hue at birth.

6 Click the Death Color swatch, and change the color to R=**180**, G=**180**, B=**180** to give the particles a light gray hue as they fade out.

● **Note:** Even though they're at the top of the Effect Controls panel, it is often easier to adjust the Longevity and Birth Rate settings after you have set the other particle properties.

7 To keep the particles from staying onscreen too long, decrease the Longevity value to **0.8** seconds.

The Faded Sphere particle type softens the look, but the particle shapes are still too sharply defined. You will fix that by blurring the layer to blend the particles with one another.

8 Hide the CC Particle Systems II effect properties.

9 Choose Effect > Blur & Sharpen > Gaussian Blur.

10 In the Gaussian Blur area of the Effect Controls panel, increase the Blurriness value to **10**. Then select Repeat Edge Pixels to keep the particles from being cropped at the edge of the frame.

Creating the sun

You will now create a bright halo of light that will go behind the particles.

1 Go to 7:00.

2 Press Ctrl+Y (Windows) or Command+Y (Mac OS) to create a new solid layer.

3 In the Solid Settings dialog box, do the following:

 • Type **Sun** in the Name box.

 • Click Make Comp Size to make the layer the same size as the composition.

 • Click the color swatch, and make the layer the same yellow as the Birth Color of the particles (**255, 200, 50**).

 • Click OK to close the Solid Settings dialog box.

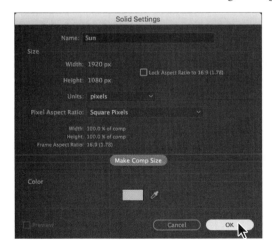

4 Drag the Sun layer below the Particles layer in the Timeline panel.

5 Select the Ellipse tool (⬤), which is hidden behind the Rectangle tool (⬛) or the Star tool (★) in the Tools panel, and Shift-drag in the Composition panel to draw a circle with a radius of roughly 100 pixels, or one-fourth the width of the composition. You've created a mask.

6 Using the Selection tool (▶), drag the mask shape to the center of the Composition panel.

7 With the Sun layer selected in the Timeline panel, press the F key to reveal its Mask Feather property. Increase the Mask Feather amount to **100, 100** pixels.

8 Press Alt+[(Windows) or Option+[(Mac OS) to set the In point of the layer to the current time.

9 Hide the properties for the Sun layer.

Lighting the darkness

Since the sun is bright, it should illuminate the surrounding darkness.

1 Make sure the current-time indicator is still at 7:00.

2 Press Ctrl+Y (Windows) or Command+Y (Mac OS) to create a new solid layer.

3 In the Solid Settings dialog box, name the layer **Background**, click the Make Comp Size button to make the layer the same size as the composition, and then click OK to create the layer.

4 In the Timeline panel, drag the Background layer to the bottom position in the layer stack.

5 With the Background layer selected in the Timeline panel, choose Effect > Generate > Gradient Ramp.

The Gradient Ramp effect creates a color gradient, blending it with the original image. You can create linear ramps or radial ramps, and vary the position and colors of the ramp over time. Use the Start Of Ramp and End Of Ramp settings to specify the start and end positions. Use the Ramp Scatter setting to disperse the ramp colors and eliminate banding.

6 In the Gradient Ramp area of the Effect Controls panel, do the following:

- Change Start Of Ramp to **960, 538** and End Of Ramp to **360, 525**.

- Choose Radial Ramp from the Ramp Shape menu.

- Click the Start Color swatch, and set the start color to dark blue (R=**0**, G=**25**, B=**135**).

- Set the End Color to black (R=**0**, G=**0**, B=**0**).

7 Press Alt+[(Windows) or Option+[(Mac OS) to set the In point of the layer to the current time.

Adding a lens flare

To tie all the elements together, you'll add a lens flare to simulate an explosion.

1 Press the Home key, or move the current-time indicator to the beginning of the time ruler.

2 Press Ctrl+Y (Windows) or Command+Y (Mac OS) to create a new solid layer.

3 In the Solid Settings dialog box, name the layer **Nova**, click the Make Comp Size button to make the layer the same size as the composition, set the Color to black (R=**0**, G=**0**, B=**0**), and then click OK.

4 Drag the Nova layer to the top of the layer stack in the Timeline panel. Then, with the Nova layer selected, choose Effect > Generate > Lens Flare.

5 In the Lens Flare area of the Effect Controls panel, do the following:

 • Change Flare Center to **960, 538**.

 • Make sure 50–300mm Zoom is selected in the Lens Type menu.

 • Decrease Flare Brightness to **0%**, and then click the Flare Brightness stopwatch icon (⏱) to create an initial keyframe.

6 Go to 0:10.

7 Increase the Flare Brightness to **240%**.

8 Go to 1:04, and decrease the Flare Brightness to **100%**.

9 With the Nova layer selected in the Timeline panel, press the U key to see the animated Lens Flare property.

About high dynamic range (HDR) footage

After Effects also supports high dynamic range (HDR) color.

The dynamic range (ratio between dark and bright regions) in the physical world far exceeds the range of human vision and of images that are printed or displayed on a monitor. But while human eyes can adapt to very different brightness levels, most cameras and computer monitors can capture and reproduce only a limited dynamic range. Photographers, motion-picture artists, and others working with digital images must be selective about what's important in a scene, because they're working with a limited dynamic range.

HDR footage opens up a world of possibilities, because it can represent a very wide dynamic range through the use of 32-bit floating-point numeric values. Floating-point numeric representations allow the same number of bits to describe a much larger range of values than integer (fixed-point) values. HDR values can contain brightness levels, including objects as bright as a candle flame or the sun, that far exceed those in 8-bit-per-channel (bpc) or 16-bpc (non-floating-point) mode. Lower dynamic range 8-bpc and 16-bpc modes can represent RGB levels only from black to white, which represents an extremely small segment of the dynamic range in the real world.

After Effects supports HDR images in a variety of ways. For example, you can create 32-bpc projects to work with HDR footage, and you can adjust the exposure, or the amount of light captured in an image, when working with HDR images in After Effects. For more information about support in After Effects for HDR images, see After Effects Help.

10 Right-click (Windows) or Control-click (Mac OS) the ending Flare Brightness keyframe, and choose Keyframe Assistant > Easy Ease In.

11 Right-click (Windows) or Control-click (Mac OS) the beginning Flare Brightness keyframe, and choose Keyframe Assistant > Easy Ease Out.

Finally, you need to make the layers under the Nova layer visible in the composition.

12 Press F2 to deselect all layers, and choose Columns > Modes from the Timeline panel menu. Then choose Screen from the Mode menu for the Nova layer.

13 Preview the movie. When you're done, press the spacebar to stop the preview.

14 Choose File > Save, and then choose File > Close Project.

Retiming playback using the Timewarp effect

The Timewarp effect in After Effects gives you precise control over a wide range of parameters when changing the playback speed of a layer, including interpolation methods, motion blur, and source cropping to eliminate unwanted artifacts.

In this exercise, you will use the Timewarp effect to change the speed of a clip for a dramatic slow-motion playback. If you haven't already watched the sample movie for this exercise, do so now.

Setting up the project

Start by launching After Effects and creating a new project.

1 If After Effects isn't open, start it, and then immediately hold down Ctrl+Alt+Shift (Windows) or Command+Option+Shift (Mac OS) to restore default preferences settings. When prompted, click OK to delete your preferences, and close the Start window.

After Effects opens to display an empty, untitled project.

2 Choose File > Save As > Save As.

3 In the Save As dialog box, navigate to the Lessons/Lesson13/ Finished_Projects folder.

4 Name the project **Lesson13_Timewarp.aep**, and then click Save.

5 Double-click an empty area of the Project panel to open the Import File dialog box. Then navigate to the Lessons/Lesson13/Assets folder on your hard disk, select the Group_Approach[DV].mov, and click Import or Open.

6 Click OK in the Interpret Footage dialog box.

Now, you'll create a new composition based on the footage item's aspect ratio and its duration.

7 Drag the Group_Approach[DV].mov file onto the Create A New Composition button (■) at the bottom of the Project panel.

After Effects creates a new composition named for the source file, and displays it in the Composition and Timeline panels.

8 Choose File > Save to save your work.

Using Timewarp

In the source footage, a group of young people approaches the camera at a steady pace. At around 2 seconds, the director would like the motion to begin to slow down to 10%, and then ramp back up to full speed at 7:00.

1 With the Group_Approach[DV] layer selected in the Timeline panel, choose Effect > Time > Timewarp.

2 In the Timewarp area of the Effect Controls panel, make sure Pixel Motion is selected in the Method menu and Speed is selected in the Adjust Time By menu.

With Pixel Motion selected, Timewarp creates new frames by analyzing the pixel movement in nearby frames and creating motion vectors. The Speed option controls the time adjustment by percentage rather than by a specific frame.

3 Go to 2:00.

4 In the Effect Controls panel, set the Speed to **100**, and click the stopwatch (⌚) to set a keyframe.

This tells Timewarp to keep the speed of the clip at 100% until the 2-second mark.

5 With the Group_Approach[DV] layer selected in the Timeline panel, press the U key to see the animated Timewarp Speed property.

6 Go to 5:00, and set the Speed to **10**. After Effects adds a keyframe.

7 Go to 7:00, and set the Speed to **100**. After Effects adds a keyframe.

● **Note:** Be patient. The first time through, After Effects is caching information in RAM. The second time it plays will provide a more accurate playback.

8 Press the Home key or move the current-time indicator to the beginning of the time ruler, and then watch a preview of the effect.

The speed adjustments are rather abrupt—not the smooth, slow-motion curve you would expect to see in a professional effect. This is because the keyframes are linear instead of curved. You'll fix that next.

9 Press the spacebar to stop playback when you're ready.

10 Click the Graph Editor button in the Timeline panel to display the Graph Editor instead of the layer bars. Make sure the Speed property name for the Group_Approach[DV] layer is selected. The Graph Editor displays its graph.

11 Click to select the first Speed keyframe (at 2:00), and then click the Easy Ease icon (⫩⫨) at the bottom of the Graph Editor.

This adjusts the influence into and out of the keyframe to smooth out sudden changes.

12 Repeat step 11 for the other two Speed keyframes in the motion graph, at 5:00 and 7:00.

▶ **Tip:** Close columns in the Timeline panel to see more icons in the Graph Editor. You can also apply an Easy Ease adjustment by pressing the F9 key.

The motion graph is now smoother, but you can tweak it even more by dragging the Bezier handles.

● **Note:** If you need a refresher on using Bezier handles, see Lesson 7, "Working with Masks."

13 Using the Bezier handles for the keyframes at 2:00 and 5:00, adjust the curve so that it resembles the following image.

14 Preview the movie again. This time, the slow-motion Timewarp effect looks professional.

15 Choose File > Save to save the project, and then choose File > Close Project.

You've now experimented with some of the advanced features in After Effects, including motion stabilization, motion tracking, particle systems, and the Timewarp effect. To render and export any or all of the projects you completed in this lesson, see Lesson 14, "Rendering and Outputting," for instructions.

Review questions

1 What is Warp Stabilizer VFX, and when do you need to use it?

2 Why might drifting occur when you're tracking an image?

3 What is the birth rate in a particle effect?

4 What does the Timewarp effect do?

Review answers

1 Shooting footage using a handheld camera typically results in shaky shots. Unless this look is intentional, you will want to stabilize the shots to eliminate unwanted motion. Warp Stabilizer VFX in After Effects analyzes the movement and rotation of the target layer, and then makes adjustments to it. When played back, the motion appears smooth, because the layer itself moves incrementally to offset the unwanted motion. You can change the way Warp Stabilizer VFX crops, scales, and performs other adjustments by modifying settings for the effect.

2 Drifting occurs when the feature region loses the feature that's being tracked. As an image moves in a shot, the lighting, surrounding objects, and angle of the object can change, making a once-distinct feature unidentifiable at the subpixel level. Even with careful planning and practice, the feature region often drifts away from the desired feature. Readjusting the feature and search regions, changing the tracking options, and trying again are all standard procedures in digital tracking.

3 The birth rate in a particle effect determines how often new particles are created.

4 The Timewarp effect gives you precise control over a wide range of parameters to change the playback speed of a layer, including interpolation methods, motion blur, and source cropping to eliminate unwanted artifacts.

14 RENDERING AND OUTPUTTING

Lesson overview

In this lesson, you'll learn how to do the following:

- Create render-settings templates for the Render Queue.
- Create output-module templates for the Render Queue.
- Output movies using Adobe Media Encoder.
- Select the appropriate compressor for your delivery format.
- Use pixel aspect ratio correction.
- Output the final composition for HDTV 1080p resolution.
- Produce a test version of a composition.
- Create custom encoding presets in Adobe Media Encoder.
- Render and output a web version of the final composition.

The total amount of time required to complete this lesson depends in part on the speed of your processor and the amount of RAM available for rendering. The amount of hands-on time required is less than an hour. Download the project files for this lesson, following the instructions in the Getting Started section under "Accessing the lesson files and Web Edition," if you haven't already done so. As you work on this lesson, you'll preserve the start files. If you need to restore the start files, download them from your Account page.

WEB

PROJECT: OUTPUTTING YOUR PROJECT FOR MULTIPLE USES

BROADCAST

The success of any project depends on your ability to deliver it in the format you need, whether it's for the web or broadcast output. Using Adobe After Effects and Adobe Media Encoder, you can render and export a final composition in a variety of formats and resolutions.

Getting started

This lesson continues from the point at which many of the preceding lessons end: when you're ready to output the final composition. In order to produce several versions of the animation for this lesson, you'll explore options available within the Render Queue panel and Adobe Media Encoder. For this lesson, we provide you with a starting project file that is essentially the final composition from Lesson 12 of this book.

1 Make sure the following files are in the Lessons/Lesson14 folder on your hard disk, or download them from your Account page at www.peachpit.com now:

- In the Assets folder: Desktop.mov, Treasures_Music.aif, Treasures_Title.psd

- In the Start_Project_File folder: Lesson14_Start.aep

- In the Sample_Movies folder: Lesson14_Final_360p_Web.mp4, Lesson14_Final_1080p.mp4, Lesson14_Final_lowres_Web.mp4, Lesson14_Final_MPEG4.mov, Lesson14_HD_test_1080p.mp4

● **Note:** The Lesson14_HD_test_1080p.mp4 file includes only the first five seconds of the movie.

2 Open and play the sample movies for Lesson 14, which represent different final versions of the movie—rendered with different quality settings—that you created in Lesson 12. When you're done viewing the sample movies, quit Windows Media Player or QuickTime Player. You may delete the sample movies from your hard disk if you have limited storage space.

As always, when you begin the lesson, restore the default application settings for After Effects. See "Restoring default preferences" on page 2.

● **Note:** Depending on which applications you have on your system, you may not be able to play the .mov file in Windows.

3 Start After Effects, and then immediately hold down Ctrl+Alt+Shift (Windows) or Command+Option+Shift (Mac OS). When prompted, click OK to delete your preferences. Close the Start window.

4 Choose File > Open Project. If the Start screen opens, click Open Project in it.

5 Navigate to the Lessons/Lesson14/Start_Project_File folder, select the Lesson14_Start.aep file, and click Open.

● **Note:** If you receive an error message about missing layer dependencies (Arial Narrow Regular), click OK.

6 Choose File > Save As > Save As.

7 In the Save As dialog box, navigate to the Lessons/Lesson14/Finished_Project folder.

8 Name the project **Lesson14_Finished.aep**, and then click Save.

9 Choose Window > Render Queue to open the Render Queue panel.

Creating templates for the Render Queue

When you output your compositions in previous lessons, you selected individual render and output-module settings. In this lesson, you'll create templates for both render settings and output-module settings. These templates are presets that you can use to streamline the setup process when you render items for the same type of delivery format. After you define templates, they appear in the Render Queue panel on the appropriate pop-up menu (Render Settings or Output Module). Then, when you're ready to render a composition, you can simply select the appropriate template for the delivery format that your job requires, and the template applies all the settings.

Creating a render-settings template for test renderings

You'll create a render-settings template, selecting settings appropriate for rendering a test version of your final movie. A test version is smaller—and therefore renders faster—than a full-resolution movie. When you work with complex compositions that take relatively long times to render, it is a good practice to render a small test version first. This helps you find any issues that you want to address before you take the time to render the final movie.

1 Choose Edit > Templates > Render Settings. The Render Settings Templates dialog box appears.

2 In the Settings area, click New to create a new template.

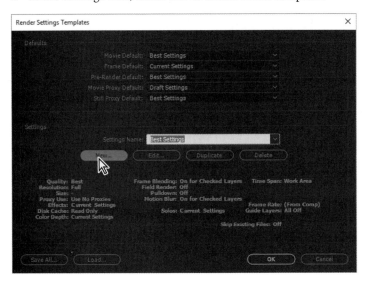

3 In the Render Settings dialog box, do the following:

- Leave Quality at Best.

- For Resolution, choose Third, which reduces the linear dimension of the composition to one-third.

4 In the Time Sampling area, do the following:

- For Frame Blending, choose Current Settings.

- For Motion Blur, choose Current Settings.

- For Time Span, choose Length Of Comp.

5 In the Frame Rate area, select Use This Frame Rate, and type **12** (fps). Then click OK to return to the Render Settings Templates dialog box.

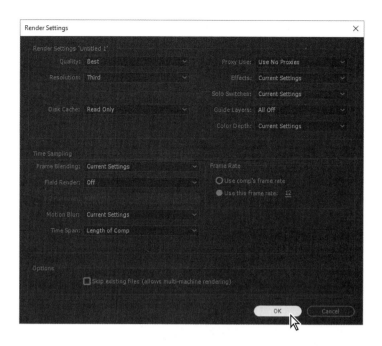

6 For Settings Name, type **Test_lowres** (for *low resolution*).

7 Examine your settings, which appear in the lower half of the dialog box.
 If you need to make any changes, click Edit to adjust the settings. Then click OK.

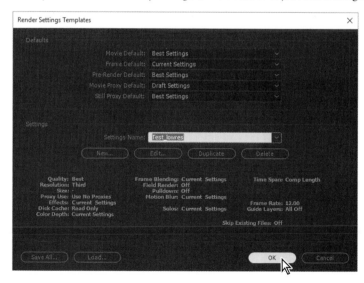

The Test_lowres option will be available on the Render Settings pop-up menu
in the Render Queue panel.

Creating templates for output modules

You'll use a similar process to create a template to use for output-module settings. Each output-module template includes unique combinations of settings appropriate for a specific type of output. You'll create one that is appropriate for a low-resolution test version of the movie, so you can quickly see a rendered version to identify any changes you want to make.

1 Choose Edit > Templates > Output Module to open the Output Module Templates dialog box.

2 In the Settings area, click New to create a new template.

3 In the Output Module Settings dialog box, choose QuickTime for Format.

4 For Post-Render Action, choose Import.

5 In the Video Output area, click Format Options.

6 Select the following settings in the QuickTime Options dialog box:

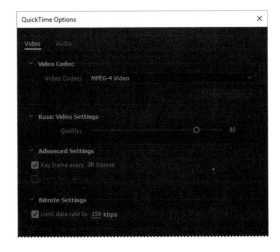

- For Video Codec, choose MPEG-4 Video. This compressor automatically determines the color depth.

- Set the Quality slider to **80**.

- In the Advanced Settings area, select Key Frame Every, and then type **30** (frames).

- In the Bitrate Settings area, select Limit Data Rate To, and type **150** (kbps).

7 Select the Audio tab, and choose IMA 4:1 from the Audio Codec menu.

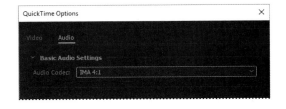

● **Note:** The IMA 4:1 compressor is commonly used when compressing audio for web or desktop playback.

8 Click OK to close the QuickTime Options dialog box and return to the Output Module Settings dialog box.

9 Choose Audio Output On from the pop-up menu at the bottom of the dialog box. Then choose the following audio settings, from left to right:

- Rate: 22.050 kHz

- Use: Stereo

10 Click OK to close the Output Module Settings dialog box.

11 In the lower half of the Output Module Templates dialog box, examine your settings, and click Edit if you need to make any changes.

About compression

Compression is essential to reduce the size of movies so that they can be stored, transmitted, and played back effectively. When exporting or rendering a movie file for playback on a specific type of device at a certain bandwidth, you choose a compressor/decompressor (also known as an encoder/decoder), or *codec*, to compress the information and generate a file that is readable by that type of device at that bandwidth.

A wide range of codecs is available; no single codec is the best for all situations. For example, the best codec for compressing cartoon animation is generally not efficient for compressing live-action video. When compressing a movie file, you can fine-tune it for the best quality playback on a computer, a video playback device, the web, or from a DVD player. Depending on which encoder you use, you may be able to reduce the size of compressed files by removing artifacts that interfere with compression, such as random camera motion and excessive film grain.

The codec you use must be available to your entire audience. For instance, if you use a hardware codec on a capture card, your audience must have the same capture card installed, or a software codec that emulates it.

For more about compression and codecs, see After Effects Help.

12 For Settings Name, type **Test_MPEG4**, and then click OK. Now this output template will be available on the Output Module pop-up menu in the Render Queue panel.

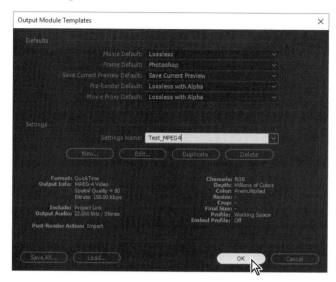

As you might expect, greater compression and lower audio sample rates create smaller file sizes, but they also reduce the quality of the output. However, this low-resolution template is fine for testing your movie before you make final edits.

Exporting using the Render Queue

Now that you have created templates for your render settings and output modules, you can use them to export the test version of your movie.

▶ **Tip:** Alternatively, you can drag the composition from the Project panel onto the Render Queue panel.

1 Select the Desktop composition in the Project panel, and choose Composition > Add To Render Queue.

In the Render Queue panel, note the default settings in the Render Settings and Output Module pop-up menus. You'll replace those settings when you select your low-resolution templates.

2 Choose Test_lowres from the Render Settings menu.

3 Choose Test_MPEG4 from the Output Module menu.

4 Click the blue words next to Output To.

5 In the Output Movie To dialog box, locate the Lessons/Lesson14 folder, and create a new folder called **Final_Movies**:

 • In Windows, click New Folder, and then type the name for the folder.

 • In Mac OS, click the New Folder button, name the folder, and click Create.

6 Open the Final_Movies folder, if it's not already open.

7 Name the file **Final_MPEG4.mov**, and then click Save to return to the Render Queue panel.

8 Choose File > Save to save your work.

● **Note:** You do not need to render a movie multiple times to export it to multiple formats with the same render settings. You can export multiple versions of the same rendered movie by adding output modules to a render item in the Render Queue panel.

9 Click the Render button in the Render Queue panel. After Effects renders the movie. If there were additional movies—or the same movie with different settings—in the queue, After Effects would render those, too.

When the processing is complete, the Final_MPEG4 movie appears in the Project panel.

● **Note:** In Windows, you may not hear the audio when you play the QuickTime movie in After Effects.

To preview the movie, double-click it in the Project panel, and then press the spacebar to view the movie.

If you need to make any final changes to the movie, reopen the composition and make those adjustments now. Remember to save your work when you finish, and then output the test movie again using the appropriate settings. After examining the test movie and making any necessary changes, you'll proceed with outputting the movie for full-resolution broadcast.

Preparing movies for mobile devices

You can create movies in After Effects for playback on mobile devices, such as tablets and smartphones. To render your movie, add the composition to the Adobe Media Encoder encoding queue, and choose an appropriate device-specific encoding preset.

For the best results, consider the limitations of mobile devices as you shoot footage and work with After Effects. For a small screen size, pay careful attention to lighting, and use a lower frame rate. See After Effects Help for more tips.

Rendering movies with Adobe Media Encoder

Your movie is ready for final output. Adobe Media Encoder, which is installed when you install After Effects, has the widest selection of codecs available for different delivery formats, including popular video services such as YouTube.

● **Note:** If Adobe Media Encoder is not currently installed on your system, install it from Creative Cloud.

Rendering a broadcast-quality movie

First, you'll select settings to render your movie in a quality suitable for broadcast.

1 In the Project panel, select the Desktop composition, and choose Composition > Add To Adobe Media Encoder Queue.

After Effects opens Adobe Media Encoder, and adds your composition with default render settings. Your default settings may vary from ours.

▶ **Tip:** You can also drag a composition into the Render Queue panel, and click Queue in AME to add it to the Adobe Media Encoder queue.

2 Click the blue link in the Preset column.

● **Note:** If you don't need to change anything else in the Export Settings dialog box, you can change the preset using the Preset pop-up menu in the Queue panel.

Adobe Media Encoder connects to the Dynamic Link server, which may take a few moments.

3 When the Export Settings dialog box appears, choose H.264 from the Format menu, and then choose HD 1080p 23.976 from the Preset menu.

Rendering the full movie with the HD 1080p 23.976 preset may take several minutes. You'll change the settings to render only the first five seconds of the movie so that you can preview the quality. You can change the range rendered using the time ruler at the bottom of the Export Settings dialog box.

4 Move the current-time indicator to 5:00, and then click the Set Out Point button (▲) to the left of the Select Zoom Level pop-up menu.

5 Click OK to close the Export Settings dialog box.

6 Click the blue link in the Output File column. Name the movie **HD-test_1080p.mp4**, and specify the Lessons/Lesson14/Final_Movies folder. Then click Save or OK.

You're ready to output this movie, but you'll set up a few additional movie options in the queue before you render it.

Adding another encoding preset to the queue

▶ **Tip:** If you render files frequently, consider setting up a "watch folder." When you place a file in the watch folder, Adobe Media Encoder automatically encodes it using the settings you've specified in the Watch Folders panel.

Adobe Media Encoder comes with dozens of built-in presets suitable for output for traditional broadcast, mobile devices, and the web. You'll output a version of your composition ready for posting to YouTube.

1 In the Preset Browser panel, navigate to Web Video > YouTube > YouTube 480p SD Wide.

2 Drag the YouTube 480p SD Wide preset onto the Desktop composition in the Queue panel.

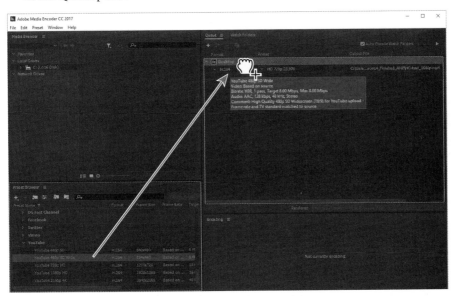

Adobe Media Encoder adds another output item to the queue.

3　Click the blue link in the Output File column for the item you just added. Then name the file **Final_Web.mp4**, specify the Lessons/Lesson14/Final_Movies folder, and click Save or OK.

Rendering movies

You've set up two versions of your movie in the queue. Now you'll render and view them. Rendering is resource-intensive, and it can take a while, depending on your system, the complexity and length of the composition, and the settings you use.

1　Click the green Start Queue button (▶) in the upper right corner of the Queue panel.

Depending on your system, this may take a while.

Adobe Media Encoder encodes the movies in the queue simultaneously, displaying a status bar, and reporting the estimated time remaining.

2 When Adobe Media Encoder has finished, navigate to the Final_Movies folder in the Finder or Explorer, and double-click your files to play them.

Creating custom presets for Adobe Media Encoder

In most cases, one of the default Adobe Media Encoder presets will be appropriate for your project. However, you can create your own encoding presets if you have specialized needs. In this case, you'll create a preset that renders a lower-resolution file for YouTube more quickly than the one you just encoded.

1 Click the Create New Preset Group button (⬛) at the top of the Preset Browser panel, and give the group a unique name, such as your name.

2 Click the Create New Preset button (✚), and choose Create Encoding Preset.

▶ **Tip:** If you forget where you saved your encoded movies, click the blue link in the Output File column next to the finished movie. Adobe Media Encoder opens a window to show you where your files were saved.

3 Do the following in the Preset Settings dialog box:

- Name the preset **Low-res_YouTube**.

- Make sure H.264 is chosen from the Format menu.

- Choose YouTube 480p SD Wide from the Based On Preset menu.

- Select the Video tab, if it's not already selected.

- For Frame Rate, deselect Based On Source.

- Choose Baseline from the Profile menu. (You may need to scroll down to see it and the following options.)

- Choose 3.0 from the Level menu.

- Make sure VBR, 1 Pass is chosen from the Bitrate Encoding menu.

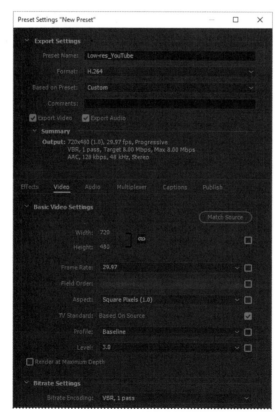

- Click the Audio tab, and choose 44100 Hz from the Sample Rate menu and Medium from the Audio Quality menu.

4 Click OK to close the Preset Settings dialog box.

5 Drag the Low_res_YouTube preset onto the Desktop composition in the Queue panel.

6 Click the blue link in the Output File column. Then name the file **Lowres_ YouTube**, specify the Lessons/Lesson14/Final_Movies folder, and click Save or OK.

7 Click the Start Queue button (▶).

With the settings in your new preset, the movie encodes more quickly. However, the quality isn't as high.

8 When Adobe Media Encoder has finished, navigate to the Final_Movies folder in Explorer or the Finder, and double-click the Lowres_YouTube movie to view it.

Preparing a movie for broadcast output

The project you're rendering in this lesson is already high-resolution and appropriate for broadcast output. However, you may need to adjust other compositions for your intended delivery format.

To change the composition size, create a new composition with the appropriate settings for your final format. Then drag the project composition into the new composition.

If you converted the composition from a square pixel aspect ratio to a nonsquare pixel aspect ratio, which is used in broadcasting, items in the Composition panel may appear wider than before. To view the video accurately, enable *pixel aspect ratio correction*. Pixel aspect ratio correction squeezes the view of the composition slightly to display the image as it will appear on a video monitor. By default, this feature is turned off, but you can easily turn it on by clicking the Toggle Pixel Aspect Ratio Correction button at the bottom of the Composition panel. The quality of the pixel aspect ratio correction for previews is affected by the Zoom Quality preference in the Previews category of the Preferences dialog box.

You have created both a web version and a broadcast version of the final composition.

Congratulations! You have completed all the lessons in *Adobe After Effects CC Classroom in a Book (2017 release)*.

While this book is intended to give you a good foundation for working with After Effects, it can't cover everything. To continue learning about After Effects, check out the resources described in the Getting Started section at the beginning of the book.

Review questions

1 Name two types of templates you can create for use in the Render Queue panel, and explain when and why to use them.

2 What is compression, and what are some things you should consider when compressing files?

3 How can you output a movie using Adobe Media Encoder?

Review answers

1 In After Effects, you can create templates for both render settings and output-module settings. These templates are presets that you can use to streamline the setup process when you render items for the same type of delivery format. After you define these templates, they appear in the Render Queue panel on the appropriate pop-up menu (Render Settings or Output Module). Then, when you're ready to render a job, you can simply select the template that is appropriate for the delivery format that your job requires, and the template applies all the settings.

2 Compression is essential to reduce the size of movies so that they can be stored, transmitted, and played back effectively. When exporting or rendering a movie file for playback on a specific type of device at a certain bandwidth, you choose a compressor/decompressor, or codec, to compress the information and generate a file readable by that type of device at that bandwidth. A wide range of codecs is available; no single codec is the best for all situations. For example, the best codec for compressing cartoon animation is generally not efficient for compressing live-action video. When compressing a movie file, you can fine-tune it for the best quality playback on a computer, a video playback device, the web, or from a DVD player. Depending on which encoder you use, you may be able to reduce the size of compressed files by removing artifacts that interfere with compression, such as random camera motion and excessive film grain.

3 To output a movie using Adobe Media Encoder, select the composition in the Project panel in After Effects, and then choose Composition > Add To Adobe Media Encoder Queue. In Adobe Media Encoder, select an encoding preset and any other settings, name the output file, and click the Start Queue button.

Appendix: General keyboard shortcuts

Result	Windows	Mac OS
Select all	Ctrl+A	Command+A
Deselect all	F2 or Ctrl+Shift+A	F2 or Command+Shift+A
Rename selected layer, composition, folder, effect, group, or mask	Enter on main keyboard	Return on main keyboard
Open selected layer, composition, or footage item	Enter on numeric keypad	Enter on numeric keypad
Move selected layers, masks, effects, or render items down (back) or up (forward) in stacking order	Ctrl+Alt+Down Arrow or Ctrl+Alt+Up Arrow	Command+Option+Down Arrow or Command+Option+Up Arrow
Move selected layers, masks, effects, or render items to bottom (back) or top (front) of stacking order	Ctrl+Alt+Shift+Down Arrow or Ctrl+Alt+Shift+Up Arrow	Command+Option+Shift+Down Arrow or Command+Option+Shift+Up Arrow
Extend selection to next item in Project panel, Render Queue panel, or Effect Controls panel	Shift+Down Arrow	Shift+Down Arrow
Extend selection to previous item in Project panel, Render Queue panel, or Effect Controls panel	Shift+Up Arrow	Shift+Up Arrow
Duplicate selected layers, masks, effects, text selectors, animators, puppet meshes, shapes, render items, output modules, or compositions	Ctrl+D	Command+D
Quit	Ctrl+Q	Command+Q
Undo	Ctrl+Z	Command+Z
Redo	Ctrl+Shift+Z	Command+Shift+Z
Purge All Memory	Ctrl+Alt+/ (on numeric keypad)	Command+Option+/ (on numeric keypad)
Interrupt running a script	Esc	Esc

INDEX

Production Notes

Adobe After Effects CC Classroom in a Book (2017 release) was created electronically using Adobe InDesign CC (2015.3 release). Art was produced using Adobe InDesign, Adobe Illustrator, and Adobe Photoshop.

References to company names in the lessons are for demonstration purposes only and are not intended to refer to any actual organization or person.

Typefaces used

Adobe Myriad Pro and Adobe Warnock Pro as well as other Adobe typefaces are used throughout the lessons. For more information about OpenType and Adobe fonts, visit www.adobe.com/type/opentype.

Team credits

The following individuals contributed to the development of *Adobe After Effects CC Classroom in a Book (2017 release)*:

- **Writer:** Brie Gyncild
- **Illustrator and Compositor:** Lisa Fridsma
- **Copyeditor and Proofreader**: Wendy Katz
- **Indexer:** Brie Gyncild
- **Keystroker:** David Van Ness
- **Cover design:** Eddie Yuen
- **Interior design:** Mimi Heft
- **Lesson Designer:** Lisa Fridsma
- **Adobe Press Executive Editor:** Nancy Davis
- **Adobe Press Production Editor:** Tracey Croom

Contributors

Mark Christiansen—Author of *After Effects CC Visual Effects and Compositing Studio Techniques* (Adobe Press), Mark has created visual effects and animations for feature films, network television, computer games, and an array of high-technology companies. Recent clients include *The Orphanage* (Dimension Films), *Telling Pictures* (The History Channel), and the Couturié Company (HBO), as well as Seagate, Sun, Intel, and Medtronic. Feature credits include *The Day After Tomorrow* and films by Robert Rodriguez.

Lee Daniels—Lee is a freelance animator, illustrator, and motion graphic artist working from his home studio in South London. Following a career in magazine design and image retouch, Lee has spent the last 10 years producing bespoke animation and visual effects for a wide range of international corporate, TV, and new media clients including Channel 4, Discovery US, National Geographic, Mirror Group, Exxon Mobile, and Cancer Research. Recently, he has worked on several newly commissioned UK TV shows for the 4oD short-form comedy platform. He generously shares tips & tricks in After Effects animation with the growing subscriber community on his LeeDanielsART YouTube channel. See more of his work at leedanielsart.com.

Takeshi Hiraoka—Plucked out of paradise, Hiraoka moved to chilly San Francisco from Honolulu, Hawaii, one cold winter day in 2002. In San Francisco, he attended the Academy of Art University, graduating in May 2004. This is where Hiraoka met Sheldon Callahan, with whom he directed and produced the feature-length DV film *Origin*. In addition to being a DV producer, Hiraoka is also a 2D and 3D animator.

Stephen Schleicher—Traveling from Kansas to Georgia to California, Stephen has worked as an editor, graphic designer, videographer, director, and producer on a variety of small and large video productions. Currently, Stephen teaches media and web development at Fort Hays State University. He also works on video and independent projects for state and local agencies and organizations, as well as his own works. Stephen is a regular contributor to Digital Media Net (www.digitalmedianet.com).

Anna Ullrich—Anna is a pale but fine digital artist based in Seattle, Washington, although her heart resides in Minnesota, where her spry and brilliant Democratic grandmother lives. Anna earned a BFA from the University of Washington in Seattle and an MFA from the University of Notre Dame in Indiana (both in photography).

Special Thanks

We offer our sincere thanks to Victoria Nece for her support and help with this project. We couldn't have done it without you!